THEMES
ON PACIFIC LANDS

THEMES
ON PACIFIC LANDS

edited by

M.C.R.EDGELL and B.H.FARRELL

Western Geographical Series, Volume 10

Department of Geography
University of Victoria
Victoria, British Columbia
Canada

1974 University of Victoria

Western Geographical Series, Volume 10

EDITORIAL ADDRESS

Harold D. Foster, Ph.D.
Department of Geography
University of Victoria
Victoria, British Columbia
Canada

ISSN 0315–2022
Library of Congress Catalog Card Number: 74-83668
ISBN 0-919838-00-6

ACKNOWLEDGMENTS

The production of this volume was made possible by a generous grant from the University of Victoria. This assistance is gratefully acknowledged.

The series editor would also like to express his sincere thanks to the many people who have combined to make the production of this volume possible. The many photographs in "Themes on Pacific Lands" were, for example, reproduced by Mr. Ian Norie who assisted Mr. John Bryant in the production of maps and diagrams. The excellent cover design was the work of Mr. Bryant. Mrs. Alison Griffith typed several rough drafts and the final copy of this volume and her hard work is warmly appreciated. Although not directly involved in the production of this book, the invaluable assistance of Mrs. Marianne Anderson in the distribution of earlier volumes deserves recognition.

Harold D. Foster

University of Victoria
Victoria, British Columbia
October, 1974

PREFACE

Themes on Pacific Lands is the first volume in the Western Geographical Series to examine problems peripheral to or outside of Canada.
In its focus on the Pacific and Canada's relations with the Pacific, the
volume reflects the interests of the Western Canada - Pacific division of
the Geography Department at the University of Victoria. All but two of
the contributors were also members of the University's Pacific Studies Programme. Most of them have lived for long periods in the areas about which
they write, and all but one of the chapters are the result of extensive field-
work beyond the borders of Canada.

The chapters have common threads providing a human connection
and a coherence, albiet one which is not defined in black and white. Some
are linked by deficiencies in the human condition, others through man's
attempts to find acceptable accommodation in, or use of, his chosen environment. In some, present day circumstances resulting from earlier
colonial domination, and often connected with multiple conflicts between
various ethnic groups, form a common theme. Man's interactions with
man or environment provide a common link in all chapters, and in some
it is shown that man's actions have led to a worsening, rather than an improvement of the quality of life and land.

Yet the topics, like the Pacific itself, are not homogenous, and
no attempt has been made by the editors to homogenise or produce uni-
formity. To have done so would have been to remove much of the freshness
from the studies. Six specialists on the Pacific are attempting to throw
light on the Pacific in their own way. The reviewer choosing to commence

"the volume is disappointingly uneven in content and style" will certainly have a field day, but hopefully those searching more deeply will also find the excursion rewarding.

M.C.R. Edgell
B.H. Farrell
October 1974

TABLE OF CONTENTS

LIST OF TABLES

LIST OF FIGURES

LIST OF PLATES

CHAPTER 1

SINGAPORE: REFLECTIONS ON A CITY STATE
IN THE TWENTIETH CENTURY

Rudolph Wikkramatileke

University of Victoria

From an obscure island possession of the Sultanate of Johore in the immediate pre-colonial period, to the most modern and vibrant but smallest national entity in Southeast Asia. This is the transformation that has been achieved in Singapore within a period of a little over one hundred and fifty years. An assessment of the phases of change and the more significant contributory factors, leads one to re-emphasize certain basic geographic concepts and at the same time to question others. In addition various economic, cultural and geo-political doctrines invite re-appraisal. Furthermore, recent developments in urban and industrial growth, provide opportunities for discussing contemporary themes in geography such as decision-making, environmental control and the quality of life.

THE CHANGING VALUE OF SPACE
AND NATURAL ENVIRONMENT

Prior to Stamford Raffles acquiring the island for Britain in 1819 from the Sultan of Johore for what is now in retrospect a paltry annual fief of 5,000 Straits dollars, Singapore was to all intents and purposes a worthless and inhospitable dot on the globe.[1] Today it ranks as one of the highest priced units of real estate in the world; land values whether for commercial or residential use are comparable to those prevailing in most urban environments of the North American continent. The main island of Singapore covers only 207 square miles, with a maximum extent from west to east of 25 miles and from north to south of 14 miles. If the off-shore islands within its territorial waters are included the total land area of the State is 224.5 square

1

miles. In a historical context, particularly in the pre-occidental contact period, the island's location at the tip of the Malay peninsula made it at best a useful landfall and an anchorage in time of distress for early Chinese, Arab and Indian mariners. There were no exotic riches to be had from the steamy tropical isle sitting just one degree north of the equator. It was no native oriental culture hearth; there was little indigenous settlement to leave an imprint of native agriculture on the landscape and there were no precious metals to be had. The legend of the thriving port of Sri Tamasek, and subsequently that of Singapura - names for the anchorage during the Indian trading empires of the seventh to tenth centuries - can hardly be given credence. Marshy estuaries, tidal mudflats and mangrove swamps extended over the island's peripheries, and here it is well to bear in mind that 64 percent of the island lies at elevations of less than 50 feet.

The inner core of higher ground was clothed in dense tropical forest; the highest point though being a mere 581 feet and rather optimistically named Bukit Timah, a 'hill of tin' in Malay. This hill has been for decades Singapore's major source of granite and it lies at the south centre of a batholitic mass of possibly Mesozoic age, which is flanked over the western sector of the island by sedimentary rocks of Permo-carboniferous age consisting of an assortment of schists, shales and sandstones. The eastern flank of the island is made up of old alluvial and marine sediments associated with an antedated drainage system from the mainland and also with changing sea levels in the Pleistocene period.[2] The impact of heavy annual rainfall, some 95 inches which usually falls in torrential doses, has led to intricate surface weathering patterns and drainage systems. Even the inland areas display a patchwork quilt made up of ground above fluvial conditions, alluvial pockets subject to periodic innundation and near perennial swamp patches.

Relatively, in terms of the time scales of other pre-developed areas of pre-occidental contact in Southeast Asia, and in respect to the value judgement of the oriental societies that inhabited them, Singapore was a

2

negative resource area. It was given to the denizens of the swamps and forest, with only meagre clusters of human predators in the form of Bugis pirates whose origins lie in the eastern Indonesian archipelago, and a sparse scatter of less adventuresome Malay fisherfolk in their wood and thatch huts sitting on stilts.

The new era of navigation, and the increased competition for the trade of the Orient between the European mercantilists at the turn of the eighteenth century placed a new focus on the island mud patch; Singapore became the linchpin of the area's narrow sea lanes. This new role strengthened through future decades was not the result of calculated design by the British, but the vision of a single individual. Raffles, an official in the service of the British East India Company, had a running battle with his superiors in the India Office and in Whitehall, to bring his views on the future importance of Singapore to fruition; for Penang (Prince of Wales Island), Malacca, Achin and Bencoelen, all with an earlier history of use had more appeal.[3] The re-appraisal of locational advantage in terms of the island's global as well as regional setting was the product of playing a scientific hunch on a long term projection based primarily on empirical grounds. This approach is not obsolescent even in these days of modern computerized quantitative analysis. Furthermore, Singapore's development in the years to follow showed the force of imagination and endeavour over environmental considerations. If only the advocates of environmental determinism could see Singapore now, the ranks of the possiblist school would be swelled by many a convert. There are now 2.1 million people in the tiny, bustling and thriving State.

THE EMERGING TOWN MORPHOLOGY AND CULTURAL SETTING

During the first three decades of Occidental impact, the early settlement initially controlled by the British East India Company and stradd-

FIGURE 1,1   Singapore: Selected Topographic Features.

4

ling the mouth of the Singapore river (Figure 1, 1), gradually spread fan-
wise into the southernmost wedge of the island. In topographic terms this
progression saw the growth of an open roadstead directly south of the Singapore
river for European clippers, Chinese junks and assorted native craft, river bank
warehousing facilities, trading establishments, merchants' residences (dominantly Chinese, Arab and Jewish), and the homes of the few British elite (administrators, custodians of the law, financiers and planters), located in relatively select and somewhat more salubrious surroundings. All of these were
overlooked rather than protected from a tactical point of view by a fort. The
latter was initially Fort Fullerton at the very mouth of the Singapore river,
but this was replaced by Fort Canning on a little knoll a bit inland. All
these features added up to the quaint and scenic but somewhat commonplace
town morphology belonging to the romantic period of modern history in the
tropics, and typical of any contemporary port town founded by the European
mercantilist. (Plates 1 and 2).

The fundamental difference was provided by the island's geographic
situation at the Indo-Pacific gateway and near midway between the two already pre-developed and flourishing Oriental culture worlds, namely that of
the Indian sub-continent and the Chinese mainland. It is from these two
sources that Singapore, the fledgeling outpost of Britain, founded with an eye
for the China trade and the maritime control of the China seas and its border-
lands, drew its exotic human resources. The peoples of China and India
proved in time to be the only real basic resource element. In 1824 the total
population was estimated at 10,683 persons. Of these 90 were Caucasians,
15 Arab, 4,850 Malay, 3,317 Chinese, 1,925 Bugis and 756 Indian.[4] But
in later decades Chinese immigrants were to swamp all the other ethnic
groups. Most of the Indians in the early decades were convicts from the
motherland, brought over as indentured labour and put to work on marsh reclamation, and the construction of roadways and quayside buildings. Many
of the Chinese were a motley lot from the grim social arena of the port-city

PLATE 1
Core of early Singapore: River mouth, boat quay, food stalls and commercial buildings.

PLATE 2
Nineteenth century Chinese merchants homes.

hinterlands of mainland China. They set to work as construction hands, squatter farmers and dealers in merchandise. They also engaged in the more exciting and seamy vocations which pandered to base human response. These two major immigrant groups, nearly all menfolk in the early years, set an unprecedented tone of endeavour under conditions of extreme hardship in a hitherto lackadaisical human setting. Even as late as the 1880's the annual death rate was 4.5 percent and infant mortality 37.7 percent, due to malaria and other endemic tropical diseases.

THE IMPRESS OF DISTINCTIVE ECONOMIC
AND SOCIAL PATTERNS

Singapore's advantageous geographic location was highlighted in the 1860's through the advent of the steamship, the opening of the Suez Canal and the maritime re-orientation of the other countries of Southeast Asia, which hitherto had been predominantly inward looking. These latter developments have been of lasting consequence because they added a growing functional economic dimension to the bald fact of the island's strategic location. The immediately peripheral territories became the sources of primary products both agricultural and mineral. Much of Sumatra's pepper and other spices for example found their way to the western world across the Malacca Straits via Singapore, as did South Johore's gambier and rattan across the Johore Straits. A pattern of barter trade, particularly between the Indonesian islands and Singapore, was thereby initiated and subsequently spiralled to comprise a significant proportion of Singapore's earnings. This inter-island and trans-peninsula trade is still of great importance. Concurrently with this emerging trade pattern the island became a haven for more immigrants. For example, during 1893 some 180,203 Chinese men and 9,640 women arrived in Singapore. This set the pattern for the dominant migration increase in population of previous decades to be gradually superseded by a natural increase within the settlement.

7

The island's total population at the same time stood at about 190,000 persons and of these only around 22,000 were women.[5] Furthermore, only 6 percent of the total population could be classed as local born and the number of persons under 16 years of age was around 10 percent. The trends of migration growth, taken in conjunction with economic growth, tend to re-emphasize a concept in geography which is of deep consequence in the developing tropics, even in relation to present-day events. Pushed or transplanted populations with a built-in fibre of initiative achieve socio-economic dominance over the 'indigene'. Traditional attitudes to a native dweller simply imply a persuance of a way of life. Tradition borne in transit more often imbues an individual with a will to live and compete more than successfully in any and every occupational field.

Meanwhile the southern town core on the right bank of the Singapore River grew in density. On the left bank with a comparative spacious layout stood the Government offices, the legislative buildings, the court house, military and police posts, churches, the Victoria memorial theatre, and the island's first major English type school, namely Raffles Institution (Plate 3). All of these came into being between the 1830's and 1860's. The aforementioned buildings fringed a broad esplanade and playing fields, with pavilions, fronting the sea. These oft repeated morphological features, typical of all cores within British established townships in the tropics, are highly symbolic both in a historical and contemporary context. They imply in turn, the arm of military might, the rule of law, the initiation of civic liberties and fundamentals of democracy, the sense of moral authority, and the elitism to be achieved through being schooled in English and the British way of life. Furthermore, the fond hope was entertained that everyone whether white, yellow or dark skinned would of necessity learn to play cricket, sip tea or nurse whiskeys and soda. These implications have been and are real, but alas a tinge of the farcial, if not downright hypocristy

PLATE 3
Colonial town morphology: Cathedral,
civic buildings, sports fields and esplanade.

PLATE 4
China Town: Two-storey
high density shop-houses.

PLATE 5
Varied land use: Modern housing (left), Chinese and Malay Kampongs (centre and right), and war memorial (top-centre).

PLATE 6
Mangrove swamp and diked-in prawn ponds around township in northeast Singapore.

has crept in periodically.

For example, west of the aforementioned morphological features
Chinatown continued its sprawl on the right bank of the river in an amal-
gam of sordid two-storeyed shop houses (Plate 4). Raffles had ruled
in the earliest years that this was to be the precinct of the Chinese,
while the Indian cantonment lay far to the east of the civic building
complex already cited. Those of Malaysian origin deployed themselves
mainly in more typical tide-water Kampongs (villages) in the hitherto
unoccupied sectors. North and northeastward but not more than four
miles from the town centre, roads fanned out to encompass the main
residential sectors of the well-to-do and associated service units.
The former were dominated by the European or Asian elite. Despite a
high level of spatial integration over the years, the basic pattern of
selective zonal ethnic density is evident even today.[6]

In the case of the Asian elite the use of the English language –
the established passport to middle class salaried employment by the
Asians – was not a necessary criterion; opulence gained through
business entrepreneurship was a sufficient substitute. However, despite the spatial concentration of elitism implied in the previous paragraph, pockets within the framework of these sophisticated areas of
domicile, harboured elements from lower social orders, such as
Chinese, Indian and Malay kampongs. Furthermore, even squalid
Indian dairy sheds as well as Chinese market gardens gradually occupied vacant ground.[7] It is this close juxtapositioning of social
strata, ethnic groups, and land use forms that has long provided the
fascinating checkerboard of varied life styles ranging from the truly
native to the ultramodernistic within even the 'urban' limits (Plate
5).

THE CHANGING CONCEPT OF HINTERLAND

The period after the 1860's till the advent of the Second World War witnessed the consolidation of the colonial administration and also high-lighted the consequences of a laissez-faire trading policy. In assessing these trends another basic geographic consideration, the changing concept of port and hinterland, is of vital concern. Initially the strict geographic hinterland of the new port town was the rustic surrounds of the island itself. In this area Chinese squatter farmers proceeded to hack down the forest for cropping gambier, pepper, nutmeg, tapioca and food crops other than rice. European planters too established estates of sugar cane.[8] The cultivated extents at peak level for the principal commercial crops were: gambier, 24,220 acres in 1840; pepper, 2,614 acres in 1848; and sugar, 400 acres in 1850. These cultivations were on the better drained terrain and made extensive inroads into the vital forest cover, took heavy toll of soil fertility and resulted in accelerated run-off. The cropping combinations referred to above were soon abandoned and much of this terrain was put under rubber at the beginning of the twentieth century and reached a maximum of 55,678 acres in 1935.

The coastal stretches away from the town perimeter could hardly be considered as part of the growing entity of Singapore during the nineteenth century. The better drained coastal patches harboured coconut palm groves and Malay peasant settlements, and the crudely diked-in swamps were given to fish and prawn culture, though there is evidence that the cultivation of rice was attempted in certain of these areas particularly in the west of the island (Plate 6). The point to be made is that the dogma of pure subsistence farming never gained a foothold in Singapore, because of the feature of a widening economic hinterland. The guiding motivation for survival among the immigrants, whether Asian or European, was not the use of island territory to live on and feed off, but rather as a location to trade from. Consequent on the forementioned, and also the minimal influence of a truly native society, there evolved a functional landscape which was essentially non-institutionalized and unfettered in terms of inflexible Oriental traditions.

Singapore from the latter half of the nineteenth century became one of the world's near unparalleled conveyor belts. It handled the pooling and transhipment of such primary products as tin and spices, as well as a wide range of oriental textiles and craft products. At the same time it became the principal port undertaking the sorting and distribution of fabricated goods from the occidental world to a wide scatter of entry points around the land areas of Southeast Asia. The story of this growing entrepôt trade can be gleaned from the following figures. In the early 1820's the value of imports and exports was around 2 million pounds sterling. By 1918 the figure was over 120 million pounds sterling. In 1869 some 99 steamers and 65 sailing ships called at the wharves, but by 1879 their numbers had risen to 541 and 91 respectively.[9] This was made possible in the first instance through the development of one of the finest sheltered alongside berthing port complexes in the tropical world. The Keppel harbour installations, on the southwest flank of the island and to the lee of Blakang Mati and Pulau Brani islands, now extending over three miles of waterfront were gradually developed from 1861. Secondly, it was Britain's consolidation of territorial control over the Malay States on the peninsula and her growing suzerainty in a more indirect manner over Sarawak, Brunei, and North Borneo that helped make Singapore the emporium for chanelling in a primary or processed state, the tin, rubber, pepper, copra, timber and oil from the forementioned territories.

The territories cited proved to be the real effective economic hinterland of Singapore. The island itself though could until the 1960's be apportioned into town and mere countryside in this specific context, with

32 square miles being within the city limits (Figure 1, 1).[10] The rest of
the land outside this perimeter could in general terms be described as rural.
The main exceptions were the British naval base flanking the eastern arm
of the Johore Straits, the scatter of air and military bases such as Changi,
Sembawang, Seletar, Tengah and Nee Soon with their associated little
townships, and a thin spread of commercial and secondary manufacturing
firms along the main road-rail link leading to the causeway joining the
island to the mainland. The latter completed in 1924 is approximately a
mile long. Elsewhere in the rural domain the occupied landscape consisted
of Chinese market gardens, which though ubiquitous, tended to show four
or five zones of marked concentration (Figure 1, 1),[11] and a few patches
of rubber on better drained ground. Both categories of land use largely
supported dispersed homesteads. The only significant native settlement
nodes throughout the rural sector were at a few select tidewater locations
which served as ferry points for local coastwise or offshore island traffic,
and as focal points for the native fishing trade. Much well drained ground
supported scrub vegetation or rank grasses, while of course certain hill-
ocks were given to the Chinese dead - the cemetery is a form of land-use,
perhaps misuse, of deep consequence both ritually and in terms of site
selectivity. Much of the coastal periphery remained in under-utilized
mangrove swamp, though the varied tree species provided pole timber,
firewood and also charcoal.

To the Chinese market gardeners, the Chinese and Malay fisherfolk,
the wide spectrum of Chinese, Indian and Malay wage earners in civic
occupations ranging from the most menial to the more dignified, and the
service operators affiliated with the British defence installations, the
functional concept of port and hinterland, or in turn the dichotomy of town
and country, took on a slightly more conventional if not narrower perspective. The Chinese market gardeners, comprising some 25,000 persons

14

utilizing about 7,500 acres of ground in the 1950's, catered to some of the
food needs of the city dweller, but nevertheless they had their eyes focussed
on the port victualling sector (Plate 7). The Chinese and Malay fisherfolk did likewise. To the workers attached to the defence establishments,
for example in the 1960's some 45,000 direct British War Department employees and perhaps another 100,000 persons in such vocations as domestic
help, cab drivers, seamstresses, laundrymen, kiosk and bar operators, the
periodic build up or decline of British strength in khaki, white or blue uni-
form through the twentieth century was of crucial concern.[12] The fortunes
of this group however were of personal concern to those involved rather
than a matter of civic anxiety in the overall scheme of things during the
colonial period.

The red lines on the atlas showing the territory of Singapore first
as a Straits Settlement and later as a Crown Colony, (both independent of
the Malay peninsula purely in administrative terms), were a mere expression
of cartographic fancy. Just as goods and services were freely moveable
across territorial boundaries, for throughout the free-trade era only opium,
gold, tobacco and alcohol were taxable, so were humans. If one could
not find work in Singapore, there were wide open avenues for employment
or personal endeavour as homesteaders in the adjacent territories of British
Southeast Asia, and also the freedom to move to them. It is this assumption
and the implication that the status quo would prevail which leads one to
dwell on the basic weakness of the colonial organizational pattern, namely
that fundamental resource use, whether natural or human, was seldom geared
to a true environmental base in terms of physical geographic entities.

RESOURCE USE ON A TRUE ECOLOGICAL BASE

The best example of the above issue is presented by a basic natural
resource need for humans and economic activity, namely, water supply.[13]

PLATE 7
Chinese market gardens: Vegetable plots, fish ponds, pig and poultry barns and farmers dwellings.

By the mid-nineteenth century the intensification of settlement within the
town limits made the domestic supply of water from wells insanitary. In 1862
the first impounding reservoir later to be known as the MacRitchie reservoir
was constructed, and was followed by the Pierce reservoir in 1900 (Figure
1,1). Both were located in the sole remaining forested high ground catchment reserve in the centre of the island. The deforestation referred to in
the earlier decades as a consequence of unbridled commerical crop cultivation had left the island with a mere 11 square miles of protected catchment. The rapid growth of population, for example 311,985 persons in 1911
to 425,912 persons by 1921, and with the water consumption component being
dominantly within the city limits for few of the rural areas had a piped water
system, and also the increased demands for water by the port led to the construction of three reservoirs in southwest Johore State in Malaya. This aug-
mentation of the island's water supply entailed a convergence of pipelines
along the causeway, thereby increasing the latter's strategic importance as
a vital artery and also set the pattern for Singapore's continuing and increasing dependence on the mainland for its water supply.

In subsequent years despite the construction of the Seletar reservoir
on the island in 1941, more extra-territorial supply points in Johore State
had to be tapped. The Tebrau River water intake system was developed in
1949 and other similar installations were to follow. Consequently, if one
were to visit Scudai for example, there is an intriguing notice board which
states 'Property of the Republic of Singapore...unauthorized personnel not
allowed' (Plate 8). It is a thought provoking example of the existence
of a physically minute but vital exclave of a tiny State as an enclave of a
neighbouring independent State of today, namely, West Malaysia. Singapore
now draws some 90 percent of its daily consumption of around 105 million
gallons of water per day from across the causeway. One may justifiably ask
whether some thought and planning should have been directed during the

colonial period to meeting Singapore's needs for water through engineering part of the western arm of the Johore Straits as a source of fresh water. The prospect would have been technically feasible though costly, and also ecologically sensible, but perhaps unnecessary from a political and economic point of view in the past. Today, Singapore continues to augment its local water supply with two new reservoirs at Kranji and Pandan, (Figure 1,1), but lives in the hope that good sense will prevail across the causeway. In the meantime as settlement expands in South Johore and the rivers disgorge an increasing amount of silt and pollutants, the physical and ecological problems of obtaining potable water from the Strait grow in dimension.

The second example of questionable use of resources during the colonial period stems from letting a port city develop within a purely pre-industrial framework. There were hardly any industrial ventures of significance in terms of employment potential till the end of the 1950's. The number of wage earners in 'industrial' plants using a labour force of more than ten persons, then numbered only 25,600 in a total population of some 1.5 million people. The bulk of these workers were in the foreign controlled petroleum industries, for example the massive Shell Company installations on Pulau Bukum, and such complexes as the Ford assembly plant and Hume Industrial works in the centre of the island. The rest of the industrial wage earners were in a wide assortment of Chinese enterprises ranging from small textile factories to oriental food processing plants. Many of the latter were in the category of under-capitalized opportunist ventures with little prospect of real growth. Consequently a high proportion of the 12 percent of the total work force deemed as being in the manufacturing sector was a floating one, and it is no wonder that manufacturing contributed no more than 5 percent of the overall domestic income till the latter 1950's. Singapore was therefore a commercial entity at best with some 75 percent of all its workers being in the tertiary sector.[14] Over 80 percent of the island's revenue came from trade, transport, storage, communications and service functions. Here it is

18

worthwhile noting that about 30 percent of the value of Singapore's import
trade was from Indonesia, and that around 8 to 10 percent of its 'national'
income depended on the Indonesian entrepôt and barter trade. The importance of trade across the causeway to and from the Malay peninsula was
literally incalculable, for such was the volume, value and the freedom of
movement.

It should not be inferred from the foregoing that the urban morphology
of the city showed little change during the first five to six decades of the
twentieth century. Far from it, for the changing skyline and the growing
urban facilities gave Singapore the look of an occidental enclave biting
into an amorphous oriental setting.[15] But all this was a change of form
rather than of function; the underlying structure of the economy remained
geared to the mobility of goods and services on an intra-regional and global
scale. And, paralleling this trend was the use of readily available and un-
organized labour at relatively cheap wages, as well as the opportunist endeavours of the wealthy strata of the populace who by and large had no
territorial roots; many a stately Chinese mansion in Kuala Lumpur or Penang,
an ostentatious Indian home in Madras or Bombay or an impressive manor on
the English landscape stands as ample testimony. Singapore during the
colonial period, despite its lack of basic natural resources, had the capacity
to industrialize. The ability to easily assemble needed raw materials, the
factor of land availability (both on the main and offshore islands), and the
adaptability of its dominant Chinese work force to technological innovation
pointed to this. The potential however was simply stifled by the inhibiting
of industrial investment by dominantly British interests preoccupied as they
were with the profits of primary and secondary import-export functions.
One must hasten to add that the Chinese and South Asian entrepreneurs too
were quick to imitate and capitalize on the situation.

A decade of startling political change, commencing in the later
1950's, however transformed the hitherto advantageous porous character of

19

Singapore's territorial boundaries to one of a consistency which implied a slow strangulation in the area of free and profitable commercial enterprise, and also raised the portent of rapidly growing physical claustrophobia for its growing number of inhabitants.

THE UNCERTAIN PATH TO NATIONAL INDENTITY

The constitutional changes of 1958 made Singapore, which had gone through the usual progressions from direct rule by the British India Office or Whitehall in the earliest periods as part of the British Straits settlements to Crown Colony status from 1867 onwards, a qualified independent State.[16] Britain though still retained control of external affairs and defence matters. One had then the peculiar situation of Singapore being politically detached from its immediate hinterland, the newly independent Federation of Malaya. The island buoyed around for nearly two years in a sea of uncertainty, under fatherly or philosophical local political figures cast either in the phlegmatic or strictly academic British mould. The eerie thoughts of the island being denied further political advancement and being put out on a limb in terms of economic growth could only serve to breed one of two things as an aftermath to colonialism, namely, unbridled leftist reaction in the socio-political arena or calculated pragmatic leadership on a more conservative basis. This situation served as a catalyst for political aspirations among the local groups on the two fronts and resulted in the emergence of the Peoples Action Party under the leadership of Prime Minister Lee Kuan Yew. This party, whose founder members were all products of high quality English academic or professional training, comprised a cross section of all the 'local' ethnic groups but with a majority of Chinese. The P.A.P., whose slogan is to build a "democratic socialist non-communist" society, has held sway since 1959 to the present day. Two interrelated issues became evident in short order. How does one go about the question of creating an awareness of

20

such highbrow political concepts as 'democratic socialism' among a multi-
ethnic population, and more particulary a plural oriental society, of which
a substantial majority remained unschooled in the English medium or un-
detribalized by British culture? And, furthermore how can one practise
socialism on 224.5 square miles of real estate with a population of 1.5 million with a growth rate of 4.3 percent per year as was the situation in
1959?

THE QUESTION OF POPULATION RESPONSE

The first issue posed in the preceding paragraph demands a fuller
appreciation of the structure of society. Of the total population, 79 percent are Chinese, 11 percent Malays, 7 percent Indians and Pakistanis,
with the balance being made up largely of Europeans, Eurasians and Cey-
lonese. With regard to the latter three groups, there are no real lines of
cleavage in respect of thought processes among any one of them, for they
have all been schooled to think in terms of western social attributes. The
stratification here is almost entirely from lower middle class to upper class,
and can be diagnosed through a simple means test related to financial stand-
ings. In the case of the Chinese, Malays, Indians and Pakistanis however,
a horizontal line of cleavage can be drawn through all four groups separating
the 'lowly proletariat' group from those comprising the lower middle class
and above. In the latter ranges the stratification is on a material index,
though it must be noted that the use of English, particularly among the
Chinese, is not necessarily a criterion of elitism. The majority of the populace from the four last mentioned ethnic groups falls into the 'proletariat'
category, and it is within this social order that vertical lines of cleavage
between the ethnic groups become abrasive. For example, those of Malay
and Pakistani stock are Muslims, but the majority of the Malays are 'rural'
orientated and use the Malay language rather than English. The Pakistani,

PLATE 8
Singapore's Scudai River
water supply plant in Johore.

PLATE 9
Modern high density State low cost housing.

who is not an indigene, is urban orientated, and though bilingual to a point, will use Urdu rather than English. Amongst the Indians, many are in the urban functional sector, but a high proportion among these adherents to the Hindu faith will only comprehend either the Tamil or Hindi dialects. The Chinese within the lower social ranges are spread over both the urban and rural scene. Though the majority practise a version of Buddhism, their sub-ethnic groupings and associated languages such as Cantonese, Hokkien, Teichu and Hakka, form significant divides. The problem here has been succinctly put as the question of 'speaking some kind of Chinese to some kind of Chinese'.[17] In short traditional life styles are starker and also linger amongst the 'proletariat', and this pattern is fostered by the differential form of educational institutions, namely those using the more progressive English media and catering to the affluent and those institutions using one of the oriental vernaculars. The latter tended not only to perpetuate the idea of communalism, but also to provide a lower level of comprehension of evolving socio-political and socio-economic processes. Of course, nearly everyone in Singapore learned in time to lapse into 'Pasar Malay'; but this low level Bazaar Malay, though often termed the 'lingua franca' of the British territories in Southeast Asia could hardly be used as the tool for engineering nationhood in the cultural environment of Singapore.

Despite the above inherent attributes of plurality described and also the apparent dichotomy between 'town' and 'country' in terms of landscape use and the nature of domiciles, there was the redeeming feature of a lack of rigid segregation in the social arena. For example, a Chinese emerging from a farmhouse, unlike the rest of his family could be a skilled mechanic or industrial technician despite his inability to converse in English. An Indian from an unpretentious home could be a rather sophisticated individual with a facile command of the English language and be a well paid clerical hand, policeman or dockyard employee, though his parents may typify the traditional Indian in regard to garb, ritualistic living and abstemious dietary

23

habits. A Malay from a wood and thatch homestead in a kampong may be a vernacular school teacher, a postman, a messenger boy, chauffeur, or seaman.

The lowly nature of domicile is not necessarily an index of a person's vocation. To summarize, one can sit down to a meal at open air pavement food stalls and take in at a single glance a wide range of ethnic groups. For example, those in complete western evening dresss, individuals in slacks, shirt and sandals, and those in a range of different traditional oriental attire related to their ethnic origins. But one's further thoughts are full of conjecture. For example, the Caucasian in fancy garb may be living on his wits or he may even be a foreign expert. The Chinese in sandals may be a millionaire, a leading surgeon, or a market gardener. The Malay may be a member of parliament, a boatman, or a chauffeur having a night out in his employer's car. The Indian may be a leading lawyer, a retailer, or a public health inspector. It is a scene which depicts a curious kind of egalitarianism, and one which is difficult to reconcile with the conventional North American view of compartmentalized Asian society. There is also the possibility (though more so in the past than now), that the quaint scene described above may be rudely interrupted by rival gangster mobs, secret society members or protection racketeers.[18] This seamy element is dominated by the Chinese but the Malays and Indians are not wholly absent.

The egalitarianism described is simply a product of Singapore's economic history and its small geographic premise; it is not hidebound by a stagnant rural subsistence framework. There is no compelling regional detachment in terms of functional form. Singapore in this context is a municipality and not a country. The proverbial carrot to improving one's level of living has been and is freely on display to all, and the wherewithal to obtain this has been and is personal endeavor. Nobody in his right mind in Singapore will wait until the coconut drops from the tree, for if he fails to pluck it first someone else will. Furthermore, there are not enough coco-

nut trees to go around in Singapore, hence the gross disparities in the ability
of the populace to satisfy a near common set of material wants, and the
attendant mad scramble to do so.

THE FORM OF GOVERNING AND DECISION MAKING

The constricted physical setting of the socio-economic problem so
far outlined has had a direct bearing on the broader scale of political man-
euvering since the initial granting of independence. One had the peculiar
situation, in the first instance, of 'independent' Singapore seeking to achieve
true independence through merger with the newly independent Federation of
Malaysia.[19] In fact the all powerful P.A.P. went to the polls again in
1963 seeking a mandate on this single issue. The fact that Singapore was
initially left apart from and out of the immediate hinterland that it had
served so well for so long can be attributed, as some have done, to simple
British neo-colonialism. On the other hand who among the Malay elite in
the peninsula would readily accept an additional 1.7 million thrusting
Chinese into its fold? The truth of the matter lay somewhere between
Britain's desire to maintain a tactical foothold, both economically and
militarily in the hub of the South China Sea and the Malay desire to preserve a hereditary life style. A combination of circumstances however led
to the fusion of Singapore with the new Federation of Malaysia in September 20, 1963.[20] The Indonesian President's (Soekarno) rantings against
the Western imperialists and his subsequent military confrontation prompted
a herd instinct among the former British territories with the exception of
Brunei. Singapore in turn needed space for its increasing population; the
wide open spaces of Malaya, Sarawak and North Borneo were indeed a
pioneer fringe for physical as well as economic deployment. Besides this,
there were kith and kin on either side of the causeway; close blood ties,
in a physical and territorial sense invariably indicate the existence of vital

25

and dense arterial economic linkages. For example, 'brother' primary producer and commercial tycoon in Malaya or the Borneo wing has always had
a heavy reliance on 'brother' financier and exporter in Singapore. It il-
lustrates yet another basic principle of geography; the art and premise of
living cannot be remoulded by summarily dismissing the imprint of history.
Singapore however had on its part to eat humble pie in this alliance. For
40 percent of its national revenue went to the Federal coffers, and its small
representation in the Federal Parliament was an insult to its numerical elect-
oral weight as well as its economic standing. But then, what good for example is a port city without water? Besides, the long range prospects in
the field of party politics for the P.A.P. and for economic gains through unfettered investment and commerce in the Malay peninsula and in the Borneo
territories proved all too inviting.

With the claustrophobic situation alleviated, the prospect of 'hunger'
appeased and thirst satisfied (the Scudai River intake in Johore was completed
as a crash program in 1963 and the mighty Johore River project put into the
blue-print stage), the human mind invariably turns to matters organizational.
And, the latter has a penetrative effect particularly if intelligence goes
hand in hand with constructive ambition. One cannot subscribe to a doctrine
of 'progressive leadership' and sit back; Premier Lee Kuan Yew and the
P.A.P. pushed hard in the Federal political scene. The climax was stub-
born reactionary ethnic-nationalism on the part of some Malay groups across
the causeway, with Singapore being compelled to withdraw from the Malaysian Federation in August 1965. This agonizing development will stand both
as a tribute to Lee Kuan Yew's drive and brilliance and a monument to his
impatience with parochial thought processes and a system of near feudal life
styles, civic and political, in the dominantly Malay territories.

With the aforementioned curtailment of expanding political and socio-
economic horizons, the instruments of government and decision making centred
compellingly once again on the island Republic. The needs, aspirations and

26

attendant restlessness of a frustrated society became the focus of attention. The government became near ruthless in its purposefulness.[21] Those entertaining thoughts of leftist (communist?) leadership on rabid lines were retired battered and bruised from the political arena, and their proletariat underlings forced to change their ways or at least to cloak them. The unsavoury gangland and delinquent elements continue to be constantly reminded by the highly regimented and growing police force that their wayward ways have no place in Singapore. There is a continuing tirade against 'yellow culture' (a rather untidy term to say the least in the ethnic context of Singapore), to decry all things of western import thought of as contributing to a weakening of moral fibre.[22] All this is possible because the P.A.P. has, despite the existence of other political parties, held all seats in parliament over the last 12 years. Is there a better platform though for an intelligent and honest group of 'non-communist democratic socialists'?

The outsider superficially surveying the subservient social scene may well raise his eyebrows and indulge in abstract liberal thoughts. He invariably fails though to diagnose the somewhat incongruous fact that it is the capitalist free enterprise base that provides the real prop. For, irrespective of one's basic income level, be it that of barrow boy, kiosk operator, or shipping magnate, the key to survival in Singapore is the art of turning 10 cents into 20 in short order. A dominantly pragmatic society of this nature induces the government to be even more so. The aesthetic attributes of the planner, the culture values of the academic and the romanticism of the intelligentzia are all sublimated to the wills of the executive. The dynamic ultra-materialistic trend of modern Singapore in every field of growth activity, from the low cost rehousing programme, urban renewal and through to industrialization and port development, is marvelled at by the visitor from the developing world. How is this possible they ask and who makes those wonderful decisions? The truth of the matter is that the decisions have been the product of expediency on the part of those select few with delegated or self appropriated powers, and the real point at which a decision is made is when a problem is blatantly obvious. That the funds, acumen and aptitudes are available to implement and bring designs to fruition is simply an interaction of two forces: a highly regimented one party executive on the one hand and geographic inertia or historical momentum on the other. As a consequence, Singapore functionally now resembles a heartless computer which has its inhabitants and activities neatly programmed.

THE EVOLVING TOPOGRAPHIC SCENE

The basic data in the computer bank is a harsh numerical reality. The island's average population density is near 10,000 persons per square mile, and within the urban limits the figure reaches 35,000 persons. A horizontal spread of population is no longer feasible; they must be stacked vertically. The mechanical monster spills out solutions in terms of density of population per cubic foot, and 35 percent of Singapore's population now lives in low cost highrise complexes built by the State Housing and Development Board.[23] (Plate 9). Residential densities in these satellite townships are in the range of 125,000 to 150,000 humans per square mile. The thatch and palm of the past has given way to the concrete and asphalt jungle, in which more persons in the future will have to attempt a new mode of life.

The data on unemployment and the prospects of continued absorption of workers in the tertiary economic sector puts the computer in near distress. Not only were there some 43,655 registered unemployed at the end of 1970, but in addition there were large numbers of under-employed.[24] Furthermore, the growing insistence on work permits for those moving to and fro across the causeway linking the island to West Malaysia led to added problems for those seeking work. And looming on the horizon was the prospect of yet another disastrous development, namely the impending withdrawal of the British from

28

PLATE 10
Sector of Jurong industrial complex.

PLATE 11
Ultra-modern commercial buildings
and hotels on outer city limits.

the military establishments on the island.[25] First, says the computer, industrialization can certainly provide part of the answer. Second, parallel development of the port installations mind you is also necessary. Third, the
C.B.D. needs to be upgraded and modernized if the anticipated spiral of
economic activity and commerce is to be suitably accommodated. Fourth,
tourism could be a fruitful area of employment potential and financial gain.
Singapore had of necessity to take up the challenge for survival or starve,
for the island is so heavily dependent on imports of food.

The first of the four above mentioned areas of growth is expressed
today on the landscape in the form of the massive Jurong Industrial Estate
in the west of the island, and numerous smaller complexes elsewhere.[26]
(Plate 10). Jurong, reclaimed from swamp in the astoundingly short
period of three to six years, is now a hive of activity. Enterprises range
from shipbreaking and shipbuilding yards (Jurong boasts the largest dry dock
facilities between the Mediterranean and Japan), through a wide variety of
petro-chemical, chemical, pharmaceutical, timber product, food processing,
car assembly and electronic plants. But Jurong was a white elephant for a
time. Local and foreign investors were wary of Singapore's economic and
political viability. A pragmatic approach to investment incentives, such
as guarantees with regard to initial tax exemptions and the disposal of profits, coupled with a high degree of civic stablility countered the initial
hesitations of would-be investors. British, French, West German, Scandina-
vian, Hong Kong and Japanese capital in particular has flooded the investment sector. What the Japanese failed to achieve through war they have
more than accomplished in peace. They are firmly entrenched in the ship-
yards at Jurong, in the recently converted facilities at the former British
naval dockyard at Sembawang and numerous other industrial ventures, (Figure 1,1).

The main port facilities at Keppel Harbour too have been developed

by leaps and bounds, and it is now the fourth largest port in the world in
terms of total inbound and outbound shipping tonnage handled. The new
berths and warehouses for handling container cargoes will place Singapore
second to Japan in the Asian Pacific margin.[27] Meanwhile urban renewal
has restructured the C.B.D. into a massive complex of giant highrise business
establishments (Plate 11). Parts of old Chinatown and many other charming buildings in the heart of the city are no more. Even Raffles Institution
(that mainspring of intellectual achievement of many a Singaporean) has
been flattened and the old 'red brick' lore recast. The pace of renewal is
near heartless, Singapore apparently is bent on making histroy by obliterating
the hitherto few visible objects of historical standing. Renewal though is
insufficient in itself to provide the required space for an integrated and en-
larged C.B.D.; new land has to be reclaimed from the sea. Consequently,
from Bedok in the southeast, through the northern part of the Kallang estu-
ary and along the southern shoreline is a major area of some six square miles
of reclamation, designed in due course to support a marine front extension
of the present C.B.D.

Modern luxury hotels, a couple even with revolving restaurants high in
the sky, and high value apartment complexes built by the private sector
have invaded the northern fringe of the urban area which five years ago
harboured a fairly placid assortment of homes with spacious gardens, small
retail stores and a sprinkling of elite residential type hotels (Plate 12).
The Paya Lebar airport is now truly in the international class and handled
the bulk of the 623,000 tourists who visited the island in 1971.[28] Those
who did so had little problem in finding accommodation, for 4 out of every
7 hotel rooms were unoccupied. And if one was astute at bargaining the
advertized rate of S.$50 per night for luxury accommodation could easily
be whittled down by 20 percent. Overzealous imitation in construction and
the brash glare of newness within the city is exciting on the one hand and

31

overpowering on the other. Despite this the record appears impressive. No country in Southeast Asia can match even remotely from a statistical view-point, the 'progress' that the city state has made in the last 12 years.

INDICES OF PROGRESS: A STATISTICAL SURVEY

In 1965, the G.N.P. was 381 million pounds sterling, the G.N.P. per capita 205 pounds sterling and the total population 1.8 million. At the end of 1971 the respective figures were 820,396, and 2.02. These reflect in turn growth rates of 13.1, 10.7, and 2.1 percent.[29] The World Bank Atlas for 1970 ranks Singapore in 35th position is assessing world per capita incomes, and also puts the country out of the category of underdeveloped countries. The island's population is at near full employment with only 8,900 persons on the dole in 1972 compared with some 27,000 persons in a similar predicament in 1964, and this despite 40,000 workers being allowed in from West Malaysia in 1971.[30] In 1970, approximately 40 percent of the 143,000 workers in manufacturing were women and the corresponding figure for women in other forms of civic and commercial employment was around 26 percent out of a total of some 399,000 persons.[31] Female occupational rates in the urban sector by age groups now approximates two-thirds of the levels reached in the developed countries of Western Europe, and in the case of the 15 to 24 year age group the figures exceed those in the U.S.A.

Between 1966-1971 the Housing and Development Board completed over 125,000 individual units in their massive highrise complexes and the rate of construction is likely to be stepped up to around 15,000 units per year. It is estimated that 75 percent of all Singaporeans will be living in low cost highrises by 1980.[32] A total of over 165,000 private automobiles, 21,000 commercial vehicles, 113,000 motorized two wheelers, and 387,000 bicycles now crowd the streets. Furthermore some 157,000 radio and television sets add to the tropical hum. In 1961 the port of Singapore handled 23,079 ships totalling 76 million net registered tons. The respective figures for 1971 were 39,426 ships and 155.9 million net registered tons.[33] The new container berths built at a cost of over S.$137 million will have a handling capacity of 1.9 million tons of cargo by 1973. Singapore made goods now have far reaching markets, and here it is worth noting that the trade surplus with South Vietnam in 1971 amounted to S.$364 million; the profits of war will no doubt extend into the 'peace'.[34] Furthermore, investors from Singapore are now busy in Indonesia and West Malaysia.

Singapore has demonstrated all too conclusively a singular moral for all developing countries. Vehement assertions on ultra-nationalistic lines should at best be a transitory part of the political game in newly emergent countries; in a functional sense the rational and rewarding follow up to colonialism is internationalism and not inward looking self-defeating nationalism. Statistical projections in respect of continuing economic advancement are in optimistic vein. 'Few people realize that by 1977 our per capita G.D.P. will be S.$6047 ...we could reach the present British per capita G.D.P. by 1977.'[35] Statistically all well and good, but, Singapore as the Britain or for that matter the Hong Kong of Southeast Asia in respect of the overall living environment by 1977? The soul of Confucius please forbid!

A NOSTALGIC RESUME

The pleasant and exotic port city atmosphere of the early 1950's no longer prevails. An excursion downtown then during even the mid-day rush hour was a pleasant interlude for the hard-pressed individual or the dreamer with time on his hands. Today, the more circumspect park their automobiles well outside the inner city perimeter and hail taxis into town. The ever changing and mileage consuming one way traffic flow patterns, the risk of

PLATE 12
Urban renewal in city core:
Note older forms at left centre.

PLATE 13
Modern roadside restaurant in Singapore.

damaged fenders and the search for and payment for parking space is all too exacting on one's nerves and pocket book. In the past one could drive leisurely on 'country' roads just outside the urban fringe, and even park awhile or picnic on the grassy verges. These routes now approximate the freeways of the American scene. And, of course traffic snarls due to flooding are more frequent than before, because surface run-off is further impounded with every increase in the expanse of concrete and asphalt.

Within the built up city core or in the congested satellite highrise townships such as Queenstown and Tao Payoh, the populace now lives in a man-made hothouse micro-climate.[36] The traditional Kampong style leisure is missed by the elders from among the proletariat in particular who have been compelled to relocate in the concrete boxes they now have to call home; this presents a sociological problem of new dimensions. They have a yearning for the cool thatch roofed hut, the shade of the jakfruit tree and the pigs and poultry in the yard. Some attempt to retain such memories by raising chickens, ducks, and pigeons, though illegally, in nooks within the highrises. The Indian dairymen and their beloved cows and buffaloes have now been banished from the urban limits into obscure locations in the northern rustic fringe of the island.

The mixture of varied oriental food aromas that wafted freely over city sidewalks are now less obvious (Plate 13). The pavement food stalls are being pushed behind doors, and those that still function outdoors have had their locales of operation and business hours progressively restricted. Anti-litter laws are scrupulously and harshly enforced and the City Health Department keeps the streets and monsoon drains clean to the point of making Singapore near sterile. But the pressure of humanity in the now congested living framework and on the sidewalks, plus the increasing levels of smog and pollution of coastal waters, tends to limit the exercise at cleanliness to just about ground level. Meanwhile the urban octopus relentlessly extends its tentacles over the remaining vacant ground, and even the Chinese market

35

gardens are compelled to relocate. The urban creep is so persistent that there is little peace for the living and less even for the dead; the once hallowed Chinese cemeteries are bing recquisitioned for other uses, even sold if the price is right, and the Chinese are now exhorted to cremate their dead.

On the other hand however, the display of material wealth is overwhelmingly impressive in Singapore. More people seem to possess the mechanical and electronic gadgets of the modern age because gross incomes are now much higher than a decade ago through all ranks of the social ladder. But, strained countenances are now more in evidence. For not only are the tensions of day to day living higher, but the capacity to save money, particularly for those in the lower income brackets, is a harder task than in the past because 'floor level' family expenditure has been greatly increased and has become less of a flexible item. Low cost State housing is comparatively cheap, (S.$40 per month for a single room unit), but one has to pay these rents regularly and meet other inevitable expenditures on electricity, water, and commuting. Furthermore, in the area of social life many amenities, for example those periodic sophisticated indulgences on a night out which made life pleasureable at comparatively little expense, are bing pushed beyond the reach of the average Singaporean. It is ironical that these particular fruits of an affluent society are today savoured increasingly by the visitor rather than by the average citizen.

The price of attemping to cast everyone in a society into the same living environmental framework is to sharpen the economic divide between the have's and have-nots. The curious and friendly egalitarian basis of the Singapore scene of the past hinged on the existence and tolerance of both varied base living patterns and different denominators for value judgements. The emergence of a common denominator in this context is not through evolution but through design if not coercion. One has to be a Singaporean these days and not merely someone who enjoys living in Singapore. On the one hand therefore there is much opportunity in Singapore and many individual constraints on the other, for examply compulsory national service, a State directed schooling system and many other regimentations in like vein. Admittedly the one cannot be provided for and maintained without the other, but this leads to a form of bottled up civic effervescence. Is this the principal reason why Singapore in the period 1971 - 1972 allocated S.$483 million of its total revenue of S.$1,400 million to internal security and defense expenditure?[37]

This high level of expenditure is hardly warranted in terms of the immediate local scene. Could it be an expression of zonal insecurity in a wider geo-political sense? British maritime supremacy in the nineteenth century placed an irritating Han beetle in the navel of the Malay world; it has since thrived exceedingly to the envy of all around. Intimidation by Malaysia and Indonesia could perhaps be considered a possibility. The sweeping tide of communism from mainland Southeast Asia could well prove a threat. On the other hand is Singapore merely attempting to safeguard its shopwindows and its emerging role as the centre of Southeast Asian trade in oil? Irrespective of the foregoing thoughts, fast changing alliances both economically and politically seem to be the order of the times. For example, the Association of Southeast Asian Nations could become a functional entity. Singapore's role in the future may then well parallel that which she played in Southeast Asia in the lucrative days of Empire, though on a more complex political and economic premise. Some might contend that to dwell on the past is to cloud the present. On the other hand to ignore the past might result in compromising the future. Singapore has always dealt from a position of strength either real or implied. The current maneuverings in the social, economic, and tactical fields are perhaps intended to keep matters just that way.

REFERENCES

1. BUCKLEY, C.B. An Anecdotal History of Old Times in Singapore 1818-1887. Kuala Lumpur: University of Malaya Press, 1965.

2. WONG, Poh Poh Modern Singapore. OOI, Jin Bee and CHIANG, Hai Ding (eds.), Singapore: University of Singapore Press, 1969, pp. 20-51.

3. SWETTENHAM, Sir Frank British Malaya. London: Allen and Unwin, 1955, p. 71.

4. MOORE, D. and MOORE, Joanna The First One Hundred and Fifty Years in Singapore. Singapore: Tien Wah Press, 1969, p. 119.

5. MOORE, D. and MOORE, Joanna op.cit., p. 472.

6. NEVILLE, R.J.W. "Singapore: Ethnic Diversity and its Implications," Annals Amer. Assoc. of Geographers, 56 (1966), pp. 236-257.

7. WIKKRAMATILEKE, R. and SINGH, K. "Tradition and Change in an Indian Dairying Community in Singapore," Annals Amer. Assoc. of Geographers, 60 (1970), pp. 717-742.

8. WHEATLEY, P. "Land Use in the Vicinity of Singapore in the Eighteen Thirties," Jour. of Tropical Geography, 2 (1954), pp. 63-66.

9. BOGAARS, G. The Tanjong Pagar Dock Company 1864-1905. Singapore: Memoirs of the Raffles Museum, No. 3, 1956.

10. DOBBY, E.H.G. "Singapore: Town and Country," Geographical Review, 30 (1940), pp. 84-99.

11. NG, Kay Fong, TAN, Chee Lian and WIKKRAMATILEKE, R. "Three Farmers of Singapore," Pacific Viewpoint, 7 (1966), pp. 169-197.

12. NEVILLE, R.J.W. "The European Military Population in Singapore," Pacific Viewpoint, 5 (1964), pp. 205-210.

13. GENO-OEHLERS, Jillian and WIKKRAMATILEKE, R. "The Water Supply of Singapore: A Fundamental Resource Problem," Institute of British Geographers. Special Publication No. 1, 1968, pp. 187-202.

14. BUCHANAN, I. Singapore in Southeast Asia. London: Bell, 1971, especially pp. 90-164.

15. WIKKRAMATILEKE, R. "Focus on Singapore, 1964," Journal of Tropical Geography, 20 (1965), pp. 73-83.

16. TURNBULL, C. Mary Modern Singapore. op.cit., pp. 181-196.

17. ENRIGHT, D.J. Figures of Speech. London: Hienamann, 1965, p. 20.

18. COOMBER, L.F. Chinese Secret Societies in Malaya. Singapore: Moore, 1957.

19. LEE, Kuan Yew The Battle for Merger. Singapore: Government Press, 1961.

20. FISHER, C.A. "The Geographic Setting of the Proposed Malaysian Federation," Journal of Tropical Geography, 17 (1963), pp. 99-115.

21. BLOODWORTH, D. An Eye for the Dragon. London: Secker and Warburg, 1970, especially pp. 304-312.

22. ENRIGHT, D.J. Memoirs of a Mendicant Professor. London: Chatto and Windus, 1969, especially pp. 124-142.

23. YEUNG, Y.M. and YEK, S.H.K. "A Shop Census in Singapore's Public Housing Estates," The Town Planning Review, 43 (1972), pp. 56-70.

24. The Straits Times, Singapore: January 1, 1972, p. 17.

25. CAMBELL, W. "Cushioning the Effects of Pull-Out," The Straits Times, Singapore: November 2, 1971, p. 4.

26. See, Annual Reports: Economic Development Board Singapore. Singapore: 1968-1972.

27. The Straits Times, (Special Supplement), Singapore: Sept. 21, 1971, pp. 1-18.

28. MABBETT, H., RICHARDS, A. and SHARP, I. "Putting Singapore in the International Class," Singapore Trade and Industry. Singapore: Oct. 1972, pp. 27-32.

29. The Straits Times, Nov. 3, 1971, p. 6.

30. The Straits Times, Apr. 8, 1972, p. 15.

31. SHARP, I. "Woman Power in Singapore," Singapore Trade and Industry. Singapore: June, 1972, pp. 2-23.

32. See, Annual Reports: Housing and Development Board. Singapore: 1968-1972.

33. See, Annual Reports: Port of Singapore Authority. Singapore: 1961-1971.

34. SIVA, M. "The War Business," Singapore Trade and Industry. Singapore: August 1972, pp. 51-55.

35. GOH, Keng Swee "When We Reach that Fateful Year," The Straits Times. Singapore: March 20, 1972, pp. 16-17.

36. NIEUWOLT, S. "The Urban Micro-climate of Singapore," Journal of Tropical Geography, 22 (1966), pp. 30-37. GREENWOOD, P.G., HILL, R.D. "Buildings and Climate in Singapore," Journal of Tropical Geography, 26 (1968), pp. 37-47.

37. See, Singapore Trade and Industry. Singapore: November 1972, p. 13.

(Processed for Publication December 1973)

CHAPTER 2

MALAYSIA: INHERENT DISPARITIES AND THE QUEST FOR STABILITY AND CONTINUED DEVELOPMENT

Rudolph Wikkramatileke

University of Victoria

In making an assessment of the contemporary Malaysian scene certain distinctive parallels are evident, in the first instance, between the two component units of the present-day Federation and the former wings of Pakistan. The Malay Peninsula or West Malaysia stands in marked contrast, in terms of basic geographic and economic considerations, to East Malaysia which comprises the territories of Sarawak and Sabah in the island of Borneo.

The physical separation between West and East Malaysia is appreciable as was the case between West and East Pakistan, and distances between selected points in the peninsula and the island territories range between 600 and 1200 miles (Figure 1,2). Furthermore, West Malaysia can be ranked as being far more advanced than East Malaysia in respect of overall economic and socio-political considerations. And, more important still, the Western unit is quite obviously the more prestigious in terms of historical perspective, civic grandeur, religious fervour and international recognition. The inference that the East sector is the poor relation of the West is implicit in the analogy.

On the other hand, however, the nature of additional geographic features and facts restricts an unqualified extension of the foregoing comparison. The combined area of the two East Malaysian units exceeds that of West Malaysia by around thirty-three percent, but the aggregate population of the East sector is far lower than that of the Western unit and comprises only twelve percent of the total population. Here it must be remembered that former East Pakistan, though much smaller than the

Western component, had the overwhelming burden of supporting the larger share of Pakistan's population, despite its making a tangible contribution to the nation's total foreign exchange earnings through its jute, tea and sugar trade in the international market. East Malaysia is, by way of contrast, much more of a pioneer fringe than West Malaysia in respect of land availability, institutionalized forms of settlement and human sophistications, and moreover it makes less of a contribution to the Federal coffers. The export earnings from tin, rubber, oil palm and timber products in West Malaysia overshadow the value of exports of rubber, timber, sago, pepper and oil from East Malaysia.

In addition, the geo-political setting of the component units in Malaysia is obviously different. The two wings of former Pakistan were separated by a vast extent of land and the teeming hearth of Indian culture, whereas the waters of the South China Sea - that much sought after international fairway with potential oil-rich surrounds - divide the Malaysian realm. But the implications of the above features and resultant fears are similar. The inevitable reaction to all of the forementioned sets of considerations is that they carry inbred elements of instability. The complications, both national and international in the Indian sub-continent, that led to the demise of former Pakistan and the formation of independent Bangladesh, and the associated problems that persist, are proof enough of this assertion. But, must such historical precedent, or the will of Allah as some would have it, be taken as prophetic of the equally Muslim State of Malaysia? Prediction, however, is likely to be unrewarding. One can only analyse the nature of the dichotomy that prevails in regard to the two halves of Malaysia, whilst probing the many disparities and even the paradoxical situations within each. The latter considerations make the initial and apparently simple concept of basic duality between the two wings even more complex.

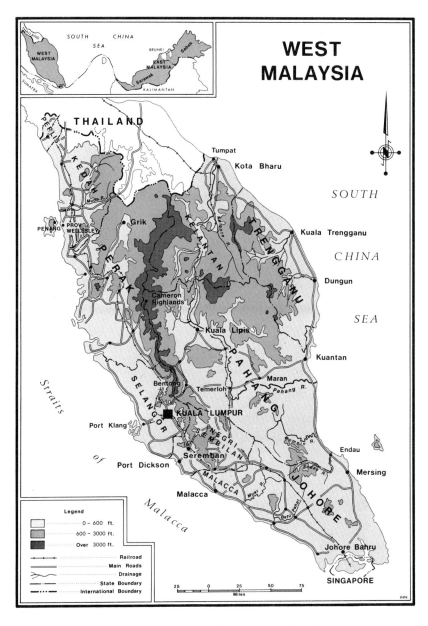

FIGURE 1,2   West Malaysia: Location Map.

43

AN ASSESSMENT OF THE WEST MALAYSIAN SETTING

The peninsula covers approximately 51,000 square miles and supports 8.8 million people. The basic layout of the country can be described in relation to three longitudinal belts, namely, the western lowlands, the medial complex of mountains, and the eastern flats. (Figure 1,2).

Factors in the Selectivity of Habitat

The terrain and lithology of the western plain is largely a product of alluvial deposition consequent on the accumulation of fluvial outwash from the mountain backbone. A good proportion of this land is well-drained, particularly inland where elevations range from 100 to 600 feet above mean sea level. On the coastal zone however, there are perennial swamps or areas subject to periodic innundation through heavy rainfall or tidal back up. The coastal fringes are festooned with mud banks and bars, and are invariably colonized by dense mangrove vegetation.[1] Because of these, the river inlets and embayments have proved difficult anchorages for vessels of appreciable draught, but a compensating factor is the somewhat sheltered character of the waters of the Malacca Straits lying to the leeward of the island of Sumatra. The anchorages of the western littoral, whether riverine or coastal, were undoubtedly the more favoured around the peninsula even during the earliest days of sail and trade. This advantage still persists, though much expenditure on dredging and other maintenance work is incurred in keeping port facilities, for example, at Port Klang (formerly Port Swettenham), Penang, Butterworth, Port Dickson and Malacca, at acceptable functional levels.[2]

Within historic times the three basic elements that have conditioned areal selectivity for indigenous settlement on a more intensive basis over the western lowlands are the lower incidence of rainfall, higher sunshine

duration and the occurrence of a predictable 'dry' season.[3] These favourable indices of seasonality, however slight their deviation from the norm
may be, are of much consequence in the more 'passive' stages of human
use of the varied terrain of the western lowlands for subsistence agriculture,
for, throughout the area the annual rainfall is between 85 and 130 inches,
and overall environmental conditions can be described as steamy, hot and
overly damp. On the foregoing basis, there are five areas that could be
classed as more 'favoured ecological niches', namely, the west and central parts of Perlis, northwest Kedah, Penang and Province Wellesley,
the western areas of Perak and Selangor with eastern extension along
sheltered valleys, and a wider tract covering the State of Malacca and
the very northwest of Johore and extending northeastward into Negri
Sembilan (Figure 1, 2). It is worthwhile noting that these areas today,
are the most productive for rice farming, though of course the subsequent
contribution of various cultural factors cannot be denied. Since the
nineteenth century however, the basic concept of 'favoured niches' in
terms of native settlement has been subject to distortion through the development of foreign enterprises such as the mining industry and the plantation economy geared particularly to perennial tree crops. Despite these
developments, the ill-drained terrain, with its cover of muck or peat
soils, still inhibits the fuller occupation of large tracts particularly in
western Johore, Selangor and Perak.

The medial mountain ranges are of massive proportions in the northern
and central parts of the peninsula, and become progressively subdued and
more broken in the southern sectors. Structurally there are seven major
longitudinal ranges. They consist of geological formations ranging through
acidic and basic granite, dolomite, sandstone and quartzite to volcanic
material. The distribution of the latter is highly selective with most of it
occurring in the eastern flanks. The northern mountain mass with peaks

45

ranging from 5,000 to 7,000 feet, and over which the yearly rainfall is a torrential 120 to 150 inches, is as yet virtually a no-man's land. Few inroads have been made into the rugged terrain with dense stands of forest dominated by tall Dipterocarp species, and the deep valleys with wildly oscillating river flow. Despite transverse breaks in the mountain back-bone in the south-central and southern parts, the nature of the relief, forest cover, inter-montane swamps, and drainage systems still inhibit movement. In early days the upper reaches of such rivers as the Muar and Batu Pahat, and those of the lower Pahang and Endau offered difficult portage points between the western and eastern flanks of the peninsula. Even today there are only three trans-peninsula roads. The first of these, a long loop from Kuala Lumpur through Bentong, Jerantut and Maran to Kuantan was in use about 1911. The second from Malacca through Kluang to Mersing was completed in 1928. The third, a quicker link from Kuala Lumpur across the mighty Pahang River at Temerloh and thence to Kuantan was completely surfaced by 1957. Even as late as 1956 a journey over the first route of about 240 miles took about ten hours of tedious driving. The medial ranges were virtually a completely effective barrier between the west and the east of the peninsula in the earlier days of settlement, and are an exacting one even at the present time. More important still, they have proved to be a 'cultural watershed' despite the inroads of settlement into the central 'waist' of the peninsula in more recent decades. The resultant dichotomy is such that the romantic in search of the 'true' Malay world is likely to realize his dream more easily in sections of the east coast plain rather than elsewhere in the peninsula.[4] (Plate 14).

The east coast plain, in contrast to the western lowlands, can be classed as a product of marine aggradation. Old beach ridges or permatungs are evident some 30 miles or more inland of the coastal fringe in sections of south Pahang. The resultant terrain is one of large scale impeded drainage,

PLATE 14
Traditional East Coast Malay fishing village.

PLATE 15
Pahang River: Levee settlements, swamp rice, marshes and swamp forest.

impressive meanders, humic soils and vast extents of inland swamp forest.
(Plate 15). These features are most in evidence where the mountain
ranges sit well back of the coast as in southeast Pahang and northeast
Johore, and the old European phrase - a 'marchland' - effectively sums
up the character of such a physical landscape. The coastal margin along
the South China Sea is fringed by a broken linear pattern of permatungs,
more recent dunes and sand bars.[5] The smaller streams break through to
the coast in intricate patterns, and the larger rivers like the Pahang and
Kelantan through a maze of distributaries. Most of the coastal inlets are
fringed by Nipah palms,[6] though in the southern sectors as around the
Endau region mangrove swamps tend to dominate. In the main soils throughout the area are either humic, or present an alternation in profile of veneers
of sand and alluvial deposits; the latter association is locally known as
bris soils. The overall lithology in essence reflects a conflict in terms
of ocean scour and marine sedimentation on the one hand and river spate
and alluvial deposition on the other. The east coast is exposed to the
strong currents of the China Sea and lashed by the winds and rains of the
northeast monsoon. From November to February most stations receive
around two-thirds of their annual rainfall varying between 100 and 150
inches, and the surface run-off is augmented through the year from rivers
discharging from the mountain interior. Through much of the year the
environment of most sectors of the east coast flats is a fluvial if not a
completely aquatic one. Anchorages are precarious and navigation up-
river is hindered by bars, wide tidal ranges and seasonal flooding. There
is only one true 'favoured ecological niche', namely the broad deltaic
region of the Kelantan River,[7] and perhaps a lesser one at the lower
reaches of the Trengganu River. But, even these are subject to the terrors
of certain flooding. On the other hand over the mid and lower reaches
of the Pahang River, which has a total catchment of over 10,000 square

miles, and others such as the Dungun, Rompin, Endau and Mersing Rivers water levels are near unmanageable. The only sectors of somewhat permanent refuge in the latter regions are the levees which extend far inland.[8]

From a physical point-of-view then East is East and West is West in West Malaysia, and this parallel may be extended into the socio-economic sphere when one considers the evolution of the overall topography of the country.[9] In so doing it is worth recounting a few significant historical highlights.

The Backdrop of History

The earliest inhabitants of the peninsula are represented even today, by such aboriginal groups as the Semang, Senoi, Temiar and Jakun. (Plate 16). Some among these have physical characteristics indicative of ancient migrations of Afro-Asian stock, whilst others bear witness to corresponding movements of early Malayo-Polynesian peoples. Their total numbers are perhaps no more than 40,000 today, and those who remain true to type dwell in widely-separated mountain fastnesses or foothill zones and retain much of their kindly and unsophisticated or, as some would have it, their primitive traits, as hunters, gatherers, rudimentary croppers and pagans.[10] Despite their small numbers they contribute to the ethnic, dialectic and social disparities within the country. They remain exotic specimens even to many of their Malay bretheren. They have paradoxically, however, proved of extreme value in recent decades in establishing national security, for many played a loyal role as trackers and couriers during the Malayan Emergency (1947-1959) and do so even now against communist guerillas in the northern border areas.[11] These simple but resilient people will long be remembered by many government officials, policemen and military personnel. The later Proto and Deutero Malay, the more direct forerunners of the Malay indigenes of today, were largely coastal or riverine folk. Their earliest resource use associations are linked

49

PLATE 16
Temiar aboriginees in West Malaysia.

PLATE 17
Rice fields and Indonesian
roofing styles in Malacca District.

to the fishing and yam-taro cultivation phase of human settlement. Subsequently, from particularly about the seventh century A.D., with increasing culture contacts with early but more advanced Siamese, Indian
and Javanese groups many of the Malay indigenes entered the more organ-
ised field of rice culture and fishing. The differential impact of these
three avenues of culture contacts is apparent even today. The orderly
wet rice landscapes of Perlis and Kelantan bear the stamp of Siamese
influence. The more productive rice fields of Kedah and Province Wellesley show the imprint of early Indian influence through the inroads of
the historic trading empires of Sri Vijaya and Majapahit, and in the
Malacca region of intensive rice farming the Javanese and Sumatran impact is obvious even to a higher degree, in terms of ethnic presence,
artifacts and house types. (Plate 17). On the other hand to the Malays
in East Pahang or East Johore, where the dominant culture contacts were
with the seafaring peoples of the East Indian archipelago, such as the
piratical Bugis and Orang Laut, rice cultivation is still an unmastered
art.[12] The basic attributes of the 'indigenous' Malay are then highly
diverse both in the strictest ethnic sense as well as in terms of culture
levels.

The two sets of developments that helped to bring about an apparent
synthesis in cultural and ethnic distinctiveness among the Malays are of
equally diverse origins. In the first instance it is the extension of the
Muslim religion from Southwest Asia and Northwest India initially through
the growing impact of Arab and Gujerati traders. This achieved recog-
nizable proportions from about 1400 A.D. with the core area of impact
being the Malacca Sultanate. Thereafter the movement gained momentum
through the habit of imitation rather than through proselytizing. For, by
this time civic organization among the Malays in the peninsula had begun
to coalesce into feudal principalities where the overlords held sway over

51

different river catchments. The highly distinctive word of the Prophet and the associated codes of everyday life related to the practice of the Muslim faith (some pandering grossly to male chauvinism) combined with the growing appreciation of the grandeur of high office in the Arab world tended to consolidate the emerging feudal pattern. The Sultans and their near kinfolk reigned supreme, and the populace became not only devotees of the Islamic faith but the camp followers of the feudal hierarchy.

The second development comprises a sequence of contacts with peoples who, in the interests of brevity, if nothing else, can be labelled the 'infidels', namely the Chinese and the European mercantalists.[13] The Chinese contacts go as far back as the other extra-regional Asian groups already mentioned. But, during these earlies periods the continued physical presence of the Chinese was of short duration and the culture impact purely mercantile, the latter centering around the trade in exotic commodities and the panning for gold, silver and tin in selected locales on the western littoral and also around Kuantan on the east coast. The influx of Chinese as residents gained momentum with the establishment of points of European contact. The Portuguese held Malacca from 1511 until the Dutch took over this historic port in 1641 (Plate 18). The impact of the Portuguese and the Dutch in West Malaya was limited in a regional sense. Socially however, the Catholic and Protestant faiths, respectively, gained their initial footings among a small proportion of the 'local' population mainly from amongst the Chinese and South Indians, and of course both European communities left behind a small minority of Eurasians with the Portuguese making the largest contribution to this particular ethnic component. On the other hand, the mercantile endeavours of the Portuguese and the Dutch highlighted the geo-political importance of Malacca as the pivot in the growing pattern of trade in Southeast Asia and the Far East. Finally, it was the acquisition of Penang (Prince of Wales Island) and Pro-

vince Wellesley by the British in 1786 , followed by the occupation of
Malacca in 1795, that opened the protective administrative umbrella
over the peninsula under which far reaching socio-political, demographic
and economic changes took place.[14]

The Chinese came in increasingly large numbers and so did the peoples from the Indian sub-continent, both Hindus and Muslims, in smaller
but significant numbers. In the initial period a very high proportion of
the Indians were either convicts or indentured workers. In the first six
decades of British authority one spoke in terms of a migration surplus of
Chinese and Indians, for although a high proportion of these migrants returned to their homelands they were replaced by larger numbers. For
example, the first decade of the twentieth century saw a migration surplus of approximately 175,000 Indians, and between 1920 and 1930 the
figure for the Chinese was about 380,000 persons.[15] But subsequently,
as the economic base broadened with the development of tin mining and
the plantation economy, and as immigration enactments became more for-
malized in the two source areas as well as in Malaya, increasing numbers
of the two principal immigrant groups considered themselves permanent
residents. Concurrently with these developments there emerged a better
balance in the sex ratios, for during the earlier decades the male component was predominant. Consequently, from 1941 onwards the growth
in the Chinese and Indian populations is to be considered near wholly a
natural increase.

Overseeing this new emerging demographic and economic structure
was the hard core of British administrators who from the latter eighteenth
century gradually began to direct the affairs of the country. Penang together with Province Wellesley and Malacca were governed directly as
Straits Settlements. The Sultanates of Perak, Selangor, Negri Sembilan,
and Pahang were designated as Federated Malay States by 1896, with the

Sultans conducting much of the affairs of State through a British resident. The other Sultanates of Kelantan, Trengganu, Kedah and Perlis were in turn granted British protection by 1909 and Johore in 1914. Collectively known as the Unfederated Malay States, their Sultans nevertheless had to accommodate the presence of British advisors. Under this calculated creep of British tutelage, stabilized by small numbers of troops both British and Indian and by a multi-racial police force, British entrepreneurs and planters as well as Chinese and Indian businessmen and other European mercantilists including even a few North American adventurers, took an overwhelming share of the mercantile and commercial sector. On the other hand the elite Malays maintained their presige through hereditary rights and as administrators using the English medium. For the proletariat, that is the majority of the Asian peoples, life continued in the vein of the traditional peasant. The end product of the foregoing sequence of events leaves one with an intriguing situation of present-day imbalances in respect of regional disparities in levels of economic development, characteristics of settlements, variable ethnic attributes and a mozaic of cultural associations. The latter in turn gives rise to fascinating social situations and behavioural patterns of curious proportions.[16] Where else in the world for example would someone proceed to order with much aplomb an imported sirloin steak, done medium rare mind you, and then smother it completely with hot chili sauce?

Regional and Socio-Economic Imbalances

Table 1,2 attempts to depict the more obvious imbalances. The disparity between the western and eastern sectors of the peninsula becomes more so if it is borne in mind that the greater weight of the statistics for Johore, and to a lesser extent for Pahang, are applicable to the western sectors of these two states. The statistics show quite convincingly that

54

PLATE 18
Core of Malacca: Portuguese,
Dutch and British period buildings.

PLATE 19
Rubber plantation and tin mines.
Inset shows tin dredge.

the bulk of the West Malaysian population is in the western sector. The figures also show the marked concentration of the Chinese and Indian communities in the western area, and in respect of crop distributions and the mining of tin a similar dominance is all too apparent. In summary, these patterns of distribution can be attributed to trends of historical impact compounding the physical environmental attractiveness of the western region as outlined in a preceding section.

The western lands have proved the more amenable to settlement.[17] Their alluvial deposits carry the world's largest accumulations of cassiterite from which tin is derived (Plate 19). The only exceptions to these are the sporadic distribution of similar deposits in Southeast Johore and west of Kuantan in Pahang, and of course there is the world's second largest load mine for tin at Sungei Lembing just north of Kuantan. Furthermore, the earliest plantations were in Penang and Province Wellesley with sugar as the principal commercial crop through the second half of the nineteenth century. The plantation economy really gained momentum with the introduction of rubber at the beginning of the twentieth century and nearly all the major estates were in the better drained terrain of the western lands. The cultivation of oil palm too made a moderate impact in the same sectors from around the 1930's. The early development in the western sector of roads, railways, bridges and ports from the mid-nineteenth century onwards further intensified the fundamental environmental advantage of this area. Even as late as 1959 only two rivers on the eastern littoral were bridged; primitive ferries doubled the duration, for example, of a journey by automobile between Kuantan and Kota Bharu at the best of times. In southeast Pahang and northeast Johore roads were non-existent till the latter 1960's. Furthermore, no railway was ever planned through the length of the eastern littoral. The cross country railway from Gemas in Johore to Tumpat in Kelantan was not completed till 1931 and is still

TABLE 1,2

WEST MALAYSIA: SELECTED DEMOGRAPHIC AND ECONOMIC STATISTICS

	Area in sq.mi.	Pop. in '000 1957	Pop. in '000 1970	Density per sq.mi. 1957	Density per sq.mi. 1970	% of Total Pop. 1957	% of Total Pop. 1970	% of Chinese 1957	% of Chinese 1970	% of Indian 1957	% of Indian 1970	Others 1957	Others 1970	% of total cult. 1970	% of cult. land	Rubber % Estate	Rubber % Smallholder	Coconut % Estate	Coconut % Smallholder	% of Rice	% of Oil Palm	% of Misc. Crop	% of Tin
Perlis	310	91	121	293	390	1.4	1.4	0.7	0.6	0.2	0.3	2.6	4.1	1.2	44.3	0.1	0.4	-	0.7	6.6	-	1.1	0.3
Kedah	3660	701	955	192	261	11.2	10.8	6.2	5.9	9.3	8.6	16.1	22.2	11.7	35.2	11.8	9.2	-³	6.1	29.2	1.0	7.5	0.9
Penang	400	570	775	1430	1939	9.1	8.8	14.0	13.9	9.6	9.6	10.7	18.7	2.3	64.3	1.2	1.6	4.1	8.0	4.0	1.0	3.3	-
Perak	7890	1221	1569	155	199	19.5	17.8	23.1	21.3	25.4	23.8	12.8	6.0	14.9	20.8	11.7	15.7	61.1	15.8	13.0	12.2	22.5	57.9
Selangor	3166	1012	1631	320	515	16.1	18.5	21.0	24.2	29.5	32.1	19.4	19.4	10.5	36.7	14.3	5.5	29.2	20.0	5.2	22.1	10.4	30.6
Negri Sembilan	2550	364	482	143	189	5.8	5.5	6.4	5.9	8.0	8.3	5.2	3.0	8.7	37.7	17.5	8.7	-	.2	3.2	3.2	3.9	1.1
Malacca	640	291	404	460	631	4.6	4.6	5.2	5.1	3.3	3.4	3.3	4.2	3.0	51.1	2.1	4.1	-	2.5	3.1	0.8	2.4	0.4
Johore	7321	927	1277	127	174	14.8	14.5	16.8	16.1	10.1	9.1	18.1	8.9	24.7	37.2	29.3	28.7	-³	28.9	2.4	34.2	20.4	3.0
Kelantan	5746	505	686	88	119	8.1	7.8	1.2	1.2	0.9	0.6	8.6	10.5	7.6	14.6	3.3	7.2	-	5.2	18.8	1.6	8.6	-
Trengganu	5050	278	405	55	80	4.4	4.6	0.8	0.7	0.4	0.3	0.8	0.7	4.9	10.7	2.0	4.8	1.8	4.0	8.8	6.1	7.1	1.9
Pahang	13873	313	505	23	36	5.0	5.7	4.6	5.1	3.3	3.9	2.4	2.3	10.5	8.3	16.7	14.1	3.3³	5.6	5.6	17.7	12.7	3.9

Sources: Population and Housing Census of Malaysia 1970, Government Press, Kuala Lumpur.
Statistical Digest, West Malaysia, Ministry of Agriculture and Lands.
Government Press, Kuala Lumpur, 1969

Note: 1. Percentages, except where otherwise indicated, are with reference to totals for all of West Malaysia.
2. Percentages refer to total cultivated area of each State.
3. Aggregate figure for the States indicated.

to be considered more as a capillary rather than a vital artery.

It is no wonder then that the Chinese, the peoples of the sub-continent of India and the Indonesians, gathered in strength in the western sector.[18] The tin mining industry utilized a dominantly Chinese work force, and the plantations provided both the Chinese and Indians with stable work opportunities. The construction of roads, railways, bridges and telecommunication lines in the same sector provided the unskilled as well as the skilled Indians, Pakistanis and Sikhs in particular with added opportunities for a profitable livelihood. The urban centres which grew up as a consequence of these developments, became lucrative domiciles of the commercial minded Chinese and Indian communities. The comparatively limited presence of the urban Malay is then a curious accident of history; the unskilled Malay is a town dweller more on sufferance and the professional Malay, overwhelmingly in the administrative cadres, is there because of the patronage of the British. A further analysis of the near self-explanatory statistics in Table 1, 2 is tantamount to an exercise in redundancy, but certain hidden implications need further elucidation.

The first of these relate to the issue of a multi-ethnic society. The presence of a variety of ethnic groups and the implications of British rule, including the use of the English language as an index to opportunity, duplicate in a sense the nature and structure of society already described in relation to Singapore. The overall parallels are there, but, a few basic differences are of significance. The first is that morphologically and functionally, unlike in Singapore, a compelling duality exists between town and country in West Malaysia. The second is that the Malay outnumbers the other Asian groups; 49 percent of the total population is Malay, 37 percent Chinese and 11 percent Indian. Third, there is the paradoxical situation that the urban centres, including the capital city of Kuala Lumpur, are functionally and economically Chinese. Furthermore, the Chinese together with Europeans are the principal operators of the large business cartels. It is also worthwhile noting then that the urban ratios, variously put at between eighteen to twenty percent, are somewhat inflated. Many of the so-called urban units have few of the amenities usually associated with towns and a large number of them are outgrowths of the 'new villages' designed as security centres during the Malayan Emergency.[19] (Plate 20). Fourth, it is the Malay hierarchy, bolstered by the Malay proletariat, that succeeded to the British tenets of administrative and political leadership when the Federation of Malay, the present day West Malaysia, won its initial independence in 1957. Fifth, there is the vital and paradoxical condition that it is the bulk of the Malays that are at the lower end of the scale of economic well being: a dominantly unrewarding commercial status simply does not provide the springboard for creative involvement in civic affairs at least in modern terms.

Besides this there is the obvious fact that the majority of the Malays in this particular context belong to a disassociated society in a spatial sense as well. Some may be of the opinion that this detachment of the Malay, is a product of a policy of 'divide and rule' by the British. The more charitable explanation is perhaps that the British had a more discerning awareness of the variance of oriental cultures than any other colonial power in the tropics. The Malay by his very nature, his unpressured pattern of life, his attitude to land as a source of sustenance rather than of profit and his Muslim faith is a vastly different individual from the more purposeful Chinese and Indian compatriots. Here it must be remembered that there were possibly no more than 250,000 peoples of Malay stock living at a leisurely pace when the British took over the Malay peninsula. In the case of the two immigrant groups, hunger, thirst and population pressure in their home domiciles had undoubtedly already

PLATE 20
Main street of Bentong, West Malaysia.

PLATE 21
Malay kampong landscape:
Rice fields, coconut and rubber.

reconditioned their life styles and attitudes towards more purposeful forms
of production.

Consequently, if one were to set aside the elite from among all the
Asian groups in West Malaysia for the moment, the following generaliz-
ations appear apt.[20] The average Chinese is a hardworking miner or lum-
berjack, a commercially-oriented rice cultivator, market gardener or
producer of rubber on well managed small-holdings, and a circumspect
salesman. In respect of truck farming the Chinese steal a march on the
other ethnic groups; pig, poultry and fish rearing are judiciously combined with vegetable growing, and organic manure including night soil
is freely used. These associations provide a closed nutrient cycle in
which every conceivable element is utilized towards maximizing production. The Indian in a similar category is a diligent wet field farmer, a
loving herdsman, a delicate-fingered rubber tapper, a hard-working labourer or gardener and a wily trader. The Malay is geared more to subsistence farming, or at best to the raising of cash to meet basic needs,
irrespective of whether he is a rice farmer, fisherman, garden cropper
or a cultivator of rubber small-holdings; the art of accumulating capital
as a means to an investment spiral is thereby compromised. Some have
over-generalized on such traits by categorizing the Malay as being in-
dolent. Nothing could be farther from the truth. The Malay through
historical circumstances is simply unsystematic, despite his putting in as
many hours of labour as the other Asians. The singular point to be made
here is that the majority of the Malays were propelled from the 'gatherer
stage' of horticulture and fishing to reliance on cash receipts from perennial tree crops, particularly haphazard plantings of rubber through a process of imitation (Plate 21). On the other hand the other Asian peasants
had evolved through all stages of more arduous food farming prior to commercial perennial tree-crop farming becoming the vogue, if not the

scourge, of Southeast Asian agrarian societies. It must also be borne in mind that the Muslim precept of the Puasa month (the period of fasting) constrains a Malay's endeavours.

The commonplace life styles and attitudes of the Chinese, Indian and Malay can perhaps best be demonstrated by the following example. Imagine a set of food stalls side by side at a roadside halt. In deference to food habits, some the product of religious scruples or for that matter the lack of them as the case may be, there are likely to be three types. The Chinese stalls are likely to display a variety of noodles and meats, including pork, together with non-alcoholic and alcoholic beverages. The Indian shops will perhaps have rice, chicken, fish, mutton, pulses, tea and milk. But beef will be absent because of the constraints of Hinduism. The Malay stalls will offer seafood, rice, beans, a variety of meats other than pork, and an assortment of sweetened non-alcoholic drinks. Pork and alcohol are taboo to adherents of the Muslim faith. A Chinese coming upon this scene is likely to stride towards a stall operated by his own kind, the Indian will hurry to his countrymen's shop and the Malay will saunter to one operated by his brethern. This is indicative of a preference born of a cultural heritage rather than of abject sectionalism. It is also important at this juncture to point out to the untravelled reader that it is not segregation but interpositioning that characterises the social scene in West Malaysia. More suggestive still the Chinese is likely to reach into his pocket for money whilst he is placing his order. This is a near common example of Chinese pragmatism and acceptance of each others' work ethics. The Indian purchaser is likely to dally around and then be invited by his compatriot to sample one of his favourite dishes, perhaps at a discount. Both parties feel they have achieved a bargain. This is the kind of transaction that typifies Indian subtlety and thrift. The Malay on the other hand is likely to inquire of his bretheren's family while re-

plenishing himself, and to offer similar hospitality in return on their meeting
again. This is a fair index of the average Malay's marked conviviality and
a living pattern based on expectancy and reciprocity. All three attitudes
have their merits in the context of the modern world. Furthermore, who is
to decide which of the three is the better?

The various associations described, ranging from basic attitudes, modes
of occupation and allied levels of earnings, need further qualification.
West Malaysian society is not only multi-ethnic but truly pluralistic, and
the economic base lacks a singular motivation for it is a dual if not a complex one. There is no clear-cut division even in an economic sense, between peasant subsistence farmer and urban producer.[21] The bulk of the
Chinese and Indians at proletariat level fall within the latter category,
the majority of the Malays find themselves between two stools. When those
from the lower strata are amalgamated with the elite or salaried workers
from among the different ethnic groups, then the present-day aspirations
as well as the motivations of decision-making in the interests of bettering
the lot of society as a whole, and of consolidating the various peoples
into a stable national entity, assume intricate proportions.

The Crucial Exercise in Democracy

At this juncture it is perhaps of value to reflect on a few important
considerations that have a bearing on the above exercise. The first of
these could be demonstrated by attempting to recast history. If the Port-
ugues had held on to the Malay Peninsula, the pattern of impact might
have had the following progression: the awe of the cross, the weight of
arms, haphazard extraction of resources, social intermingling and implied
assimilation, leisure leading to lethargy and ultimate petrification. It
is worthwhile noting here that Portugal remains the only real colonial
power based on the old world order in the 1970's, and Portuguese Timor,

within the seething Indonesian realm, is a stark reminder; even the Indonesians have apparently not woken up to the existence of this sleepy residual. On the other hand if it were the Dutch who dominated Malaya, then one could visualize a progression of pompous authority, the dream of a home from home (there were over 250,000 Dutch in the East Indies at the heyday of Empire), the quest for infinite profit, ambivalence when the latter was not possible and a legacy of an administrative and executive vacuum in the end. But it was the British that gained and held the Malay peninsula until the end of colonial rule in 1957. They did so with a judicious mixture of power tinged with benevolence, and with an exhibition of calculated appreciation of local situations softening the appropriation of all things of consequence. The pattern of administration, social values, and the economic framework were converted to the British mould where and when it mattered most; it was the stylish thing to do. For example, the Malay Sultans were shown their place but allowed to keep it, together with their privileged trappings of civic authority and their feudal domains. The rank and file from among the Malay proletariat were allowed to go their own way with unoccupied lands adjacent to traditional settlements being demarcated as Malay Reservations for their future use, while the emerging Malay bureaucrat schooled in English was carefully worked in as a servicing link. The Chinese traits of astute mercantilism at all social levels were recognised and then procured for further capital gains, and the Indian's attributes of studied loyalty were capitalized upon both at professional and more menial levels. All untenured land was expropriated as Crown Land; vast extents remained as forest reserves, others alienated to plantation interests, and the remainder left as potential forestry reserves or as agricultural land. There was nothing very wrong in doing so was there? More so because as the beginning of the nineteenth century not more than three percent of the land area was settled.

The second point of consequence is that more peoples of Malay stock entered the country from the East Indian archipelago under the British umbrella then were there previously. Census reports up to the 1950's attempted to differentiate between Aboriginee, Malay and Indonesian elements. Current census reports amalgamate these groups under the single category of Malaysians. If not for this exercise in semantics the oft-emphasized dominance of the 'true' Malay in the demographic structure of West Malaysia would be somewhat diluted. The situation here depicted has some deep socio-political consequences. Current ardour in the nationalistic context is more often than not expressed in terms of the Malays - the Malay language, Malay life styles and the Muslim faith. But many persons from the Indian subcontinent and mainland China have equal claims to being considered Bumi Putras or 'sons of the soil' through longer periods of residence than some Malays. However, fair-minded the leading politicians and elite of the day (irrespective of their ethnic heritage) may be, the point under consideration becomes an abrasive one at the more common social levels of allegiance to a cause or to authority. In this latter human setting the situation becomes even more complex owing to the existence of a dual heirarchy. On the one hand the rural Malay tends to focus one eye on the old-order feudal ladder which extends from the Penghulu (Village Headmen), to the Mentri Besar (Chief State Executive) and then to the Sultan. Here it has to be noted that the titular sovereign head of Malaysia (the Agong) is now elected from among the Sultans in turn. On the other hand, the rural Malay tends to focus the other eye on his local political representative, on his representative in the State Assembly, and thence on his idol in the Federal Legislature. The latter sequence is a product of British tutelage and represents an exercise in government based on classical party politics. If one had a truly egalitarian society the thought processes essential to the

65

latter would have had more substance. But, since gross economic disparities aligned to ethnic cleavages are obvious the exercise in democracy
turns itself into a game in ethnocentric fraternalism. Consequently, when
it comes to a question of a quest for advancement, or self-preservation,
the political system as it stands invariably tends to breed communalism.
In turn, communalism if unduly frustrated leads to marked social discord.

A SUMMARY OF THE EAST MALAYSIAN SETTING

In comparison to the relatively developed landscapes of West Malaysia,
the topography of a high proportion of Sarawak and Sabah can be characterized as 'green desert'. The compactness and comparatively massive nature
of the island of Borneo makes it a virtual equatorial exclave from an ecological point of view, rather than a unit typical of the monsoon lands of
Southeast Asia. It is a land of sparse populations and of highly secluded
indigenous groups. The distinctiveness of these groups is emphasized through
the separation of their traditional habitats by environmental frontiers such
as swamps inland of coastal flats, imposing interfluve areas between one
catchment and another, and rugged crests isolating interior basins and plains.
Sarawak extending over 48,000 square miles has a population of approximately 976,000 persons, while Sabah with an area of a little over 29,000
square miles has about 654,000 people. The average population densities
for these two States are therefore 20 and 23 per square mile respectively,
and contrasts markedly with the overall figure of 174 persons per square
mile for West Malaysia.

The evolution of the topographic scene in both East Malaysian territories until recently is best explained by the statement that 'contacts were
peripheral and interests centrifugal'.[22] The island of Borneo, parts of
which in early times were under the overlordshp of the Sultanate of Brunei,
was situated well away from the 'pre-developed' Southeast Asian culture

66

hearths of that area.[23] Even pre-occidental contacts by Indian and Arab groups were emphemeral, while Chinese traders sought profit in such curious items as monkeys' gallstones, rhinoceros horns and hornbill casques. Certainly a few Chinese did settle in some coastal niches, and the Muslim faith spread to the elite Brunei Malays and some indigenes such as the Melanau in Sarawak, as was the case in West Malaysia but with much less penetrative effect. During the subsequent phase of initial European mercantilism Borneo was incidental to the evolving pattern of trade routes between the occident and the orient. Furthermore, even when the phase of territorial apportioning necessarily emerged the island of Borneo became a bone of contention between the chief protagonists, Britain and Holland, more as an alternative to leaving a vacuum than as a compulsive need for acquisition.

Following the Anglo-Dutch Treaty of 1824, the southern portion of Borneo (now Indonesian Kalimantan) came under the purview of the Dutch, and North Borneo (now Sabah), Sarawak and the little enclave of Brunei (now the independent Sultanate of Brunei) were in due course to become a loose preserve of the British (Figure 2,2). But the British lion had apparently spent its strength, because other than for the establishment of a naval outpost on the island of Labuan off the northwest coast of Borneo in 1847 and the later extension of protection over the Sultanate of Brunei, North Borneo and Sarawak in contrast to Malaya and Singapore remained in a state of limbo. Consequently there emerged two unique examples of territorial management in Southeast Asia in respect of the two orphans. Sarawak became the domain of James Brooke in 1841 and remained a family possession until after the second world war,[24] and North Borneo came under the North Borneo Chartered Company in 1881.[25]

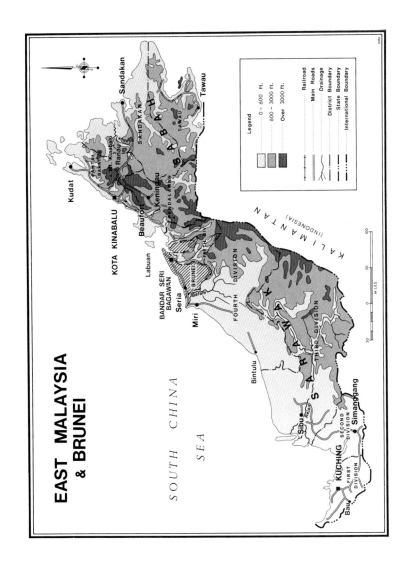

FIGURE 2,2   East Malaysia: Location Map.

From the Brookes to Colonial Status in Sarawak

The acquisition of Sarawak by James Brooke reads almost like a fairy tale. A tract smaller than the present First Division of Sarawak around Kuching, came into the hands of the adventurous Britisher on his quelling a revolt which flared up against the then ineffective Sultan of Brunei, though not without a show of force by a unit of the Royal Navy. Said the Sultan, 'if you will stay and help me I will give you the country...its government and trade shall be yours, and you will have the title of Rajah.'[26] From then on the Brooke family extended its suzerainty over all of the native tribal chiefs and their peoples. They did so with a curious blend of benevolent feudal patronage, an eye for pecuniary gain and extraction of tribute, and harsh parental authority. For example, the placid Land Dyaks were protected from the inroads of the Chinese miners. The latter in turn contributed a share of the antimony and gold to the 'White Rajah's coffers. The adventurous Sea Dyaks (Ibans) were subjected to periodic punitive expeditions by the Brookes; the Ibans penchant for pirating and head hunting was no doubt out of step with the quest for orderly extension of prestige and also contrary to Christian ethic.

Once law and order had been introduced the motto for economic gain was to 'proceed at the pace of the natives'. Sarawak therefore remained in essence the preserve of a wide array of fascinating native cultures, each with a fairly specific regional distribution.[27] (Table 2,2). These groups form the real Bumi-Putras of Sarawak: primitive yet charming, initially suspicious but subsequently loyal, animists by and large but with folklore and dance that is intriguing, underclad longhouse dwellers perhaps but with a local civic sense far surpassing that of many so-called sophisticated urbanites anywhere in the world.[28] (Plate 22).

Over one hundred years of Brooks family rule left a quaint and rustic world in the interior and a disorderly semi-urban and rural morphology along

TABLE 2, 2
EAST MALAYSIA: SELECTED DEMOGRAPHIC STATISTICS BY DISTRICTS AND ETHNIC GROUPS[1]
SARAWAK

Ethnic Group	Melanau		Sea Dayaks		Land Dayaks		Other Indigenes		Malay		Chinese		Others		Total	
	No.	%	No.	%	No.	%	No.	%	No.	%	No.	%	No.	%	No.	%
Division																
First	427	.04	27,927	2.8	81,263	8.3	559	.1	99,990	10.2	129,961	13.3	7,036	.7	346,973	35.5
Second	102	.01	84,263	8.6	325	.03	436	.04	36,347	3.7	15,258	1.6	169	.01	137,260	14.1
Third	44,802	4.6	138,356	14.2	953	.1	8,064	.8	16,288	1.7	109,440	11.2	1,133	.1	319,036	32.7
Fourth	7,837	.8	47,544	4.9	645	.1	27,;44	2.8	17,371	1.8	34,230	3.5	1,147	.1	135,918	13.9
Fifth	66	0	4,734	.5	90	0	13,747	1.4	12,713	1.3	5,131	.5	250	.02	36,731	3.8
Total:	53,234	5.5	302,984	31.0	83,276	8.6	49,960	5.1	182,709	18.7	294,020	30.1	9,735	1.0	975,918	100.0

SABAH

Ethnic Group	Kadazan		Murut		Bajau		Other Indigenes		Malays		Chinese		Indonesians		Others		Total	
	No.	%	No.	%	No.	%	No.	%	No.	%	No.	%	No.	%	No.	%	No.	%
District																		
Tawau	4,434	.7	850	.1	22,783	3.5	12,299	1.9	3,375	.5	29,172	4.5	22,519	3.4	18,729	2.9	114,161	17.5
Sandakan	11,693	1.8	464	.1	4,403	.7	35,221	5.4	4,365	.6	38,541	5.9	9,413	1.5	9,691	1.5	113,791	17.4
Pantai Barat	129,008	19.7	904	.1	48,290	7.3	40,367	6.2	4,936	.8	52,754	8.1	3,992	.6	6,836	1.0	287,087	43.9
Pendalaman	38,838	5.9	29,010	4.4	1,702	.3	31,768	4.9	1,279	.2	14,243	2.2	2,993	.5	1,203	.2	121,036	18.5
Labuan	539	.1	71	.01	93	.01	5,976	.8	4,410	.7	4,799	.7	609	.1	692	.1	17,189	2.7
Total:	184,512	28.2	31,299	4.8	77,271	11.8	125,631	19.2	18,365	2.8	139,509	21.4	39,526	6.1	37,151	5.7	653,264	100.0

Source: Population and Housing Census of Malaysia, 1970, Government Press, Kuala Lumpur.
Note: All percentages are with reference to aggregate fitures for Sabah and Sarawak respectively.

PLATE 22
Longhouses, home-crafts and native attire in Sarawak.

PLATE 23
Coastal kampong of Melanau peoples.

PLATE 24
Expanses of shifting cultivation
in Iban territory.

PLATE 25
Docks at up-river port of Sibu.

the lower riverine and coastal reaches. The inland ranges of mass shifting cultivation, the hill padi plots and the longhouses of the largely animistic Ibans presented an entirely different world when compared with the coastal linear patterns of stilt-houses, the sago plots and fishing gear of the Muslim Melanau. (Plates 23 and 24). The primitive units of horticulture, rudimentary swamp padi plots and haphazard rubber groves of the Land Dyaks immediately back of the coast in south Sarawak were a far cry away from the blow pipe and poisoned darts of the wandering Punan in the deep interior.[29] The exotic but shabby upriver port towns of Kuching and more so Sibu, dominated by the Chinese, stood apart from the unruly mining towns such as Bahu as well as from the orderly pepper vine plots and rubber small-holdings operated by members of the same community. The Muslim Malay sauntered in and out of the rurban fringe and later made his presence felt in the emerging bureaucratic machine.

There were only a handful of small rubber estates, a minimal town road net with no real through linkages and no railways. As a consequence there was the conspicuous absence of the Indian. Most traffic was by boat; exhilarating journeys along swirling rivers such as the Rejan and Baram into the interior, or anxious ones from point to point along the coast for nasty currents, storms and pirates prevailed. Land tenure systems and crop-use patterns were chaotic. The former ranged from undefinable though recognized tribal land, through vaguely demarcated though gazetted forest reserves and legally assessed private holdings. For no part of Sarawak were there topographic maps to match the quality and detail of those available for the Malay peninsula, nor were cadastral maps available for much of the permanently settled area. It is for these reasons that agricultural statistics, comparable to those in Table 1, 2 could not be set out in Table 2, 2 Sarawak even today can be described as a land of random harvests. In general terms about 20 percent of the terrain can be classified as agricult-

73

ural land. Of this total about 60 percent is under rubber small-holdings,
5 percent under other permanent use such as rubber estates, padi fields
and pepper groves, and the balance under non-permanent tillage with
shifting cultivation being dominant (Plate 24). The only tangible
aspects of early modernism were the oil fields at Miri developed in 1912,
the limited port facilities at Kuching and Sibu (Plate 25), the few
limousines of the wealthy traversing the restricted road net enclaves, and
of course the Christian missions. The latter, particularly the Jesuits and
their so-called detribalized wards, mainly from among the Chinese and a
lesser number of indigenes were dominant in the few townships and areas
inland of them.

Modernism as one has come to accept the term in respect of contemporary Southeast Asia is the product initially of the second world war.
Guns and grenades came before land use capability surveys, British bully
beef and the Japanese variety of hard tack before reliable yields from well
organized rice fields, and military aircraft made their impact prior to more
civic if not civil modes of overland transport. The Brookes left a land of
petulant 'polyglot' opportunists in the towns, and a much larger family of
doting and civil mystics in the vast interior. The Japanese left a befuddled
populace and a disarrayed economy. The old order had changed and it
was beyond the scope of the Brookes to remuster. The financial outlays for
reconstruction were beyond them and the mood of the post-war world was
irreconcilable with the past. Private estates the size of Sarawak were no
longer fashionable, though the allegiance of the indigenous chiefs and
their peoples remained as sentimental as ever. Sarawak was ceded by the
last 'White Rajah' to Britain and became a Crown Colony in 1946. Ironically it was one of the last accretions to the British Raj when the Empire
itself was beginning to wilt elsewhere. The second addition was North
Borneo.

From Company Management to Colony in North Borneo

The story of the emergence of Chartered Company rule necessarily concerns itself at first with the activities of a batch of goblins.[30] The Sultan of Sulu had laid claims to a fair proportion of the land held by the Sultan of Brunei. The Portuguese, Spanish, Germans and Americans too were inquisitive. Ultimately it was left to an American 'consul' (?) in Manila to obtain a lease from the Sultan of Brunei with mercenary intent, for the final lessee was to be the American Trading Company then based in Hong Kong. Ultimately it was an Englishman who won the claim on behalf of a shadowy Anglo-Austrian consortium, with the consent of both the Sultans of Brunei and Sulu in 1878. This led to a Royal Charter being granted in 1881; a stamp of legality being put as it were on a questionable sequence of manipulations.

The activities of the Company could be likened, in a loose manner, to those of the Hudson's Bay Company in Canada. The quest for trade and profits through exploitation was the main motivation, and restricted modernism by way of port towns and the circumscribed, if not distressing acculturization of the indigenes, then numbering only about 100,000 persons, the end result. The Company paved the way for speculators. Dutch and German pioneers tried their hand at tobacco growing in the eastern districts in the latter nineteenth century and British interests opened rubber plantations in the western districts in the early twentieth century. The Chinese, mainly the Hakka community, were encouraged into the wild land in large numbers. It was they who helped build the port towns of Jesselton (now Kota Kinabalu), Kudat, Sandakan and Tawau, the few roads, and the railway from Jesselton through the main rubber plantation tract to Beaufort, Tenom and Weston (Figure 2,2). A thin scatter of Indians, including Sikhs, then helped service the railway and the telecommunications. From humble beginnings the Chinese prospered in time to match their occidental masters in commerce and oppulence. Many of the richest tycoons in the country today are Chinese rubber and timber barons. In the wake of increased opportunity there was also an influx of Indonesians (particularly Javanese) and Filipinos (Table 2, 2). They augmented the labour supply needed for the plantations as well as the timber, sago and fishing trades. Enterprising Englishmen ventured into the interior and organized outposts of territorial control.

The alien reigned supreme; they let down roots while the indigene was uprooted. For example the Kadazans (Dusun) of the western littoral became near lifeless appendages of the new plantation cum town complexes. The Muruts fell prey to new strains of malaria brought in by the Javanese, and the numbers of these interior folk declined steadily. Rural depopulation became an obvious trend through much of the hinterland. The small percentage of coastal Malays remained dormant and their practice of the Muslim faith, as well as by small numbers of Kadazan and Bajau converts, displayed widely different levels of orthodoxy. The Christian missions, of course, achieved most success amongst the Chinese, though converts there were from among the indigenes.

North Borneo in contrast to Sarawak provided handsome profits in time to cartels and individuals. The harvests of rubber, timber, coconut, tobacco, sago and hemp, were by no means random. These provided frontiers of opportunity to the honourably industrious a well as to wiley manipulators. Over 50 percent of the total of approximately 180,000 acres of rubber today are under plantation management. These acreages plus those under coconut, wet rice fields, village gardens and other permanent cropland comprise only about 6 percent of the total land area.[31] Over 75 percent of the rugged interior eastward of the Crocker range, capped by 13,450 foot Mt. Kinabalu, is largely forest and therein lies the mainstream of wealth in the country; Sandakan can be put among the world's leading timber ports. Elsewhere in the interior, hill padi and shifting cultivation, covers around 12 percent of the land and supports the way of life of the inland native. On the other hand the principal ports and interior towns provided more amenities than like locales in Sarawak. Jessleton, Sandakan and Tawau were not only boom towns, but also rather picturesque ones at that, when compared to Kuching, Sibu or Bintulu, (Figure 2,2), because of the less swampy and more scenic coastal physiography of much of North Borneo (Plate 26). Furthermore, the greater presence of European planters and British administrators meant that occidental facilities and furbishings peripheral, to say tennis, became near essentials irrespective of whether the game was played in Kudat or Beaufort.

The demise of Company rule can be explained in terms of considerations similar to those that affected Sarawak during and after the Japanese occupation. Jesselton, Sandakan and Tawau for example, were in shambles. They were key locations which felt the weight of allied bombs during the closing stages of the British comeback, and the Japanese invader in turn vented his frustations on structures or equipment of any economic value when further resistance proved futile. North Borneo, a war-torn land, was also handed over to Britain in 1946. Unlike the Brookes in Sarawak, however, the Chartered Company left a legacy of a higher level of private enterprise geared to shades of British administrative procedures, the framework of a superior land communication system and a fundamentally more productive commercial agricultural base. On the other hand, the indigenous tribal groups were left as less cohesive entities. The Brookes for the most part dealt with ethnic groups, and through their leaders. The Company, by and large, dealt in land and labour; the latter being dominantly alien. The plight of the indigenes who did not fall into the scheme of things in North Borneo can be likened, though in an obviously different context and with less intensity, to that of the Canadian Indian.

FROM COLONIAL RULE TO THE MALAYSIAN ASSOCIATION

The first fifteen years of rule by the Colonial Office (1946-1960), in the two Borneo territories were devoted to programmes of economic re-construction and human rehabilitation.[32] Large amounts of money and material, as well as British administrative and technical personnel, were utilized to restore the image of Britain in the 'Far East'. The port towns were redeveloped, communications restored and agricultural settlement schemes for the peasantry were initiated particularly in North Borneo, for example, in the Keningau plains to the west and Labuk Valley in the east.[33] But progress was inevitably slow on account of the vastness of the territories and the high degree of inaccessibility. Furthermore, though qualified personnel were recruited in increasing numbers, their presence in the rural areas was thin and despite their efforts there was really little tangible improvement in the overall economic status of the colonies.

The somewhat stagnant position could in part be attributed to the fluctuating and often unrewarding prices for rubber, copra and sago in the world market. In fact the only enterprise which showed an upward progression was the timber trade. It is true that outboard motors and transistor radios became commonplace items in, for example, the eyes of the Muruts and Ibans, but these simply meant on the one hand that the mobility of the upriver trader was increased, and on the other, that the 'bright lights' of the coastal towns came within easier reach of the longhouse dweller. Consequently, in many an instance, slacks, brassieres and lipstick exemplified the beginnings of modernism. They were mere concessions though to the issue of development rather than worthwhile instruments. The indigenes became tied to two worlds, the old and the new, and were ill at ease with both.

The vital flimsy link in the anticipated chain of development, namely a comprehension of economic principles and attendant socio-political innovations, could not be improved upon in short order. Though the latter years of Chartered Company rule had introduced the limited elite from among the Chinese, Eurasians, Indian and Malays (of both early Brunei and Philippine lineage) to some of the rudimentary techniques of self-expression and self-determinism, the latter considerations were as has been the case in most 'developing' societies, revamped to serve the interests of group preservation. In Sarawak there were even fewer articulate local people. As far as the true indigenes in both territories were concerned, their brand of filial loyalty and traditional etiquette simply made them either curious onlookers or ambivalent participants. Even after fifteen years of colonial rule the legislatures of both territories consisted of nominated and ex-officio members, with the latter being dominantly British. This is to be taken as simple fact and not as a dart against the regime. One could perhaps make simple robots in fifteen years, but not those with even a fair degree of political awareness. Furthermore, when it came to even contemplating the necessary prerequisite of democracy, namely the exercising of a universal franchise the problem was near insurmountable. In Borneo, most people did not as yet make up their minds and speak for they were accustomed to speaking until their minds were made up; a ballot paper was neither significant nor even symbolic to the many who continued to live so very close to nature.

It was a voice from Kuala Lumpur, namely that of Malaya's first Prime Minister Tunku Abdul Rahman, with perhaps an echo from Whitehall, that thrust the Borneo territories into the era of modern socio-politics. What were the thoughts in the mind of the father figure of the Malayan Federation, which had gained its independence in 1957, when he first proposed the Malaysian Federation in 1961? Was it a mere premonition that all the Briish territories in Southeast Asia would do well to knit themselves together? There was a precedent in the West Indies, and besides there was the prospect of an ideological buffer against the inroads of communism from the north of the Asian mainland. If Britain was indeed going to pull out – post war colonies were truly expensive propositions – would not it be expedient to gather the apparently more pliable and dominantly non-Chinese peoples of Borneo into the fold? And, here it seemed profitable to include the oil rich Sultanate of Brunei, though it was administered in the manner of a resplendent sheikdom dominated by a multi-million dollar mosque built of Italian marble, and very reminiscent in an overall social sense of the features set out in a certain work.[34] After all, despite the ethnic complexities, the life styles in general of the peoples in the three States of Borneo were more akin to the basically 'land-oriented' peoples of Malaya than to the boisterous urban world of dominantly Chinese Singapore.[35] Even if Singapore had to be included, as was the case later on, though only for a short period, would it not have been nice if Whitehall held onto this unit for a bit longer even as a memento of past prestige? There was much to be gained in having a breathing space whilst replacing British tutelage in Borneo with socio-political schooling from Kuala Lumpur, before the inevitable union of the entire British realm in this part of the world took place. To any right-thinking person the historic, commercial and financial linkages, as well of those of kith and kin would make it so.[36]

Kuala Lumpur had its say, but the developments that were not anticipated were the bitter and harsh attitude of the Indonesians under Soekarno against so called British neo-colonialism, the Philippine reaction of resurrecting their claim to parts of North Borneo,[37] and the attempted coup in Brunei by an organization calling itself the North Kalimantan National Army which banked on support from Indonesia.[38] These factors hustled the timing of the creation of the new Federation and also affected its compo-

PLATE 26
Kota Kinabalu: Sector of port and town.

PLATE 27
Peasant land colonization project
under oil palm.

sition. Singapore hurried to join the new political entity, whilst Brunei remained the odd man out in September 1963. The Sultan of Brunei no doubt had second thoughts induced not only by the abortive rebellion, but also because he would obviously have to funnel in a high proportion of his substantial oil revenues into the coffers of the new Federation. Besides this, he was not at all certain of his own ranking in comparison to the other Sultans in Malaya; the titular sovereign head of the new Federation was to be chosen in turn from among the traditional rulers.

Through all this though, it was the British governors of Sarawak and North Borneo who acted as the spokesmen for the Bornean peoples; such was the general level of socio-political simplicity if not immaturity. If developments in West Malaysia had propelled the traditional peasantry from a state of long standing lethargy into the vibrancy of the mid-twentieth century, in Borneo they were thrown from seclusion into an era of confusion. Two stories bear repetition in this context. First, when a British parliamentary mission visited Sarawak prior to the cession to Britain in 1946 the following questions were reportedly asked of its members by local tribal leaders. Does the king intend to live in Kuching? If not, what would the cost be of getting to London to obtain a hearing?[39] Secondly, a decade or so later when Prince Philip visited North Borneo another source relates that the Chiefs of the Muruts and the women folk of the tribe alarmed by lowered birth rates, were prepared to extend their 'traditional open polygamous hospitality' to the visitor, and would have done so if not for the intervention of a timorous if not officious British bureaucrat![40] The foregoing should not be interpreted though as being indicative of a static level of appreciation. Given due time the indigene is highly adaptable to change. For example the Ibans in Sarawak have proved this by their contribution to the Sarawak Rangers one of the finest military units in Southeast Asia, by their work in the Miri oil fields and their competence in handling heavy mechanized road building equipment.

In a comparative sense then, whereas political awareness preceded or ran concurrently with the attainment of independence in what is now West Malaysia, the attempt at injecting this comprehension was made hurriedly in the East Malaysia of today once the Federation of Malaysia was thought of as being a near certainty. In this light and in a strictly academic sense the Borneo territories could be viewed as the 'African States' of Malaysia. The latter, when it was formed, was more an 'adhocracy' than a democracy. In such a pioneer situation self-determinism in Borneo began to exhibit itself in ethnic arrogance as was displayed by a few local sophisticates, and then in anti-British expatriate feelings. When the British expatriate was necessarily replaced by administrators technicians, teachers, police and army personnel from the Federation of Malaya (West Malaysia), they in turn were looked upon as 'coloured' expatriates. The end product has been a brand of Bornean chauvinism which still tends to persist.[41] The background of the successive Chief Ministers of Sabah to date is highly illuminative in this respect. The first was of Caucasian lineage who developed strong affinities with the Kadazans; this was an extension of the shadow of the Chartered Company perhaps! The second was Chinese and this could be taken as indicative of the intrinsic economic and implied political prestige of this community. The current incumbent is a very orthodox Muslim, Malay, but with his heritage harking back to the Sulu Islands, and this could be taken as a resurgence of the glory of the Muslim hierarchy of old. In both wings of Malaysia then, the multi-ethnic ethic, has shown a tendency from time to time to degenerate into exhibitions of cultural and also regional ethnocentricity. But despite these apparent notes of social and political discord the country still hangs together.

ACHIEVEMENTS IN THE FACE OF DISQUIET

For a 'developing' country the levels of achievement in many areas
of economic growth are indeed impressive. Within the scope of this paper,
however, it is possible to draw attention only to the more significant of
these. In the agricultural sector there has been a staggering extension of
state-sponsored, rural, peasant land colonization. In West Malaysia for
example, approximately 450,000 acres of new ground had been brought
under cultivation with high yield rubber and oil palm by 1973, and about
27,000 families settled on 120 colonization projects throughout the country
(Plate 27). This aspect of settlement is under the direction of the
Federal Land Development Authority.[42] The pride of this programme is the
Jengka Triangle regional project.[43] Further large schemes of a like nature
are to be implemented in the southeast sectors of both Pahang and Johore.
In East Malaysia, similar programmes are being carried out by local land
development boards, though the rate of development is not as impressive
largely because of the difficulties of communications and the paucity of
trained personnel. Much attention though, has to be given in this wing
to replanting existing old rubber small-holdings with new high yield vari-
eties. In addition to the extension of perennial tree crop farming, there
have been significant advances in implementing irrigated rice farming projects for the peasantry in West Malaysia. The most impressive of these is
the combined Muda and Pedu River projects in upper Kedah (Figure 1, 2).
This enterprise costing over M.$ 228 million has brought over 260,000
acres of padi lands in Kedah and Perlis under double-cropping for the
benefit of an estimated 325,000 peasant farm population.[44] A like project, though of smaller proportions, is now underway at Kemubu on the
lower Kelantan River. In East Malaysia strenuous efforts are being made
to increase production on existing rice acreages with government aid to
farmers. This infrastructure includes monetary subsidies, supply of high-

yield seed, fertilizers and even small motorized implements.[45] Large-scale
new irrigation and drainage projects however will take time to develop because the problems of hydraulic engineering in these pioneer territories
assume massive proportions.

Developments with regard to communications are no less impressive.
Here again West Malaysia takes pride of place. A journey through the
length of the east coast of the peninsula is no longer tedious, for all rivers
southward from Kelantan, inclusive of the mighty Pahang River have been
bridged. This programme left only two major rivers on the east coast, namely
the Rompin and Endau with ferry crossings in 1973. In addition a major trunk
road from Grik in North Perak through the northern mountain wilderness to
Kelantan is under construction. In East Malaysia the major developments
in the same field are the Simangang-Sibu link in Sarawak and the Ranau-
Sandakan one in Sabah. These endeavours will be overshadowed when the
trans East Malaysian road through the Crocker range, now under construction, is completed.[46] Considerable headway has also been made with regard
to port development. The new facilities at Port Klang (formerly Port Swettenham) provide for container traffic, and a new port is under construction
on the eastern arm of the Johore Strait. Sabah and Sarawak too are pro-
ceeding with port improvements and Kota Kinabalu and Sandakan in particular have achieved a new look. Air transportation is a vital link between
the two wings of Malaysia and all existing airfields in both areas have been
much improved, and a new international airport complementing that at
Subang, west of Kuala Lumpur, has now been completed at Senai, north of
Johore Bahru.

Industrial growth has up to now been largely restricted to West Malaysia. Petaling Jaya situated just west of Kuala Lumpur is the most significant complex, while others at Seremban and Johore Bahru are reaching
appreciable levels. (Plate 28). In addition new large-scale timber

and plywood factories and paper mills are being established in many areas. The principal ones in this respect are in Jengka, Kota Bahru and Kuala Trengganu. In regard to energy supplies, oil has been struck in the South China Sea immediately off Kuantan and preliminary drilling indicate worthwhile reserves.[47] In addition the Japanese are in the process of developing facilities for shipping liquified natural gas from the Miri fields in Sarawak.[48] Furthermore, West Malaysia boasts one of the largest capacity hydro-electric power stations in Southeast Asia which is located in the Cameron Highlands,[49] and yet another is being built at Temendor on the Upper Perak River with Canadian aid.[50] In East Malaysia a net of mini-hydroelectric plants are to be sited along the Rejan River.

From an overall point of view there is no denying that much progress has been made in developing the economy of both wings in Malaysia. But, East Malaysia is still not only an area of formidable challenges but a deficit area as well, with a generally unfavourable balance of trade.[51] It is also of importance to note that of the forty percent requirement of rice imports into Malaysia, thirty percent goes to the East wing. What is really significant though is that progress has been made despite the persistence of social disquiet.

Through the 1960's, sporadic instances of racial strife occurred in some locales in the peninsula and the climax was reached with the tragic civic disorders which followed the general elections of 1969. This led to a hiatus in the tempo of economic development and the harshness of the social situation prompted many an observer to predict dire forebodings for the future of Malaysia.[52] In Malaysia religion is apparently being used as a catalyst towards the achieving of a national identity; mass conversions of Kadazans and other indigenes in Sabah to the Muslim faith have been reported.[53] The following extract from the proceedings of the Chinese Muslim Association in Penang is also thought provoking: "...65 percent of the Malayan population were

Muslims in 1921. But this had dropped to 46 percent in 1970."[54] In one sense the call for increased participation in the Muslim faith can be looked upon as reasonable, for religion if soberly channeled could be a strong and positive motivating force in an entity such as Malaysia. On the other hand, when one considers the reported hindrances placed in the path of the Christian clergy, for example in Sabah in the latter part of 1973, then the Muslim movement lends itself to being labelled as near proselytism.[55] Furthermore, when questions pertaining to the foregoing were asked in the Federal Legislature in Kuala Lumpur it was obvious that the right hand (the West) was not aware of what the left (the East) was doing. To top it all there has been a marked resurgence of communist guerilla activity in the northern border regions of West Malaysia and in Sarawak. In the latter area many prominent Chinese businessmen and professionals were arrested in September 1973, for alleged dealings with the insurgents.

Despite the tremors referred to above, however, there are many redeeming features in the country. For example, the leading political party, namely the United Malay National Organization (U.M.N.O.) continues to work together with the Malayan Chinese Association and the Malayan Indian Congress. Furthermore, the extremist Pan Malayan Islamic Party, once the bane of U.M.N.O., is now back in the fold after adopting 'splinter tactics' in West Malaysia over many years. One can indeed take heart from developments such as these and hope that Bornean chauvinism too, will also disappear. Differences of opinion, and tricky if not distasteful situations of the kind outlined, will no doubt continue to arise from time to time, but there is hope for the future. In this respect the following anecdote attributed to Malaysia's first Prime Minister, that gentleman of uncommon common sense, seems appropriate. In recounting this however one hopes that Muslim readers will not take it literally or too seriously for that matter. Tunku Abdul Rahman once reportedly remarked to a gathering in Kuala Lumpur, from all the ethnic groups as well as from all social levels, that what the country needed most were 'more good Muslims who could also eat pork and drink brandy'. This statement had everyone reeling with laughter. There is much food for thought in the foregoing. First, it does imply categorically that all Malaysians, by virtue of their history of settlement, must necessarily be committed to the multi-ethnic ethic regardless of the disparities in levels of living between each other. Second, the statement suggests that the economic gap between the rank and file of the Malays and other indigenes on the one hand and their compatriots on the other needs to be narrowed, and that this should be the goal of all the peoples of the country. Third, the reaction of the gathering does illustrate the fact that Malaysians in general are peoples of basically good humour.

The fundamental problem in Malaysia today is not what has to be done or what is being done to lessen disparities, but the way things are done. Anyone in his right mind is agreed on the former, but there is a degree of insecurity when it comes to the latter. It is one thing, for example, to say that the Malays should have a greater share in commerce and industry as opportunities open up. It is an entirely different proposition to declare that entrepreneurs will not be allowed a factory licence unless they employ forty percent Malay workers. Most of the problems are in fact caused through misrepresentation of rational intent by lesser politicians who hurriedly attempt to tinker with the minds of the less sophisticated sectors of their electorates (Plate 29). Within such a society where admirable natural social graces are germane to all peoples and far in advance of their ability to cope with complicated administrative, economic and executive concepts, it seems fitting to venture the opinion that good humour, the basis of progress and stability in the cultural and territorial setting under review, must necessarily come from the heart and not the mind.

PLATE 28
Johore Bahru: New industrial and urban development, and causeway to Singapore.

PLATE 29
The multi-ethnic proletariat of West Malaysia.

A SPECULATIVE CONCLUSION

Will the two wings of Malaysia go the way of the former wings of Pakistan? In the latter situation the emergence of Bangladesh could in large part be attributed to the culminative effects of an inordinately long history of diverse traditions and the weight of man on the land. Egocentricism in West Pakistan finally induced ethnocentricism in Bangladesh. Though there is a diversity of traditions between West and East Malaysia it is in a nascent stage and both are essentially pioneer areas. This is both a source of strength and a sign of weakness, but with the former conditions currently outweighing the latter because there is a high level of interdependence. At the present time the East does lean more heavily on the West for economic advancement, but in the process of both partners growing up there is the prospect that an equalization rather than a separatist movement would take place.

One final conjecture is perhaps permissible. Will the maturing process extend itself to cover the Malaysia that might have been? Singaporeans need land and more flexible work opportunities to alleviate an increasing claustrophobic situation. West Malaysia could well economize, for instance, by taking more advantage of the established port of Singapore as an alternative to incurring huge expenses in promoting its own harbours. The oil, and also the revenues so derived, from Brunei would undoubtedly enhance the overall economic pattern. Furthermore, both the Sultanate and East Malaysia would profit from the administrative and technical expertise as well as the readily adaptable general labour supply available in Singapore and West Malaysia. The shortage of personnel in all categories is a critical problem in East Malaysia.

At the present time however much that is trivial, and perhaps even petty, seems to prevail. For example the once thriving Malaysia-Singapore Airlines has been broken up into two independent national airlines. The 'joint' currency system which prevailed for so long is no more, and the rubber market and stock exchanges have been separated. The mile long causeway between Singapore and West Malaysia is a traveller's nightmare; million-dollar establishments at each end now oversee the irritating procedures related to work permits, passports and customs inspection. Again, when Johore placed an export tariff on unprocessed timber to Singapore, the latter retaliated with an embargo on that not-too-easily-indulged-in but locally-appreciated fruit, the Durian. Consequently, the Malay peasantry in whose backyards this seasonal fruit grows bountifully were left with a reduced income and some Singaporeans possibly grew weaker; the Durian is believed to have aphrodisiac properties.

Hindrances of many kinds, the duplication of effort in many fields of economic growth and an uneconomic channelling of funds for civic and military purposes, are the obvious concommitants of the individualistic phase of history among the units of the former British realm in Southeast Asia. But underneath it all the territories are still interdependent to a high degree. Pronouncements to the contrary more often than not simply make waves from time to time. The fish of various hues, particularly the big ones, in the old and profitable pool encompassed by the Straits of Malacca and the South China Sea, still continue to swim placidly underwater. They may however surface together in due time for history is indeed cyclic.

REFERENCES

1. CARTER, Jean "Mangrove Succession and Coastal Change in South-west Malaya," Transactions and Papers. Institute of British Geographers, No. 26, 1959, pp. 79-88.

2. WARD, Marion "Port Swettenham and its Hinterland, 1900-1960," The Journal of Tropical Geography, 19 (1964), pp. 69-78.

3. DALE, W.L. "The Rainfall of Malaya," The Journal of Tropical Geography, 13 (1959), pp. 23-37 and 14 (1960), pp. 11-28.

4. ROFF, W.R. (ed.) Stories by Sir Hugh Clifford. Oxford University Press, 1966, especially pp. 14 and 15.

5. NOSSIN, J.J. "Relief and Coastal Development in Northeastern Johore," The Journal of Tropical Geography, 15 (1961), pp. 27-38.

6. WYATT-SMITH, J. "A Preliminary Vegetation Map of Malaya with Descriptions of the Vegetation Types," The Journal of Tropical Geography, 18 (1964), pp. 200-213.

7. DOBBY, E.H.G. "The Kelantan Delta," The Geographical Review, 41 (1951), pp. 226-255.

8. WIKKRAMATILEKE, R. "Mukim Pulau Rusa: Land Use in a Malayan Riverine Settlement," Journal of Tropical Geography, 11 (1958), pp. 1-31.

9. WARD, Marion "A Review of Problems and Achievements in the Economic Development of Independent Malaya," Economic Geography, 44 (1968), pp. 326-342.

10. SLIMMING, J. Temiar Jungle. London: John Murray, 1958. HOLMAN, D. Noone of the Ulu. London: W. Heinemann, 1958.

11. BARBER, N. War of the Running Dogs: Malaya 1948-1960. London: W. Collins, 1971.

12. WIKKRAMATILEKE, R. "Trends in Settlement and Economic Development in Eastern Malaya," Pacific Viewpoint, 3 (1962), pp. 27-50.

13. WHEELER, L.R. The Modern Malay. London: Allen and Unwin, 1928, especially pp. 118-145.

14. SWETTENHAM, F. British Malaya. London: Allen and Unwin, 1906.

15. OOI, Jin Bee Land, People and Economy in Malaya. London: Longmans, especially pp. 106-125.

16. BURGESS, A. The Malayan Trilogy. London: Penguin Books, 1973.

17. COURTENAY, P.P. A Geography of Trade and Development in Malaya. London: Bell, 1972, especially pp. 62-114.

18. SANDHU, K.S. "Chinese Colonization of Malacca," Journal of Tropical Geography, 15 (1961), pp. 1-26. "The Population of Malaya," Journal of Tropical Geography, 15 (1961), pp. 82-96.

19. SANDHU, K.S. "Emergency Resettlement in Malaya," Journal of Tropical Geography, 18 (1964), pp. 158-183.

20. WIKKRAMATILEKE, R. "Variable Ethnic Attributes in Malayan Rural Land Development," Pacific Viewpoint, 5 (1964), pp. 35-50.

21. FRYER, D.W. and JACKSON, J.C. "Peasant Producers or Urban Planters?" Pacific Viewpoint, 7 (1966), pp. 198-228.

22. DOBBY, E.H.G. Southeast Asia. London: University of London Press, 1954, p. 245.

23. BUCHANAN, K. The Southeast Asian World. London: Bell, 1965, especially pp. 77-78.

24. RUNCIMAN, O. The White Rajahs: A History of Sarawak. London: Cambridge University Press, 1965.

25. TREGONNING, K.G. Under Chartered Company Rule, North Borneo 1891-1946. Singapore: 1958.

26. RAWLINS, Joan Sarawak, 1839-1963. London: Macmillan and Company, 1965, p. 19.

27. LENG, Lee Yong Population and Settlement in Sarawak. Singapore: Asia Pacific Press, 1970, especially pp. 55-118.

28. MacDONALD, M. Borneo People. New York: A. Knoft Inc., 1958. GEDDES, W.R. Nine Dyak Nights. London: Oxford University Press, 1957.

29. VILLARD, M. My Friends the Punan. Singapore: Straits Times Annual, 1970, pp. 54-59.

30. FISHER, C.A. Southeast Asia. London: Methuen, 1967, p. 669.

31. LENG, Lee Yong North Borneo. Singapore: Eastern Universities Press, 1965, especially pp. 118-130.

32. HODDER, B.W. The Economic Development of Sarawak. Geographical Studies, 3 (1956), pp. 71-84.

33. LENG, Lee Yong "Land Settlement for Agriculture in North Borneo," Tijdschrift Voor Econ. En Soc. Geografie. July 1961, pp. 184-191.

34. BURGESS, A. A Devil of a State. London: Heineman, 1961.

35. McKIE, R. Malaysia in Focus. London: Angus and Robertson, 1963, especially pp. 182-184.

36. FISHER, C.A. "The Geographical Basis of the Proposed Malaysian Federation," Journal of Tropical Geography, 17 (1963), pp. 99-115.

37. LIEFER, M. The Philippine Claim to Sabah. Hull Monographs on Southeast Asia, University of Hull, 1968.

38. United States Government, Area Handbook for Malaysia. Washington: Government Printing Office, 1970, pp. 65-66.

39. RAWLINS, Joan op.cit., p. 144.

40. BLOODWORTH, D. An Eye for the Dragon. London: Secker and Warburg, 1970, p. 39.

41. ONGKILI, J.P. Modernization in East Malaysia 1960-1970. Kuala Lumpur: Oxford Press, 1972, especially pp. 56-78.

42. WIKKRAMATILEKE, R. "State Aided Rural Land Colonization in Malaya: An Appraisal of the F.L.D.A. Program," Annals, Assoc. of Amer. Geographers, 55 (1965), pp. 377-403. WIKKRAMATILEKE, R. "Federal Land Development in West Malaysia, 1957-1971," Pacific Viewpoint, 13 (1972), pp. 62-86.

43. WIKKRAMATILEKE, R. "The Jengka Triangle, West Malaysia: A Regional Development Project," Geographical Review, 62 (1972), pp. 479-500.

44. The Straits Times, Singapore: April 1, 1972, pp. 17-18.

45. The Straits Times, Singapore: June 22, 1972, pp. 1-10.

46. HARBUTT, C. "Trans Sabah Road," The Straits Times Annual. 1972, pp. 123-125.

47. The Straits Times, Singapore: May 5, 1973, p. 24.

48. The Straits Times, Singapore: July 24, 1973, p. 6.

49. BURNS, R.S. "The Cameron Highlands Hydro-Electric Power Scheme," Geography, 51 (1966), pp. 61-64.

50. The Straits Times, Singapore: October 9, 1971, p. 8.

51. JACKSON, J.C. Sarawak: A Geographical Survey of a Developing State. University of London, 1968, especially pp. 202-205.

52. SLIMMING, J. Malaysia: Death of a Democracy. London: John Murray, 1969.

53. The Straits Times, Singapore: April 22, 1972, p. 7, and June 9, 1973, p. 8.

54. The Straits Times, Singapore: July 4, 1972, p. 6.

55. The Straits Times, Singapore: December 19, 1972, p. 1, December
19, 1972, p. 19 and March 20, 1973, p. 30.

(Processed for Publication, December 1973)

CHAPTER 3

FIJIAN LAND:
A BASIS FOR INTER-CULTURAL VARIANCE

Bryan H. Farrell

University of California, Santa Cruz

Most readers will be more familiar with Hawaii than with Fiji; consequently an introduction to the land problems of Fiji in the South Pacific
might profitably start with an analogy from the more visited territory in the
North Pacific. Both groups have had much in common. Each, in precontact
times, supported indigenous people with roughly similar agriculture; in each,
war was an important element of life; each was settled by Caucasian outsiders at approximately the same time; in each a powerful chiefly elite exerted substantial but varying control over the allocation of lands, and in
each there was a deep spirituality residing in the land. European avarice
concerning land was common to both, and to solve what were thought to be
significant economic and social problems, Asians were brought into these
tropical islands to provide agricultural plantation labour. In each territory,
however, the impact of the determining elements was not the same, nor were
all the elements – the emphases were subtly and sometimes markedly different.
The Fijians were governed by the white intruder paternalistically, with indigenous rights protected at every turn. The Hawaiians ultimately were
culturally overwhelmed by the Caucasian and retention of land was of little
concern to the alien. Both however were afforded a local status much higher
than the imported labour. In the south, corporate land management gave way
to Asian peasantry; in the north there was a mild move towards small-holder
farming, but ultimately large-scale corporate land management prevailed.[1]
It is commonly alleged that in one, the welfare of the indigenous inhabitants
gave major direction to government policy; in the other that the inhabitants

were treated miserably and in a cavalier manner. Yet it can be argued today that the poorly-treated are prosperous and the well-treated, poor. Here the analogy must rest but a detailed study of common and contrasting themes in the two areas would make a fascinating exercise. The greatest disparity tends now to be political, with economic and social costs and benefits stemming in the one, from intimate and integral association with one of the world's richest nations, the United States; and in the other, from the frustrations and problems of national independence, cultural accommodation, and in comparison, a low national income.

Given some of the same basic ingredients of Hawaii but very different attitudes and behaviour patterns, an attempt will be made to show changing attitudes and conflicts concerning land, from precontact to the present in Fiji. The resolution of present problems and the rational management of land for multiple use, especially agriculture and leisure, is without a doubt a key to Fiji's future. Geographical change a by-product of changing culture, reflects more the ravages of conflicting values rather than those elements usually considered by geographers.

No attempt will be made to give a summary of the geography of Fiji (Figure 1,3) nor the Fijian way of life. This is done most adequately elsewhere.[2] Reference must be made however to the dominance of Indians (Indo-Fijians) as a component of population; the startling disparities between used and unused land, conserved and depleted land; the importance of sugar as an Indian-grown crop on land Indians will possibly never own; the "subsistence affluence" (a term coined by Fisk)[3] of the Fijians who own eighty-three percent of the land yet show limited interest in commercial agriculture; and the manner in which policy makers have lionised the Fijians while treating Indians at times with contempt, frequently as a distasteful, but ever-so-necessary adjunct to the extemely important, but shaky, sugar industry.

These, and, a number of other characteristics of today's Fiji result

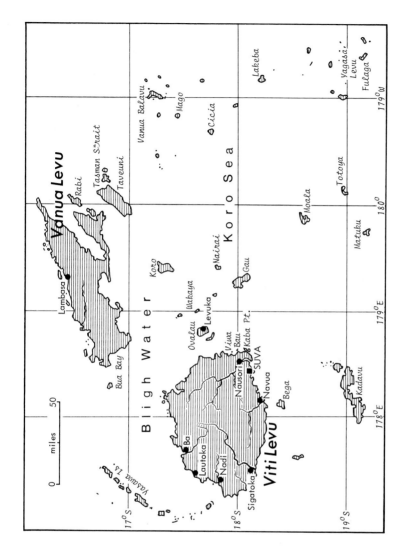

FIGURE 1,3   The Fijian Islands.

99

largely from prejudice, former colonialism with excessive paternalism, and the interplay of three major cultures - Fijian, Indian and English. To this must be added the activities of numerous interest groups and most importantly, the administration's attitudes prevailing at the end of the last century. Together they have had a profound bearing on land.

EARLY RELATIONS WITH THE LAND

Much attention must be paid to the Fijian's early relations with land. For the most part, precontact land tenure and group links with territory are known only vaguely. At the time of earliest post-contact, colonial land legislation, the intricacies of Fijian land relationships were known in a general way, even less than they are today, and herein lie the seeds of one of Fiji's major current problems. Land meant many things to the pre-contact Fijian, but early observers, using the perceptions of Western Europeans towards land, failed to see the shadowy areas and nuances in the evidence before them. Their own blinkered perceptions led only in one direction and caused most to seek evidence largely in terms only of real property, ownership, and legally-defined bounded areas. There was much to be gained by some aliens in so doing. It appeared to make administration of land straightforward, and it obviously brought such exotic and inviting territories closer to the market place. But to be fair, rather than critical with enlightened hindsight, most outsiders viewed land in terms of the values of the day, and were ignorant of the possibility of other view-points. Many aliens, influenced as they may have been, were equally as ignorant as the indigenes were naive.

Land provided a place of origin, a place in which to live, a territory possibly worthy of defending and a source of subsistence. Shifting bush-fallow or swidden agriculture was practised. The territorial boundaries were vague. Outstanding places for dalo (taro) or yam production were better-known and extended family garden areas (qele) were well-known and outlined

100

by recognized natural points of interest. Persons had rights towards crops they grew and to trees which had been planted. An individual could have rights to a tree directly surrounded by root crops for which rights were held by others.

War was always present and the territory-group relationship was usually temporary except for the strongest tribe, which at best could not expect to occupy its place indefinitely. Wars were expected, inevitable events never associated with great bloodshed but rather concerned with the sacking of villages, the subjection of the conquered, or the migration of groups to unoccupied, and less desirable land.

Brewster, an early observer of hill tribes sums up the situation as follows:

> I have managed with great difficulty to piece together [three hundred years of] history...[records] relating to a period of almost unbroken warfare [in which] little blood was actually shed. [Warriors] harried and chased each other, frequently burning villages which were speedily replaced by others...the land was but sparsely populated and there was plenty of uninhabited country for fugitives to take refuge in. The impression in my mind after some study of their folklore stories is that life in the hills in the old times was like a huge game of hide-and-seek. Communities would build houses, become prosperous and arrogant, and excite the jealously of their neighbours, who would then enter into alliances with other clans and attack...their enemy ...the weaker side would flee further back into the ...hills.[4]

Although it was difficult to think of people apart from land, Nayacakalou, along with others, felt that the notion of territoriality, a concept so popularly borrowed from ethology today, was probably a weaker driving force for war than revenge.[5] People on the attack were more interested in conquering people than territory, although land may have provided those attacked with characteristics found to be extremely offensive by the attackers. Nevertheless a de facto unity of people and land existed and a group once conquered was completely subjugated along with the group area's soil, plants and animals. To symbolise the cessation of warfare (or a voluntary submission to another group) the vanquished presented the conquerors (or the new overlord as the case may be) with a basket of earth from the surrendered territory. This extended well into post-contact Fijian history.[6]

In 1880 in an attempt to define areas, rationalize territorial interrelations and ostensibly to understand the occupation of land by Fijians, each group visited by the Native Land Commission gave specific evidence as well as relating its history. These records, tukutuku raramba, were written in longhand and filed in Suva. Because there seems little reason for falsification, the portions of the tukutuku raramba which included these rambling narratives are probably correct and cross-checking confirms this. They tell of former village sites, areas previously occupied, defeats, victories, groups begging for land, land distribution to the vanquished, and the accommodation of refugees. France states that out of six hundred tukutuku raramba only twenty-one are concerned with claiming in the late nineteenth century, the site on which the group was founded, or in other words only a little more than three percent of groups still occupied the "initial" ancestral land upon which the group based its founding.[7]

Tukutuku raramba noted "peace" as a special interlude between wars. When a tribe settled for any length of time in one place without fighting, the fact appeared worthy of note. Nayacakalou shades this a little differently using information from extremely old chiefs who remembered being told of times when there was no fighting and many groups were more or less settled for relatively long periods on their lands.

Groups of people were constantly amalgamating into federations or splitting into smaller groups as the result of politics, local dissension of demographic change. Sometimes cohesion was temporary, sometimes more permanent. Groups occupying territory ran the whole spectral gamut from large

102

political federations amalgamated perhaps only occasionally for an emergency or defence, to small, dejected, wandering splinter groups who might ultimately be absorbed by a sympathetic larger group in another territory. Movement and flexible relationships were characteristics.

Each group was descended patrilineally from an initial deified ancestor-founder, vu. The smallest group (in some areas called i tokatoka) was the extended family, several extended families made a mataqali and these in turn amalgamated to constitute yet a third and major lineage, the yavusa. This rather simplistic scheme has been roundly debated and will be referred to later.[8] Interlinked kin groups ideally occupied villages or groups of villages. In theory at least the yavusa was more localized initially than later, but there was no understood rule that a particular group should occupy a specific village. As the result of fission, fusion, migration and warfare, ultimately and sometimes frequently, groups at various levels, would be split between villages. At the whim of a chief, as the result of population growth, from political dissension, or through war or the the threat of war, the entire group or a part of it would move to new territory either forceably propelled, or as the result of voluntary decision. As recently as 1951 Belshaw reports that people from the village of Natawa removed themselves from their village site because malign spirits had caused five deaths in one month.[9]

The actual landholding unit differed from area to area and group links with land varied locationally with respect to house site, garden, and forest. The most exclusive rights were associated with a house site, yavu and arable land, qele, the most inclusive with veikau or wasteland. Interest in wastelands, for example, was a corporate affair concerning the village or whatever larger group was prepared to defend it. Agriculture was the concern of the individual within the family and most likely never communal.[10] Like other aspects of Fijian life, land tenure practices were flexible and probably in a state of constant change. Special rocks, tree groves and other natural

objects were sacred, sava tambu.[11] In addition a most sacred and tabu place
was the yavutu, a place where it was believed that the original ancestral
group lived or at least the earliest pioneer ancestors of the present territory
had lived.[12] To most persons the most precious land was that point – rather
than area – where the founder arose.[13]

Mataqali tended to assume specialised roles within the community, and
their attitudes and relations with the land reflected the service performed:
defence, building, fishing or farming and so on. Land meant more to a food
producing mataqali than to others and obviously land farmed for its production
had a value status greater than land which was barren. Places of special
value, either larger useful tracts or smaller areas were named. Implicitly,
areas big or small, which were named meant more to occupiers than areas
whose roles was so inconsequential they lacked names. A deeper-than-normal
attachment to land may very well have come as the result of a group which
was probably strong occupying a territory for a long period of time.

Each group had a chiefly leader whose status depended on the military
strength of the group he led and also on the status of the founder. Chiefly
titles were frequently associated with land and the chief was not only in
charge of sacred land, but was also identified with it. As the most sacred
land lay where the founder arose, the chief was identified intimately with
this most-important-of-all deified ancestors. The image of the founder then,
was imbued with a spirituality carried also by the chief, his living representative. The deity's spirituality was intimately linked with the land and consequently all important events concerning land and its production required
ceremonial communication through priest or chief.

It was normal then, that first-fruits (sevu) of harvest were presented to
the deities through the chief. After contact, first-fruits ceremonies were known
to be directed also towards missionaries and representatives of the colonial
governments. This was probably a convenient manner of showing ceremonial

104

respect rather than actual belief that recipients were connected in the tra-ditional customary way with land.[14] The chief could also grant the use of wastelands not only to his own followers but also to outsiders who hence-forth would provide him with gifts and services while the land was being used. The chief, as spokesman for and leader of the group, became land-lord as well and accepted rent in kind from his alien tenants. Use of land by outsiders for a "fee", was not unknown to early Fijians.

In summary then, prior to the first European contact land had a variety of meanings for the early Fijian. It meant first of all a place providing food. It did not have economic value as Westerners know it, but labour applied to land and the things it produced, did. It was the residing place of all ancestral spirits and consequently parts, places or points could have a deep emotive and religious connotation. A territory defended successfully over many generations would have greater significance for its occupiers than lands continually occupied and evacuated which for some was the rule. Unless land had strategic importance, supported valuable fruit trees or salt pans, the loss of which would be considerable, it was usually per se, of little account. On the other hand the products of human industry such as wells, crops, and specially nurtured trees were of particular importance. Conversely, successive movement and impermanence of tenure allowed little time for enterprise and for an abiding affection towards the land to develop.

Because they received service and gifts from group members and could allocate waste land for rental to refugees from elsewhere, chiefs had a per-sonal interest in land greater than the common man, a powerful chief more than a lesser one. The fact that land could be gifted and confiscated as re-ward or punishment, suggests it had other values difficult to define.

Places rather than tracts were known, points rather than boundaries de-fined places. No point had greater significance than that where the deified founder of each kin group arose, or was more inviolate to the individual than a house site. Further complicating, although completely understandable and

logical factors interposed themselves between the more 'legitimate' group
member and land. As time progressed many more than those with patrilineages
flowing back to the founder developed legitimate rights regarding land which
were recognized in social custom, if not in law. Today some concessions are
made towards what the law calls 'dependents'. Patrilineal descent was not
the only condition for membership of a group.[15]

Under certain circumstances persons acquired rights of mataqali membership through co-residence or through their mother's group relationships; others
were admitted as a recompense for giving valuable service, or in charity as
refugees. Some qualified by virtue of distant kinship. Consequently strangers
eventually gained full rights to land with the passage of time, by achievement and the development of loyalty to the host group, rather than by more
traditional customary descent. Thompson summed up the situation as follows:

> The Fijians had no territorial roots. It is not too
> much to say that no tribe now [1908] occupies the
> land held by its fathers two centuries ago. They
> are united by consanguinity, not by joint owner-
> ship of the soil. But the longer they stay upon
> the land, the stronger becomes their connection
> with it, until at last it becomes the basis of
> brotherhood, and the adoption of a stranger con-
> fers nearly the same priviledges as those enjoyed
> by fullborn members of the tribe.[16]

For particular purposes yavusa would cooperate and this would also provide loose intervillage ties. Although such alliances were usually weak they
could provide a mild extension of a group's vision of land, and on the occasion
of yavusa working together as a wider political unit (a vanua) this too must
have at least temporarily extended spatial perception. The amalgamation of
vanua into wider, militarily powerful, socio-economic associations of States,
matanitu, close to the time of first European contact must have developed at
least temporarily a real sense of territoriality unknown previously by the

106

smaller, more traditional group.[17]

CONTACT: THE FIRST SEVENTY YEARS

During the first decade of the nineteenth century, ships arrived in
Fiji for cargoes of sandalwood. The wood, highly valued by Chinese, was
first taken in 1804 from Vanua Levu. The main island, Viti Levu, remained
unknown as a source of sandalwood for another decade.[18] A cargo bought
from Fijians for fifty dollars could be sold for twenty thousand dollars on the
China market. By the second decade of the century ships seeking bêche-
de-mer (Holothuriod spp., sea-cucumber or sea slug) were contracting with
chiefs along coastal Viti Levu to collect the organism. Wherever contact
was made, exploitive activity followed. To cure bêche-de-mer, large,
deeply-trenched drying sheds were necessary and these were fired with great
quantities of timber.[19] Whether it was for the sandalwood or the bêche-de-
mer trade, during periods of peace between fighting, forests fell at the hands
of primitive loggers. In some areas the resource base had virtually widened
overnight and land assumed a new significance. Its trees directly or indirectly
bought arms, tools, trade goods and 'superiority' in relation to other groups
for the short period that exploitation lasted. Strangely enough, despite an
early start, the real potentiality of land to grow trees other than the coconut
has yet to be developed even today, in more than a tentative manner.

Many Fijian villages at the time were located in out-of-the way places,
frequently sited on a ridge or prominence to allow sentries to watch carefully
for the approach of enemies. Where this was not possible, especially on lowlands, villages were guarded by moats or fortified pallisades. Taro and yams
were grown by a cultivator in the nearest secluded patch which would allow
a quick-return to the village in emergencies. Cultivations then, could be a
matter of only some hundreds of feet from a fortified village. A wide variety
of techniques including terracing, water reservoirs, ditches and bamboo pipe-

PLATE 30
A modern variation of traditional swidden agriculture: a clearing awaiting planting.

PLATE 31
The Sigatoka Valley today: leased land under commercial cultivation.

lines allowed such places as the Sigatoka valley to support extremely large populations over the centuries.[20] (Plates 30 and 31).

Following the sandalwood and bêche-de-mer trade, missionaries, adventurers and entrepreneurs of all types arrived in Fiji. Missionaries were granted land by chiefs for house sites and Pritchard cites some who made land purchases for purely secular purposes.[21] Probably more important was the fact that missionary teaching gradually eroded the Fijian view of the essential spiritual association between the deities and the land and the temple site disappeared from the village plan.[22] Fijians must have been confused by the ambiguity and contradictions of European attitudes. Early nineteenth century European viewpoints were represented by entrepreneurs and potential agriculturalists intent on buying land for the cheapest possible price. Missionaries, on the other hand, at times proved to be a levelling influence. No group, as a whole, was able to understand the perceptions of the frequently naive Fijian 'vendor'. Many individuals were unwilling to try.

It was obvious that conflicts over lands had to be uneven and it says much for later administrators, despite their shortcomings, that in their own way they realised something of the enormity of the problems which would be created if conditions continued as they were before the islands were ceded to Great Britain. White settlers had an eye for land in a content of Western commercial agriculture, elementary rules set up for its purchase were theirs, and later when sales were adjudicated by a court or a land commission, judgements too had to be made within the context of Western perceptions of land. Nowhere was there real appreciation of a Fijian view. Nevertheless, despite inexperience of European wiles, even at this early date, there were some Fijians learning very quickly to manipulate the system, one of the limited options available to the indigene.

Fijian farming was not understood by early Europeans. Land being rehabilitated under customary bush fallow farming or as yet uncleared, appeared vacant, unused and following the Western train of thought, available for appropriation. This is a charitable interpretation. Another is that they felt convinced that they could use the land to better effect and this warranted the ousting of the rightful occupiers. As in Hawaii it was difficult to ascertain just what current land practices were and if land were to be alienated, who was the person or persons in whom authority was vested and who could be party to a 'legal contract'. Again, like Hawaii where it appears there have been several land tenure systems depending on the time, place and chiefly influence, so too was the situation in Fiji. Systems varied from place to place; all were subject to change. The power of chiefs varied from absolute to minimal, and rights concerning land varied in different places under different conditions. As alienation and the concept of land as a commodity was unknown, no one in reality had experience under custom to transact the sort of business the European sought. In all probability, at least in most matters, a strong chief probably spoke for everybody, but this was a most unsatisfactory basis for negotiations, where neither side clearly understood the perceptions, values and aspirations of the other. To Europeans, chiefs appeared to have had the authority to provide plantation labour; so why not to sell land as well?

For many Fijians there was little understanding that a 'sale' was also a message to 'vacate'. A confusing point was that this was not invariably the case. R.A. Smythe in a report to the Colonial Office, probably in the late 1850's says that early white purchasers did not evict Fijians from 'alienated' land. This came later when whites arrived with the intention of setting up cotton plantations.[23] In general, many Fijians felt that the 'sale' of land meant 'permission to use for a consideration', a concept quite compatible with Fijian custom. This had never before meant eviction and the cancellation for ever of traditional rights. By the late 1860's, due

110

to hints of annexation, threats of possible land confiscation and the high price of cotton, it was reported that demand for plantation land was great and sales boomed. There was also a degree of correlation between sales and warfare.[24]

Sales of sandalwood, bêche-de-mer and later land, frequently provided the means for the purchase of arms and powder. Sales of land in the Dreketi River district of Vanua Levu were made directly by chiefs who seldom hesitated to sell land in the common interests of tribe or matanitu to procure arms for war. This intensified fighting and proved devastating. The imagined invulnerability of certain leaders when not armed with western weapons was demolished overnight, and war became deadly serious, not a game. Important as well as unimportant people were killed indescriminately and the role of fighting changed immeasurably.

Had warfare not been stopped in the late 1870's it would probably have caused its own destruction soon after. The point however, is that land sales became a useful instrument of war and a means, in other intriguing ways, of gaining advantage.[25] Soon after a series of wars in the Sigatoka district, fifteen land sales were made in five months in 1868. All were sold by chiefs. One piece of land was sold to two different people within the space of a few days and in another case the Chief Nagadru hurriedly sold land he suspected Ratu Kini would sell the following day.[26] If the sale of land was unable to win a war by the provision of newer and deadly weapons, its sale postwar might inflict telling personal damage of a sort previously unknown.

Pritchard notes that Fijians were willing to sell lands between rival districts, contentious lands, and lands that had been frequently battle fields. In these cases it was necessary to pay both parties who were only too glad to place a neutral zone between them. He went on to say that when land was sold the Fijian occupiers frequently expected to be employed by the

111

buyer. "Indeed they not infrequently [sold] merely to bring a white man into their neighbourhood, and so get employment under him, whenever they [wanted] a knife or a yard of cloth."[27] Land had, through sales, become the means to rather dubious ends.

A defence of the Fijians changing attitude towards land was written in an early report of the Land Commissioners:

> A large proportion of the sales were affected in order to obtain arms and ammunition...the inequity of the transactions rested chiefly with those...who first introduced such means of warfare into the country then in a state of rampant savageness and cannibalism. When guns fell thus into the hands of a tribe, upon whose shores the vessel containing the first fire arms was anchored, their neighbours were soon to discover that it was a matter of life and death that they should likewise procure the same means of defence and when land buying commenced what was easier than to sell a portion of the land upon the desire of a white to buy...By Fijian custom, that is by Fijian law, the absolute alienation of land as understood by us was unknown...it cannot be doubted [the Fijians] had a perfect right and common prudence to procure by any means in their power the safety of their lives and the lives of their wives, and families. Where would be the utility of preserving land when by so doing they subjected themselves to extinction altogether and consequently left no posterity to enjoy the lands thus spared by a too-rigid adherence to their old customs.[28]

THE COLONY'S EARLY YEARS AND THE LAND COMMISSIONS

In the mid 1870's numbers of land sales usually by chiefs had taken place and it was generally understood by outsiders that chiefs were entitled to negotiate in these matters. Like Hawaii in the days of King Kamehameha, a powerful chief's word was law. On the eve of cession to Great Britain, Sir Hercules Robinson, Governor of New South Wales, who had been sent to Fiji for the purpose, talked to the leading chief of Bau, Cakobau on board H.M.S. Dido. Cakobau said :

> Giving the country up to England is merely a matter
> of word. All our people obey us and the greater part
> of the chiefs will think what I do is right...my de-
> cision in the matter will be for the good of the people
> and of Fiji.

It seemed obvious that Cakobau believed, like his colleagues that the lands of Fiji were vested in the ruling chiefs. Sir Hercules reply was also interesting:

> What has occurred to me as the fairest way of
> arranging this matter...is that all lands which
> can be shown to have been fairly and honestly
> acquired by whites shall be secured to them,
> that all lands which now in the actual use or
> occupation of any chief or tribe and such lands
> as may be necessary for the probably future
> support and maintenance of any chief or tribe
> shall be set apart for them, and that all the
> residue of the land shall go to the Government,
> not for the personal advantage of Her Majesty,
> or the members of any Government but for the
> general good - for the purpose of rule and order.
> The more public land there is, the less necessity
> for taxation and the less burdensome to the peo-
> ple will be the maintenance of policies of ad-
> ministration of justice, the building of hospitals
> and other places of public charity.[29]

There appeared an acceptance by representatives of H.M. Government at this time that land titles, as well as sovereignty, were transferrable to Her Majesty. Fijian people were only entitled to hold sufficient land for their maintenance. After cession this theory, it is alleged, was accepted

by Sir Arthur Gordon, the first Colonial Governor, because under his direction sales were made as if the Crown were proprietor and in public
speeches in England he invited 'capitalists' to buy Fijian land from the
Crown.[30]

In a Fiji Argus editorial of June 11, 1875, Sir Hercules Robinson was
quoted as saying:

> ...three things are necessary for a valid sale to
> Europeans: first a fair consideration for the value
> of the land, secondly that 'all parties whose assent
> was necessary to the validity of the transfer were
> duly represented and were aware of the nature of
> the transaction and of the boundaries of the land'
> to be sold, and thirdly, the sale was registered in
> one of the consulates in the manner required by the
> Land Regulations.

Within this ambiguous statement lay the seeds of a conflict which has never
really been resolved except by the law as promulgated later. What parties
were necessary for assent to be given? Could either party ever be really
aware of the nature of the transaction as seen through the eyes of the other
party? Was either party capable of thinking in terms of precise boundaries
which would be sustained in court and if so, was the delineation of one
group, ever really understandable by the other?

In October 1874, Fiji was ceded to Great Britain, and at this time after
seventy years of contact and two decades of active land sales, conflicting
viewpoints had already emerged between settlers, Fijians and the representatives of the Colonial Government. The English administrator was to some
degree pitying, protective, paternal and concerned to bring about only
enlightened, cautious change, with the absolute minimum of disruption.
To him the 'noble savage' had evolved to a certain stage, and it was arrogantly
thought that with careful nurturing he would reach the exalted level of the
administrator himself in time. This might even include individual land holding

like the white settler himself, a possibility mentioned later. There is no doubt that this view was sincere. By 1874 much, if not all of the choice land, had been claimed by European buyers. Already Fijian links with land had weathered more than half a century of alien incursion and had changed considerably. One might assume that cultural flexibility had always been characteristic of the Fijian way of life, but the European agent of change was certainly the most traumatic.

Article Four and Five of the Deed of Cession focussed specifically and emphatically on land. It reflected the view of Sir Hercules Robinson already noted. Article Four stated:

> ...that the absolute proprietorship of all lands not [shown to be legitimately the bona fide property of aliens] or not now in the actual use or occupation of some chief or tribe or not actually required for the probable future support or maintenance of some chief or tribe, should be and is hereby declared to be vested in her said Majesty, her heirs and successors. [31]

In December 1875, the Land Claims Commission was set up to look at the validity of land claims. Relatively few of these, less than fifty percent of the area claimed, were allowed, but included some of the best land in Fiji. No sale or transfer of land was to be allowed until after the Commission had finished its work (1882) and "all dealings in land between Europeans and natives shall be invalid...and forbidden." [32] Sir Arthur Gordon's instructions from Downing Street implied future sales, but in reality only for three years after 1905 was further alienation allowed. The instruction read:

> Whenever a European desires to purchase native land his application must be addressed to the Colonial Government. If it is believed the purchaser should be authorized, it shall acquire the land itself and fix a

price at which it shall be granted by the Crown to
the applicant.

Further instructions, somewhat contradictory, advised him to disturb as little
as possible existing tenures.[33]

One obvious result of the Land Claims Commission was that it brought
into conflict the views of opposing Europeans as well as Fijians. It highlighted the malpractices of many Europeans and as well focussed from time
to time on the deceits of 'vendors' or their representatives. It also gave
the new government time to consider the administration of land, both
native and alienated. The records of the Commission must have given pause
to a number of more sensitive or aware individuals as well as those with
vested interests. A number of persons, from altruistic, administrative national or personal interests were at pains to reconstruct a traditional land
tenure system as a basis for the deliberations of the Land Claims Commission,
for future land legislation, and as a basis for a Native Land Commission
which was ultimately to investigate and register every Fijian parcel of land
in the group.

Among the contestants, as authorities on native land custom were Mr.
John Thurston, Sir Arthur Gordon himself, and missionaries W.T. Pritchard
and Lorimer Fison.[34] In their submissions to the Commission European land
claimants attempted to demonstrate that the proprietary unit for land in
Fijian custom was the individual **chief** , and in the case of the claim under
consideration, the chief who had signed the documents the buyer held. On
the other hand the Fijian people, including many chiefs, were becoming
more aware of the enormity of the land issue and the potentialities land may
hold for them in the generations to come. In contradistinction to the claimants they were at pains now, if not earlier, to show that land was vested in
the people and that chiefs acted ultra vires in selling it.[35] This was
an expedient view reflecting contemporaneous conflict between parties
rather than a true reflection of belief regarding pre-contact land tenure.

Because a minority of claims were being upheld, a substantial number of influential aliens now found themselves in conflict as well with the Commission. But the implications moved far beyond the individuals involved - Great Britain stood in judgement of the transactions not only of its own subjects but of Germans and Americans as well, with the result that international politics became a new dimension characterized by official protests and negotiations.

All views of Fijian land practices in reality had to be distorted at this time. Evidence to support one view or another embellished certain aspects, neglected others. More than three-quarters of a century of acculturation had taken place. Fijians had modified their views and way of life as the result of alien intrusion. Some degree of cultural change had taken place, as would be normal, without the aid of an outside stimulus. Change had taken place in the past and must have been operating at the time of contact as the result of numerous Polynesian intrusions from the east. This does not mean that Fijians were static and did not themselves make excursions leading to change elsewhere.

The English planter, the missionary, the foreign consul and the administrator were all imbued with Western ideas of social stratification; to look on a chief as the true representative of the people was consequently second nature. Pritchard and others with knowledge of Polynesia where social stratification and degrees of feudalism were prevalent would look for and find similar signs in the Fijian social fabric. All, if they chose to ask questions about Fijian society, were likely to seek a chief as an informant and this could add to the possibility of biasing newly formed opinions. Fison understood this and consequently paid attention more to the commoner or taukei as a source of information. To listen to only one side was wrong but whether or not there was a person capable of putting both sides together in the context of constant social change in which the function of a chief waxed and waned is debatable. It is also unlikely that a trained social

117

scientist with some academic or social axe to grind would do a better job by retrospection at a later date.

Fison disputed the Cakobau Rex theory of land proprietorship by ruling chiefs under a feudal system which had existed from time immemorial, a system very similar to that generally serving as a reconstruction of conditions in Hawaii at the time of contact. This, he said, was obviously the theory held by Sir Hercules Robinson and Sir Arthur Gordon. Land title and sovereignty had been transferred to Her Majesty by the chiefs and the people were only entitled to sufficient land for their maintenance. Sir Arthur Gordon, he went on, had authorized sales as if the Crown were proprietor.

"Land tenure in Fiji," said Fison, "is tribal. Title is vested in all full born members of the tribe commoners as well as chiefs; not in any one individual nor in any class of individuals." Fison's view undoubtedly made a very great impact. Sir Arthur Gordon, who considered himself as something of an amateur anthropologist, was impressed. Fison's views were set out publicly in the Journal of the Anthropological Society, reprinted by the Colonial Office, and reprinted again in the Memorial of the United States in Support of the Claims of Fiji Lands...[36] That they had profound effect on at least some members of the Commission and the public is shown in the remarks of Victor Williamson, a former Land Commissioner.

> The ignorance of most of the colonists in Fiji of the natives and their customs is almost incredible, and I can only ascribe it to the contemptuous indifference with which such are regarded by the 'superior race'. I believe the lecture of the Reverend L. Fison on land tenure in Fiji delivered at Levuka on April 15, 1880, operated quite as a revelation to the European population.[37]

It is obvious that the European needed some sort of revelation, but what was being sought by Fison, Gordon and others was something of a will-o-

the-wisp. The difference between the Fison theory and the <u>Cakobau Rex</u>
theory could be a matter only of scale, a perceptual conflict stemming from
persons looking at the same thing or different things (thinking they are the
same) through different eyes. It has been suggested that in the past links
between groups and between groups and land have been a matter of constant fission and fusion, and changing land relationships and practices.
With regard to later written (or spoken) records of Westerners, not only
did much depend on the perceptions of the observer but also upon the place
of observation. Was the informant chief or commoner? Did the investigation take place in an area ruled by a chief of great power, or by a man
of limited consequence? Chief-commoner land relationships varied considerably with local circumstance, and without doubt valid examples could
be found which would have supported any one of the theories or their
spokesmen. The complexity of the situation is suggested by Thomson who
states that "in the narrow areas formed by the watershed on the eastern
part of Viti Levu no less than eight systems of [land] tenure [had]... been
found to exist."[38]

The early European settlement took place and their attitudes were formed
within the sphere of influence of the powerful Bauan chief Cakombau. The
land tenure terms ultimately used by administrators were Bauan and so too
were the concepts. Besides Cakombau, another powerful chief signing
the Deed of Cession was Ma'afu, a chief of Tongan background who ruled
the Lau Confederacy Taveuni and the greater part of Vanua Levu. This
serves to introduce a fact essential to an understanding of Fiji. Fiji
structurally in many ways is typically Melanesian; in other ways, especially in the behaviour of chiefs and nobility it appears essentially Polynesian. The tide of Polynesian influence waxed and waned and its influence varied territorially. Was there ever a 'true and pure' Fijian
society free from local variation and evolution, unmodified to some degree
by Polynesia, and were those changes wrought in the nineteenth century

following contact any different in principle from those of past centuries?

If the structure of Fijian society related closely to Melanesian, one would expect to find what Kirchoff calls unilateral exogamous clans, a relevant characteristic of which is that complete equality rules among members and individuals are always subordinate to the clan as a whole. The appropriate elements of Polynesian structure, on the other hand emphasise descent (patrilineal, matrilineal or both) from a superior god-like ancestor. The aristoi, those closest to the centre-line of descent, occupy the leading economic, social and religious functions of society. The nearer an individual is to the god-ancestor, the greater his potential for power and for social and economic recognition.[39] At the time of contact one can surmise that regions of Fiji reflected to some degree both Melanesian equality and Polynesian elitism. This situation depended on the quality and amount of past, outside, intrusion and regional in loco social evolution. Fijian society then, lying transitional to Melanesia and Polynesia at the time of contact, defied any neat, facile classification of society, land practices, or a number of other cultural attributes. Despite increasing hints of the real situation which must have vexed some persons, Sir Arthur Gordon believed there was indeed a single unitary system worth seeking which would be found beneath any local overlay and would provide a basis for understanding Fijian society.

Sir Arthur Gordon's personality dominates early legislation and administrative attitudes. Peter France shows him to be egotistical, arrogant, a self-appraised intellectual, a protector of indigenous institutions and a champion of the alien-exploited underdog, a role he had played previously in Mauritius.[40] His views, and those which continued beyond his time, contained invalid assumptions, inconsistencies, ambiguities, and a fair degree of ambivalence. The Native Land Ordinance of 1880 reflects this latter duality. It confirmed that Fijian land should be inalienable and that the mataqali should be the proprietorial unit. Simultaneoulsy provision was made for land ultimately to be divided among individual members of a mataqali, each with a Native Certificate of Title, implying that the preservation of the reconstructed rural organization and management was not to continue in perpetuity. Ancient custom would remain "until the native race was ripe for a division of such community rights among individuals." For some this could theoretically mean a virtual freehold Crown Grant of an individual's portion of land five years after having received a Certificate.[41] This of course never came to pass. Gordon's views were to become less obscure and obtuse with time. Communal ownership (the Fison view) he felt, would make alienation difficult if not impossible and would help to preserve Fijian institutions. But while seeking from the Council of Fijian Chiefs, the 'true nature' of Fijian land tenure he was prepared without this external knowledge believed to be in no way superior to his own, to support the Land Claims Commission in their rather arbitrary and ad hoc decisions. The fact that official policy was not clear on critical aspects of social structure was not allowed to impede their deliberations. It could be argued perhaps, that intimate knowledge of Fijian land custom was less necessary for these earlier deliberations than it was for those following tardily in 1890 under the aegis of the Native Land Commission, which had been authorized a decade earlier.

Gordon has been commended for the fact that in an effort to maintain Fijian institutions he placed considerable reliance on the Fijian hierarchy, especially the Council of Chiefs. Three times the Council of Chiefs was asked to rule on Fijian land tenure. The first of three meetings was in 1876, the last in 1880. It is relevant to note that this was at a crucial period in Fijian history. The hearings of the Land Claims Commission were in progress and a decision by the Council one way or another could, and did, have long term effects on their own Fijian people. If a particular decision could help the Fijian cause, the Council of Chiefs, like most human beings, would be unconsciously or consciously drawn in that direction. Another complicating factor was that after Gordon's Little War of 1876, fighting ceased and the relationship between Chiefs and people, and Chiefs and land changed markedly. This too could affect decisions made about land. Perhaps it is too much and too early to believe that they had become already aware that "the functions of the Chief as a real leader...[were losing] much of their point with the suppression of warfare and the introduction of machinery to settle land disputes (Spate),"[42] but the implications of a changing function and status must have been dawning and would very likely colour deliberations.

During the first two meetings the Chiefs, like the Native Land Commissioners later, were unable to come to any definite conclusions. Procedures and practices in one district were totally different from those in another and Fijian terms meant one thing in one area and something quite different in another. In some there were critical concepts and practices unknown in another. Meetings were characterised by complete confusion and an inability to communicate because of a lack of common ground. The Council recommended, at the end of the first meeting, that there should be numerous ways of holding, managing and organizing land, and the "accepted" way should depend on local wishes. This was entirely unacceptable. What Gordon was looking for was a blueprint from the past to be applied in the future. After much presure the Chiefs finally spoke with one voice, unanimously making the statement Gordon wanted to hear, that the true ownership of the land rested with the mataqali and that Fijian land was inalienable. That this was a decision made under psychological duress and within the exigencies of the times was obvious. These were the same Chiefs who, less than a decade earlier had sold land to Europeans under an authority they believed was theirs to use and it was the same group, if not the same members, who in 1914 stated quite deliberately that "Chiefs alone are the owners of the lands and that inferior members of the tribe only own the land with their permission."[43] Even if the white establishment had been successfully brain-washed

122

four decades after Cession, the Fijian establishment was not, and was certainly prepared to have second thoughts on the matter.

If confusion appeared to reign during Gordon's period of office, the situation did not become any clearer during the remainder of the century and during the first decade of the next, in which time various Governors, Councils-of-Chiefs and Native Land Commissioners struggled with the knotty problem of land tenure, the recording of land occupying units and the delineation of boundaries of land so occupied. Some found the job impossible, other were ambivalent and amazing in the extent of their mental dexterity. Despite finding in the field what appeared to be anomaly after anomaly, and incensing Fijian groups with whom they came into contact, administrative officers were usually unwilling to budge from their own self-imposed scheme for Fijian land and society. If they were willing to be more flexible, questioning and even critical, they invariably found themselves ultimately running headlong into the intransigence of officials at a more elevated level within the colonial hierarchy. Although Commissioners knew most operational land-occupying units were not mataqali they continued to record mataqali units which, in many areas had no utility or meaning while ignoring and not recording those units and the areas they occupied which were essential to the functioning of Fijian Society.[44] By World War I any opposition on the part of well-meaning colonial officers in the field had subsided, individuals fighting their losing battle had withdrawn and the Fijians, who were forced to live with the system, ignored.

The events, attitudes and administrative activities embodied in the foregoing discussion laid the basis for intercultural conflict, the point of this paper. The stage was set by Sir Arthur Gordon but there were many actors in this play, a classic of perceptual dissonance and insensitive ethnocentricity. The major elements have already been noted: the colonial administrator, the European settlers, the Fijian elite and the indigenous commoners. Ethnically this can be boiled down to Fijian and European. One further, and now an

123

essential element of the Fijian fabric, the Indian, needs to be introduced.

THE INDIAN FARMER

In the 1870's the demand for plantation labour was strong and the Governor, again Sir Arthur Gordon, insisted that it was undesirable for Fijians to be separated from their lands and villages. In this contention he was supported by the Chiefs who did not want their people working for planters, or for Fijian society to be drastically changed. This it would have to be if commercial agriculture were to be served. In 1879, to provide for the growing labour deficit, a programme of indentured Indian labour was started, which ultimately introduced 60,000 persons, and which remained with regular immigration until the second decade of the twentieth century. By this time sugar was not grown on estates but was produced by Indian peasant farmers who had chosen to remain in Fiji. Nearly 25,000 had been repatriated under indenture contracts.

The Indian labourer eventually became the small holder sugar producer who leased either freehold land from the Colonial Sugar Refining Company or Fijian land from mataqali. During forty years of living in Fiji the Indian, after travelling unsegregated to Fiji, and being treated ignominiously by both recruiters and planters, became culturally disoriented and casteless, an outcast with reference to his origianl society. With this background he developed in his new surroundings fresh, and peculiarly Indo-Fijian, values.[45] The Indian had fought and beaten the indenture system and the commercial estate system, and had learned that sugar grown in Fiji on a ten-acre farm could provide him with a better living than anything practicable in India. This was cold comfort to some immigrants who knew psychologically and culturally that it was inappropriate and perhaps impossible for them to return anyway. On the other side of the coin there was no compulsion whatever for an Indian to return, and this must have appealed to some who had found an attractive niche in Fiji.[46]

The Indians knew that their rapidly growing population, which today constitutes more than half of the total, although providing security in a social sense, would antagonise Fijians. They quickly learned also that if no provision were made to supply more land for leasing, the competition for good sugar land would become unbearable. The fact too, that Europeans looked upon Indians as insensitives coolies while treating the land-owning Fijians with paternal beneficence contributed still further to a trying situation. These elements, among others, helped develop a distinctive Indo-Fijian attitude towards the land of Fiji. Their expertise and success in the sugar industry rested to some extent with Western technology and the careful supervision of Australian field staff, but to this they added dogged perseverance and commendable energy.

THREE CULTURE INTERACTION

As the threat of growing Indian population became greater the Government saw its responsibility to the Fijians grow proportionally. At the beginning of the century there still remained a possibility that land surplus to Fijian use which could be claimed by the Crown under the Deed of Cession, would be held for future use. For a short period in 1905-1908, a little further alienation was allowed before it was stopped for all time. From then on, constant assurances were given that Fijian land was forever inviolable. An exception was the land of an extinct mataqali. No attempts were made to take for the Crown land not used by Fijians, a definite understanding at the time of Cession, nor did later governments venture to suggest that there be the merest threat to lands considered by the Fijians as their own. This was the result of developing policy which placed successive governments in an increasingly protective role, a stance which undoubtedly bears on the introduction of the Indian, his growing numbers and the prevailing attitudes toward him by virtually all non-Indian groups.

But Fijians did have land surplus to their needs which had previously
been allocated for temporary use according to custom. As mid-century
approached it was obvious that a degree of rationalization was required to
bring custom in line with practice "by law decreed". In 1940 the Native
Land Trust Ordinance provided for a Native Land Trust Board to negotiate
all leases for Fijian owners outside the mataqali group, Indian, European
or other Fijian. The Board was authorised to use up to twenty-five percent
of the income for administration purposes. A percentage was distributed
to chiefs at different levels and the remainder to mataqali members. This
provided for a registered lease on a business-like basis and a possible extended period of tenure to 30 years. The Ordinance also provided for the
delineation of reserves, areas not currently used by mataqali but mapped
and set aside as land banks for use in the foreseeable future. Reserves
provided a source of further conflict and an irritant for the Indians who probably stimulated governmental thinking about reserves in the first place.
Prior agreements were terminated for non-mataqali members as the law stated
that reserve land could not be used by persons outside the mataqali owners.
Like the original registering of mataqali land in the past, the reserving of
land was to have taken two years but was still incomplete by the end of the
third decade. Land formerly leased by Indians and reverting to Fijian reserve fell into disuse. Land destined for reserve but not yet surveyed could
not be leased.

Some mataqali did not, (and this is still the case), wish to lose twenty-
five percent of their rental income to the Native Land Trust Board and consequently arranged illegal leases. This is still a problem. An associated
problem is that Indian tenure of Fijian land, outside or on the edge of sugar-
growing areas is frequently insecure. Indian farmers pay under-the-counter
deals both to get and to keep the land and this, together with high rents
virtually forces him to ravage the land in an attempt to get a return before

126

possible eviction.[47]

Land leased from Fijians sometimes means the paying of premiums and gifts by an Indian lessee at the outset, then further gifts to the land owners who might jeopardize the renewal of the lease ten years later. Under the Agricultural Landlord and Tenant Ordinance of 1966 a first or second ten year extension may not be given the tenant if one or more of the owners requires the land for his own use "and [if] greater hardship would be caused by granting an extension than by refusing it."[48] The threat of a contest at the end of ten years by the lessors could result in an out-of-court settlement by the tenant. The alternative to making some sort of payment, and a worse threat, could be a disastrous fire in the lessees cane crop. Some Fijians, informants state, quickly learned the art of extortion. Prevailing racial attitudes suggested too that Indians were fair game. English administrators created the instrument which gave to Fijians wide power over Indians, yet despite discrimination which has not disappeared with Independence in 1970, each, the Fijian and the Indian, is de jure, if not de facto, equal.

During 1968, the tempers of both Indians and Fijians were running high because of the implementation of the Landlord and Tenant Ordinance introduced mainly to protect tenants of any group from rapacious landlords, mostly European.[49] Few persons had praise for the legislation. Indians felt that it was used against them, and when aspects of the legislation were contested by Fijian owners before the Agricultural Tribunal it was strongly felt that decisions invariably favoured the Indian. In addition, the Native Land Trust Board fell into disfavour. At Agricultural Tribunals it would not speak on behalf of the owners, yet the original leases had to be arranged through the Native Land Trust Board whom mataqali members felt should act as their agent. This one piece of legislation, no less mindless than a number concerning land enacted over the past century, brought Colonial Government, Indian tenant, Fijian landowners, the Agricultural Tribunal and the

Native Land Trust Board into potentially violent conflict. Despite the actions and best intentions on the part of many persons, tensions deriving from the land were ill-disguised and at best were hidden barely beneath the surface.

Both Fijian and Indian have undergone traumatic changes of culture and attitude. The Fijian saw his relationships towards land forcibly changed by the imposition of outsiders, or as France says "by law established". The power of chiefs diminished, yet in compensation they derived, and still do, special extra economic benefits from rentals not given mataqali members. Changes of course, have not stopped and increasingly Fijians are being affected by the influences of a market economy which causes new links to be forged with the land. In the sugar area there is a growing awareness by Fijians of the economic value of land and the potential of commercial production. Cases may be cited of Fijians undergoing radical change, moving from affluent subsistence and mataqali landlordism to membership in the market economy.[50] In this case the diffusion of new views of land has flowed from Australian supervisors, through Indian tenants and ultimately to indigenous Fijian landowners. Normally, one might expect the owners rather than the tenants to be innovators.

In a preliminary analysis of the responses of 291 sixteen-year-old Fijian high school students the author found a number of noteworthy present-day attitudes concerning land. When asked questions about the meaning of land to them today, more persons thought in terms of economic development of Fiji than in terms of cultural continuities or anything else. With justification, three-quarters of the respondents believed that the best land had been taken from the Fijian by the Europeans, and interestingly three-quarters believed land should be individualised among mataqali members who should have absolute and complete control over their share. It was generally agreed that Fijian farming could stand much improvement and although Indians were exceedingly hardworking their desire for land was excessive. Around two-thirds admitted that Fijians rejoice in sole proprietorship over land even if

PLATE 32
Indian-grown irrigated rice,
lower Navua Valley.

PLATE 33
Indian family home and rice mill,
Rewa River.

PLATE 34
Early tourist accommodation in traditional Fijian bure, Nasilai village.

PLATE 35
Modern Caucasian response to the tourist trade: the Fijian Resort Hotel, Yanuca Island.

large areas remain idle, and consistent with this there was general agreement that reserves should remain. Despite the ructions of 1968, views asked for in 1970 on the Landlord and Tenant Act were not decisive in any particular direction.

Indians too were questioned and 422 replies in the preliminary run were tabulated. On a number of questions responses were much more decisive than Fijians. Obviously they too believed Indians worked hard and provided a good example of how land should be used. In sampling views of what land meant to the individual, fewer Indians than Fijians noted land as a key to economic development but it still ranked high. On the other hand land as "a place giving a family or a group a sense of security" was much more important to Indians than Fijians. In general Indians maintained that Fijians made poor use of land while they themselves provided a model. As many Indians wanted Fijian reserves abolished as Fijians wanted them retained, (61 percent) and whereas Fijians were indecisive about equal rights for all races concerning land, Indians overwhelmingly sought this option. Three-quarters of both Fijians and Indians regarded large numbers of Indian dependents in one house and on one farm a significant contemporary problem. Although data remains to be analysed and explained, the above tabulated opinions confirm what one might expect from experience in the area and careful observations in the field. The Indian smarts under conditions of extreme land shortage, the Fijians rejoices in the fact that he still has title to his land. Both agree that the Indian diligently tills the soil, (Plates 32 and 33), that the Fijian has a lot to learn concerning farming (commercial farming by implication) and that the European skimmed the cream of the best land in the past. Initially, cursory inspection of the data points to a greater Fijian economic orientation rather than the traditional view one might expect.[51]

Whereas land provides a degree of security in perpetuity for the Fijian, the Indian's lack of land makes its possession, even under the most insecure tenure, a valuable acquisition. It provides cash, security, and a place for an ever-growing augmented family.[52] There is indeed nowhere else other than existing farms for relatives to go if they wish to remain with their kin in the rural area. Land is also a means of earning dowry money, supporting an extravagant wedding, providing for the education of children and a source of constant conflict. Because of a lack of ownership the Indian is very much more vulnerable to economic change than the Fijian. A possibility of a close down in the South Pacific Sugar Mills in the early 1970's, if no solution had been found to continue milling, would have affected disastrously, and severed the land-ties, of no fewer than 31,000 sub-tenants and their families.

Little has been done to change law concerning land, and commissions of enquiry have suggested only mild modifications and revisions. As insurance against the inroads of aliens, the Council of Chiefs has always reaffirmed land regulations. But former aliens are no longer aliens. With independence granted in 1970, Indo-Fijians and Fijians are acceptable equally as citizens of the new Dominion, yet one group takes great pride in having the land which the other cannot possess. As a consequence, Indians dominate all non-farm employment. Paradoxically, Indians who do not own land certainly occupy the very best land, while Fijians who are touted as having almost all the land have relatively little of high quality. This issue is not simple.

In the future, development of Fiji tourism will undoubtedly be of great importance, (Plates 34 and 35), widening perception of land and possibly increasing the gap between owners and non-owners of land. Freehold land has already been used for tourist development but many attractive prime coastal areas belong to Fijian owners. Over the past five years companies have negotiated with the Native Land Trust Board with a view to developing Fijian land, and in one contract the eleven mataqali members owning the 128 acres to be developed, will share two and a half percent of gross takings in the hotel development - a sign of the time and enough to have Gordon and Fison turn in their graves.

CONCLUSION

A number of contemporary workers have written scholarly papers and books on Fiji. Gillion, Derrick, France, Mayer, Spate, Watters, and Ward are recent writers of books who warrant mention. This paper has no intention of duplicating the themes of any writer, and the names of numerous fine writers have been omitted. The intention of the present work is to focus specifically on the changing relationships, some real, others reconstructed (but hopefully close to the "truth") between man of various cultures and the land of Fiji.

The most intriguing aspect of the study from an intellectual point of view has been the interacting and vacillating viewpoints of Fijian and European. The most distressing in terms of emotional response has been the conflict between the European-manipulated Fijian and the European-introduced Indian, where neither party is in a position of its own creation and both are where they are as the result of the machinations a third party.

Charitably one may say that Britain in its own fashion attempted to preserve the Fijian way of life and institutions in their most "pure" form. In what one must consider to be a sincere attempt to do this, it wrought monumental changes, imposed a new system of land holding by law, and manipulated the Fijians in such a way that the wounds of cultural interference may not have healed centuries from now.

Of the three parties Britain is present now only residually, and to be fair, a high degree of both respect and affection is accorded that country. But recorders of history must consider cultural interchange of this sort an inevitablity, as well as a reflection, of the times in which they took place. Similar cultural confrontations will inevitably take place in the future. In the meantime Fiji finds itself a very pleasant land occupied unequally by

133

two races. For successful accommodation of one by the other, dramatic compromises must take place.

What has been written here is account by one, who although concerned is only capable really of a Western perception despite his sincere attempt to see important questions through the eyes of other cultures. Lasaqa, has recently, with justification taken exception to some of the attitudes and approaches of Western scholars. One can only feel sympathetic to his view, while at the same time pointing out that in the realm of perception there is no one absolute truth. There are indeed a number of perceived realities. Together these make for a deeper and more sensitive understanding of the entire question. Lasaqa makes an eloquent plea for a Fijian appreciation of the issues involved and this is a point well taken. In the absence of more than one or two Fijian evaluations, and possibly fewer Indian assessments, it is hoped that a relatively detached outside view may contribute something of a constructive nature while awaiting indigenous histories able to rectify the present imbalance.

REFERENCES

1. MELLER, N. and HORWITZ, R.H. "Hawaii: Themes in Land Mono-
    poly," pp. 25-42 in CROCOMBE, R. G. (ed.) Land Tenure
    in the Pacific Islands. Melbourne: Oxford University Press,
    1970.

2. See, WARD, R.G. Land Use and Population in Fiji. London: Her
    Majesty's Stationery Office, 1965. WATTERS, R. Coro.
    London: Oxford University Press, 1969. SPATE, O.H.K.
    The Fijian People. Suva: Legislative Council Paper No. 13,
    1959. ROTH, G.K. Fijian Way of Life. London: Oxford
    University Press, 1953. DERRICK, R.A. A History of Fiji.
    Suva: Government Press, 1950.

3. FISK, E.K. The Political Economy of Independent Fiji. Wellington:
    AH & AW REED, 1970, pp. 23.

4. BREWSTER, A.B. The Hill Tribes of Fiji. Philadelphia: J.B.
    Lippincott Co. 1922, p. 59.

5. Personal communication with the late Fijian anthropologist, Rusiate
    Nayacakalou. Suva: 1969.

6. Ibid. Robert Swanston, tells of the Tawaki of Ba who surrendered
    his lands with a symbolic gift of soil to Cakombau who in return
    secured the Ba district and set Tawaki up as the paramount
    chief, Tui Ba. This is cited on p. 183 "Affidavit from Mr.
    Robert S. Swanston, British Subject residing in Fiji June 15,
    1892," part of Memoirs of the United States in Support of
    Claims of Fiji Land by George Rodney Burt, Burt Robert Henry,
    John B. Williams and Isaac M. Brower," Suva: N.D. (1902?)

7. FRANCE, P. The Charter of the Land: Custom and Colonization.
    Melbourne: Oxford University Press, 1969, pp. 11-13.

8. See, GROVES, M. "The Nature of Fijian Society: A Review Article,"
    Journal Polynesian Society, 72, No. 3 (1963), pp. 272-291;
    NAYACAKALOU, R.R. "Fiji: Manipulating the System," in
    CROCOMBE, R.G. (ed.) Land Tenure in the Pacific. Mel-
    bourne: Oxford University Press, 1971, pp. 206-226; SAHLINS,
    M.D. Moala: Culture and Nature on a Fijian Island. Seattle:

135

University of Washington Press, 1962, 453 pp., FRANCE, P. op.cit., THOMSON, B. The Fijians: A Study of the Decay of Custom. London: William Heinemann, 1908, 396 pp.

9.   BELSHAW, C.S. Under the Ivi Tree: Society and Economic Growth in Rural Fiji. Berkeley: University of California Press, 1964, p. 183.

10.   Ibid., p. 185.

11.   BERTHOLD, S. Viti: An Account of a Government Mission. Cambridge: Macmillan and Company, 1862, pp. 87, 89.

12.   PARK, A. Personal communication, 1969, Formerly Assistant Chief Secretary to the Government of Fiji.

13.   HOCART, A.M. "The Northern States of Fiji," London: Occasional Paper, No. 11, Royal Anthropological Institute, 1952, p. 16. HOCART, A.M. p. 16-24, pays more than usual attention to the spirituality of land. PRITCHARD, W.T. Polynesian Reminiscences or Life in the South Pacific Islands. London: Chapman and Hall, 1866, p. 242, notes contrary to the writers conclusion that "every parcel or tract of land in Fiji has a name and the boundaries are defined and well known." The present writer feels Pritchard derived his information from informants in well-settled areas with names and that at the time his observations were made Fijians probably were beginning to be wary about questioning concerning land. Without a doubt with the continuation of European occupation Fijians became more sensitive about the importance of labelling and defining land other than that which had traditionally meant much to them.

14.   BREWSTER, A.B. op.cit., p. 290.

15.   NAYACAKALOU, R.R. op.cit., p. 211. Persons and their issue at the time of Cession accepted into another tribe were known legally as dependants. They and descendants received some consideration under law but not the full rights which would have been granted under customary law. See, Government of Fiji, The Laws of Fiji: Native Lands. Ordinances, Chapter 114 (1967), pp. 1522, and 1528.

16.   THOMSON, B. op.cit., p. 355.

17. NAYACAKALOU, R.R. "Nature of Changes in Living Patterns of Pacific Island Man," in FOSBERG, F.R. (ed.), Man's Place in the Island Ecosystem. Honolulu: Bishop Museum Press, 1963, p. 176.

18. IM THURN, Sir Everard, The Journal of William Lockerby - Sandalwood Trader in Fiji 1808-1809. London: Leonard C. Wharton, 1925, p. 8.

19. WARD, R.G. The Pacific Bêche-de-Mer Trade and its Consequences. Paper presented to Pacific Science Congress, Tokyo: August-September 1966. See also, WALLIS, M.D. Life in Fejee. London: William Heath, 1851, p. 97, and WILLIAMS, T. "The Islands and their Inhabitants," Vol. 1 of George S. Rowe (ed.), Fiji and the Fijians. London: Alexander Haylin, 1858, p. 84.

20. Present day air photographs show remains of complicated earth systems. Personal communication with Martin Adams, Pedologist, Department of Agriculture. See, IM THURN, op.cit., p. 28-30 where descriptions of early agriculture and fortifications are given and also WARD, R.G. "Village Agriculture in Viti Levu, Fiji." New Zealand Geographer, April 1960, pp. 36-37.

21. PRITCHARD, W.T. op.cit., p. 245.

22. CARGILL, D. The Memoirs of Mrs. Margaret Cargill. London: John Mason, 1841, p. 117.

23. SMYTHE, R.A. appendix to Seemann, op.cit., p. 427.

24. General Report of Messrs. Williamson and Carew on Lands in the Sigatoka District. Report No. 706 Levuka, April 1880. For an excellent summary of events in the period See, WARD, R.G. "Land use and Alienation in Fiji to 1885," Second Waigani Seminar, Port Moresby: 1968.

25. WILLIAMS, J.B. op.cit., p. 42. Various examples of land trickery are listed in the Fiji Argus, June 25, 1875.

26. General Report of Messrs. Williamson and Carew. op.cit., p. 183.

27. PRITCHARD, W.T. op.cit., pp. 250-252, and "Extract from Final Report of the Land Commissioners Showing the Necessity to the

Natives of Arms and Ammunition," part of Memorial of the United States in Support of the Claims of Fiji Land, etc. op.cit., Also published earlier in Parliamentary Paper C 3584 1883.

28. "Report of the Land Commissioners – Extract Showing the necessity to Natives of Arms and Ammunition," Memorial of the United States... op.cit., p. 225-226, and C 3584, p. 31.

29. "Conversation Sir Hercules Robinson and Cakobau on H.M.S. Dido, September 25, 1874," Parliamentary Papers, C1114, 1875, p. 8.

30. Memorial of the United States in Support of the Claims of Fiji Land. op.cit., p. 7.

31. Parliamentary Papers, C1114, op.cit., p. 19.

32. "Instructions of the Earl of Carnarvon to Sir Arthur Gordon, as to Land Titles and a Land Commission, March 4, 1875, Downing Street," Parliamentary Papers, C3584, 1883, pp. 107. About 400,000 acres out of 850,000 acres were allowed. These were henceforth known as Crown Grants.

33. "Instructions of the Earl of Carnarvon...", op.cit., pp. 107.

34. PRITCHARD, W.T. op.cit., LORIMER, F. "Land Tenure in Fiji," Journal of the Anthropological Sec. April 15, 1880. Parliamentary Paper C3584, 1883, pp. 67-77. THURSTON, J.B. "Upon the Native Ownership of Land in Fiji," Parliamentary Paper C1114, 1875, pp. 55-58.

35. FISON, L. op.cit., p. 67.

36. Ibid., and Memorial of the United States etc., op.cit.,

37. "Remarks Made 1882 by Mr. Victor A. Williamson, former land Commissioner on a petition of colonists and land owners in Fiji," Parliamentary Paper C3584, 1883, p. 60, op.cit.

38. THOMSON, B. op.cit., p. 357.

39. KIRCHOFF, P. "The Principles of Clanship in Human Society," in FRIED, M. (ed.), Readings in Anthropology, Cultural Anthropology, New York: Thomas Y. Crowell, 2 (1959), pp. 259-

270.

40. FRANCE, P. The Charter of the Land. op.cit., pp. 102-110.

41. WARD, R.G. Land Use and Population in Fiji. op.cit., p. 116.

42. SPATE, O.H.K. op.cit., pp. 5 and 6.

43. Council of Chiefs, (Minutes of Proceedings) Records of the Native
    Land Court 1914, cited in France, op.cit., p. 169.

44. For a detailed account of this fascinating period in Fijian history one
    could do no better than read Peter France's outstanding book,
    op.cit.

45. For accounts of Indians in Fiji see: MAYER, A.C. Peasants in the
    Pacific. London: Routledge and Keagan P. (1961). Indians
    in Fiji. London: Oxford University Press (1963), and GILLION,
    K.L. Fiji's Indian Migrants. Melbourne: Oxford University
    Press

46. MAYER, A.C. Indians in Fiji. op.cit., p. 12.

47. Information regarding leases comes from field interviews with author-
    itative Indians and Fijians.

48. Government of Fiji: Agricultural Landlord and Tenant Ordinance
    No. 23, 1966, Title XLI, Cap. 242, Suva: 1967, p. 3266.

49. Personal communications in 1969 with A. Park op.cit., Justin Lewis,
    Attorney General; John Gilmore, Native Land Trust Board;
    and Joketani Cokanasiga, Assistant Secretary, Fijian Affairs.

50. ANDERSON, A.G. "Quality in Indo-Fijian Small Farming," in
    BASSETT, I.G. (ed.) Pacific Peasantry. Palmerston North,
    N.Z.: Geographical Society, 1969, p. 24; Indian Small-
    Farming in Fiji: The Significance of Off-Farm Employment
    Pacific Viewpoint, 9 (1968), No. 1 p. 19.

51. The survey referred to was conducted with the generous cooperation of
    the Fiji Department of Education. Over seven hundred students
    in a large number of both government and private schools in
    Viti Levu and Vanua Levu were questioned in 1970. There
    were approximately 60 variables. A later study will be con-

cerned with correlation and other analyses of the data. Fourth-form students were chosen because it was considered that they were young enought to still reflect the views of parents and old and experienced enough to complete questionnaires. It was assumed that the general level of education of the students was much higher than the parents they represented who could not have been questioned the same way. To arrive at the questions asked approximately one hundred Indian and Fijian adults were interviewed individually.

52. For the importance of off-farm employment by farm dwellers see ANDERSON, A.G. "Indian Small-Farming in Fiji." op.cit.

53. LASAQA, I. "Geography and Geographers in the Changing Pacific: an Islanders View," in BROOKFIELD, H. (ed.) The Pacific in Transition. London: Edward Arnold, 1973, pp. 299-312.

CHAPTER 4

HUMAN CROWDING IN HONG KONG:
A STUDY OF ITS EARLIEST TYPE OF PUBLIC HOUSING[1]

Chuen-Yan David Lai

University of Victoria

Two prominent features within the urban scene in many developing

countries are squatter settlements and overcrowding, both of which are

harrowing and rapidly increasing but challenging forms of city life in the

contemporary world. They are products of two basic considerations, namely,

an enormous influx of people and an inadequate provision of housing. Squat-

ter settlements invariably result in the illegal occupation of government or

private land by poverty-stricken immigrants in their desperate struggle for

space and shelter. Squatters make up a significant percentage of the pop-

ulation of many Asian cities throughout the Pacific rim. For example, they

constitute 15 percent of the population in Singapore and at least over 20

percent in both Djarkarta and Manila. In Hong Kong, the squatter popula-

tion in 1973 was estimated at about 281,000 persons or 7 percent of the

Colony's four million people[2] but this is a comparatively low figure when

compared with the 500,000 squatters or 14 percent of the Colony's popula-

tion in 1965. The reduction is largely due to the government's active pro-

grammes of squatter control, clearance and resettlement. Since 1954, the

Hong Kong government has built hundreds of multi-storey blocks in various

resettlement estates in order to rehouse as many squatters as possible. All

resettlement has been achieved through the use of high-density housing.

The other common feature in Asian cities is overcrowding which may

be expressed in terms of the amount of living space in square feet per per-

son within a single dwelling unit. This ratio was estimated in 1968 by Mitchell

at 135 in Malaysia, 111 in Singapore, 96 in Taipei, 84 in Bangkok and 43

141

in Hong Kong.[3] The last figure masks the specific crowding in many resettlement blocks in Hong Kong because squatters have been rehoused there
at a standard rate of 24 square feet of living space per 'adult', two children under ten years of age being equivalent to an 'adult'.[4] In other words,
a standard room of about 120 square feet (9' 6" x 12' 6") in a resettlement
block will accommodate a family with a possible maximum of eight persons.
This may include a man, his wife and six children under ten years of age.
Such high-density living is unthinkable to many western town planners.

In the past decade, the concern of social scientists has been growing
rapidly for the consequences of high density and overcrowding. The detrimental effects of crowding upon animal populations were demonstrated by
experiments on rats carried out by Calhoun and his associates,[5] and on deer
by Christian, Flyger and Davis.[6] The findings of many studies on human
population display conceptual ambiguities related to definitions of pathology, density and crowding. This confounds any inquiry into the adverse
effects of high population densities on the quality of life.[7] Jacobs, for example, pointed out that overcrowding was different from high density and
asserted that it was the former rather than the latter that might be associated
with high death, disease and social disorganization rates.[8] Population densities are usually expressed in dwelling units or persons per unit ground area
but crowding is defined as the number of persons per bed, the number of
people per room, residential floor area per person, or by other measures.
Therefore, high densities do not indicate the extent of overcrowding and
vice versa. The effects of crowding on people may also vary from persons
of lower socioeconomic status to those of higher socioeconomic status, from
one ethnic group to another, from one city to another, between individuals
and between groups with different attitudes. For instance, Winsborough's
study revealed that the population density in Chicago had a positive correlation with five measures, namely, infant mortality rate, public assistance to persons under eighteen years of age, overall death rate, tuberculosis

rate, and overall public assistance.[9] However, after he removed the effects of migration, quality of housing and socioeconomic status upon these five measures by performing partial correlations, he discovered that high population density still had a positive correlation with the first measure but it had no association with the second measure and had a negative association with each of the last three measures. His findings therefore suggested that the association of high density with urban ills was contingent upon the effects of the three variables of migration, housing quality and socioeconomic status. Newman's study indicated that the crime rate in New York City increased proportionately to building height,[10] and Schmitt's study also revealed that the population density in Honolulu had a positive correlation with its criminal or delinquent behaviour, suicide rate and other social and mental breakdown.[11] However, his study of Hong Kong revealed that Hong Kong, unlike congested areas in the United States, had relatively low death, disease and social disorganization rates.[12] Mitchell's surveys provided further evidence that high densities in Hong Kong did not affect "deeper and more basic levels of emotional strain and hostility, but they affected two superficial manifestations of emotional strain, namely, worry and unhappiness."[13] He also pointed out that "it is necessary to statistically control for other stresses producing these strains. When one (but only one) of these controls is applied (poverty), these two superficial strains still respond to high densities, but they do so only for the poorest members of the communities surveyed in the study."[14] His surveys also showed that although Hong Kong people seemed to have less joy and happiness in life, they did not worry as much as peoples in Southeast Asia who lived at much lower densities.[15] The Thais in Bangkok, and Malays and Indians in Singapore and Malaysia, for, example, had higher levels of emotional strain. Except for Chinese in Bangkok, Chinese people in Malaysia, Singapore and Hong Kong had the lowest levels of emotional illness.[16]

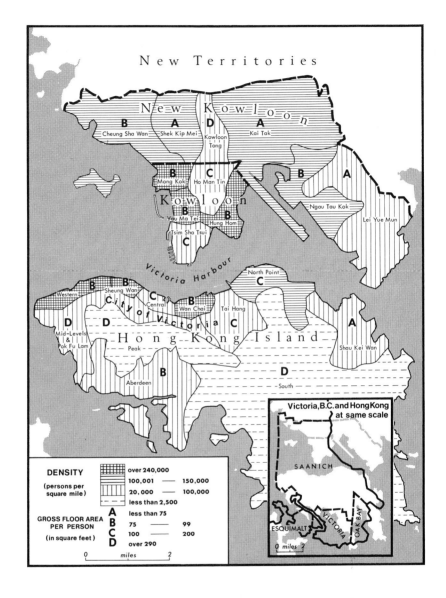

FIGURE 1,4   Population densities and crowding in the urban census
districts of Hong Kong's City proper, 1971.

144

This paper is a study of the overcrowding conditions in the earliest type of Hong Kong's public housing, namely, the Mark I and Mark II Resettlement Domestic Blocks. A seven-storey Mark I Block in Chai Wan Estate was examined as a sample of human crowding in Hong Kong. This paper investigates how families have used their limited space and reveals that although overcrowding is deleterious, it is mainly limited space, poor housing conditions, sub-standard provisions, and the attitudes and behaviour of resettlement residents that have contributed to social conflicts and environmental degradation.

HIGH DENSITY AND OVERCROWDING

The Colony of Hong Kong has a land area of about 408 square miles. The city proper which includes Hong Kong Island, Kowloon Peninsula and New Kowloon, comprises about 50 square miles and covers a slightly smaller area than Greater Victoria, British Columbia, (Table 1,4).

In 1971, the city proper of Hong Kong had nearly 3.2 million people or about three-quarters of the Colony's population, and its average density of 63,314 persons per square mile was about two and a half times greater than the average density of Tokyo (25,200) or Osaka (24,300), and over twenty times that of Greater Victoria (3,047). But this amazing density figure for Hong Kong is an overall mean and fails to indicate the even higher densities of its urban census districts such as Mong Kok, Yau Ma Tei, Hung Hom, Wan Chai, Sheung Wan and the Western District, each of which had a density of over 240,000 persons per square mile (Figure 1,4).[17] Mong Kok, for example, the most densely peopled district, on 0.43 square miles, had a population of 171,692 or a density of over 400,000 persons per square mile (Plates 36 and 37). A similar demographic concentration could be simulated if the entire population of Metropolitan Victoria (195,800) were to be crammed into multi-storey buildings confined within the campus of the University of Victoria which has an area of 0.58 square mile.[18] This would

145

PLATE 36
An aerial view of the
northwestern part of Kowloon.

Hong Kong Government Ph

TABLE 1,4

AREA AND POPULATION OF HONG KONG'S CITY PROPER AND GREATER VICTORIA, 1971

Districts	Area square miles	Population	Density per square mile
Greater Victoria:			
City of Victoria	7.25	61,760	8,518
Saanich	38.08	65,040	1,708
Oak Bay	4.01	18,430	4,607
Esquimalt	2.58	12,925	5,009
Total	51.92	158,155	3,047
Hong Kong's City Proper:			
Hong Kong Island	30.38	996,183	33,157
Kowloon Peninsula	3.56	716,272	90,940
New Kowloon	16.45	1,478,581	203,861
Total	50.39	3,191,036	63,314

Source: Census and Statistics Department, Hong Kong Population and Housing Census, 1971 Main Report. Hong Kong: 1973. Statistics Canada, Victoria Population and Housing Characteristics by Census Tracts, 1971 Census. Ottawa: 1973.

be equivalent to about 340,000 persons per square mile and still less than the density figure for Mong Kok District.

The degree of overcrowding in Hong Kong can be measured in terms of the number of people per bed, or the residential floor area per person. Accordingly to Mitchell's sample surveys, "...28 percent of the adult Hong Kong population sleep 3 or more to a bed and 13 percent sleep four or more to a bed at one time."[19] The 1971 census reported that the four most crowded districts, namely, Skek Kip Mei, Kai Tak, Lei Yue Mun, and Shau Kei Wan, had an average of about 62 square feet of gross residential floor area

PLATE 37
A common street scene in Kowloon.

per person (Figure 1, 4). However it should be noted that these four districts were not the most densely peopled districts, and their average net floor density or actual living space for a person was in fact only 31 square feet.[20] Even this figure underrated the extent of crowding in many resettlement estates, where in March, 1973, a total of about 51,000 families comprising over 377,000 persons lived in conditions below the original space standard of 24 square feet per 'adult'.[21] With this amount of living space per 'adult', about 80 percent of the 18,430 residents in the Oak Bay municipality in Victoria, could be accommodated in the Empress Hotel, the city's largest hotel.[22] Such a density would be more or less equivalent to the crowding in an old resettlement block in Hong Kong.

RESETTLEMENT ESTATES AND BLOCKS

In 1972, there were four kinds of public housing, namely resettlement blocks, government low cost housing units, dwellings of the Hong Kong Housing Authority and those of the Hong Kong Housing Society, which together provided accommodation for nearly two-fifths of the Colony's population.[23] (Table 2,4). In March, 1973, there were twenty-five resettlement estates consisting of 515 multi-storey blocks which have housed over 1.2 million former squatters and others.[24] Twenty of these resettlement estates are situated within the city proper of Hong Kong (Figure 2,4). Each estate is in fact an urban community by itself because it has a great concentration of people and variety of industrial and commercial activities. The average population of each estate is above 50,000 but a few have more than 100,000 persons. For example, Tsz Wan Shan Estate which covers about 100 acres or 0.16 square miles has a population of nearly 150,000 which is only about 8,000 persons less than the population of Greater Victoria.

In each resettlement estate there are different types of multi-storey blocks which can be broadly classified into three main groups.[25] The first group is

149

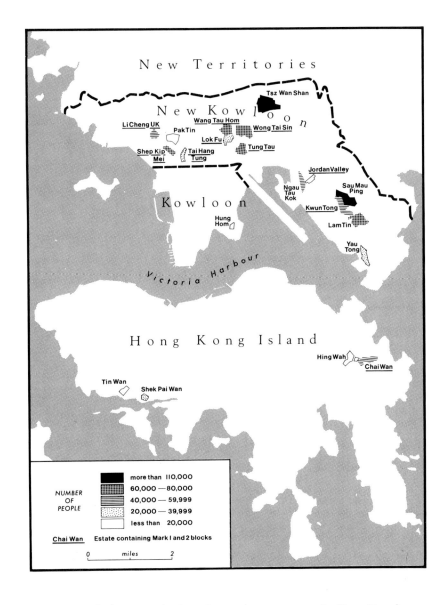

FIGURE 2,4   Distribution of resettlement estates in Hong Kong's
City proper, 1973

150

TABLE 2,4

GOVERNMENT AND GOVERNMENT-AIDED HOUSING,
HONG KONG 1972

Kind	Family Income-Limit $HK Per Month[a]	Standard Space Allocation sq. ft. per adult	Population Estimated	Percentage of Hong Kong's Population
Resettlement Blocks	No limit	24 - 25	1,049,900[d]	25
Government Low Cost Housing Units	Less than $500[b]	35	231,400	6
Housing Authority Dwellings	$400-$900[c]	35	201,900	5
Housing Society Dwellings	Less than $1,000[c]	35	115,000	3

Source: Report of the Housing Board, Hong Kong Government, 1972, pp. 17-18.

(a) $HK5 is equivalent to $Cdn1 or roughly equivalent to $US1.

(b) $600 a month for Kwai Chung Estate.

(c) Up to $1,250 a month for high rent units.

(d) The population figure published by the Resettlement Department was 1,205,085.

the earliest type of resettlement buildings known as Mark I and Mark II blocks. These are six, seven, or eight-storey buildings constructed between 1955 and 1964 (Plate 38).[26] Most of them are H-shaped, but some I-shaped blocks have been built on sites where space limitations or site characteristics have precluded the use of a standard 'H' block. Communal latrines, bathrooms, and washing places are provided, and dwelling units are accessible from a public external balcony corridor which skirts the outside of each floor (Figure 3,4). The standard size of a room is about 120 square feet housing four to five 'adults'. The second group of resettlement

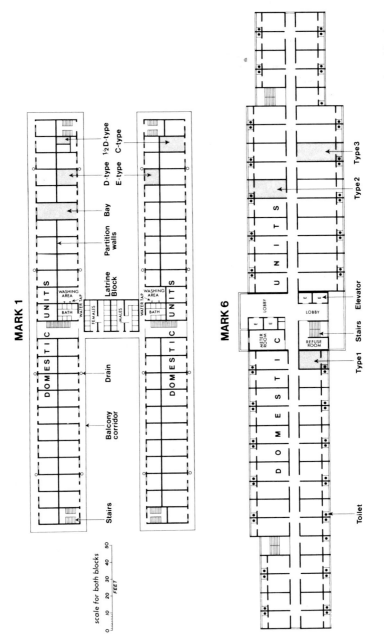

MARK 1

Stairs

Balcony
corridor

Drain

DOMESTIC UNITS

DOMESTIC UNITS

WASHING
AREA

BATH

WATER TAP

FEMALES

MALES

Latrine
Block

WASHING
AREA

WATER TAP

BATH

Partition
walls

Bay

D-type   ½D-type   C-type
E-type

scale for both blocks

0 10 20 30 40 50
FEET

MARK 6

DOMESTIC

UNITS

METER
ROOM

E

E

LOBBY

E

E

LOBBY

REFUSE
ROOM

Toilet

Type1   Stairs   Elevator

Type2   Type3

FIGURE 3,4   Floor plans of Mark I and Mark VI resettlement domestic blocks. Mark IV and Mark V blocks are basically similar in design.

152

PLATE 38
Typical H-shaped Mark I and II blocks
in Wong Tai Sin resettlement estate.

Hong Kong Government Photo

153

buildings range from the eight-storey Mark III to sixteen-storey Mark IV and V blocks, which were constructed between 1964 and 1970 (Plate 39). They are completely different in design from the first group because their dwelling rooms are accessible from internal corridors and each room has its own private balcony, water tap, internal electrical wiring and private lavatory or a lavatory shared between two or three rooms (Figure 3,4). Refuse chutes are provided in each corridor. The standard room size varies from 129 to 135 square feet and is therefore slightly larger than that of the first group. The last group, the most recent highrise buildings, consists of the sixteen-storey Mark VI blocks which were built after 1970. They are basically similar to the Mark V in design but their rooms are longer so as to permit a more generous allocation of space at 35 square feet per 'adult'. The standard room is therefore 140 square feet for four 'adults', and this space allocation is similar to that found in improved government low-cost housing units.

In March, 1973 the earliest group of resettlement blocks housed 525,641, the middle or intermediate group 630,580 and the latest group 27,456 people.[27] In other words, nearly half of the resettlement population still live in the first group where the poor living environment can be exemplified by an in-depth study of a Mark I block in Chai Wan Estate. This estate was developed in 1958 and is situated at the northeastern corner of Hong Kong Island. It is medium-sized, covers an area of about twenty-seven acres and had a population of 55,550 in March 1973 (Plate 40). The estate contains twenty-six blocks, of which its twelve Mark I and II blocks housed 27,426 and its fourteen Mark III and IV blocks housed 28,124 people.[28] Similar to other old resettlement estates in Hong Kong, Chai Wan Estate is confronted with the problem of overcrowding. In May, 1973, over 24,000 or 43 percent of its population did not have a living space at the standard rate of 24 square feet per 'adult' (Table 3, 4). Previously if families reached

154

PLATE 39
Typical sixteen-story Mark IV and V blocks in Ngau Tau Kok resettlement estate.

155

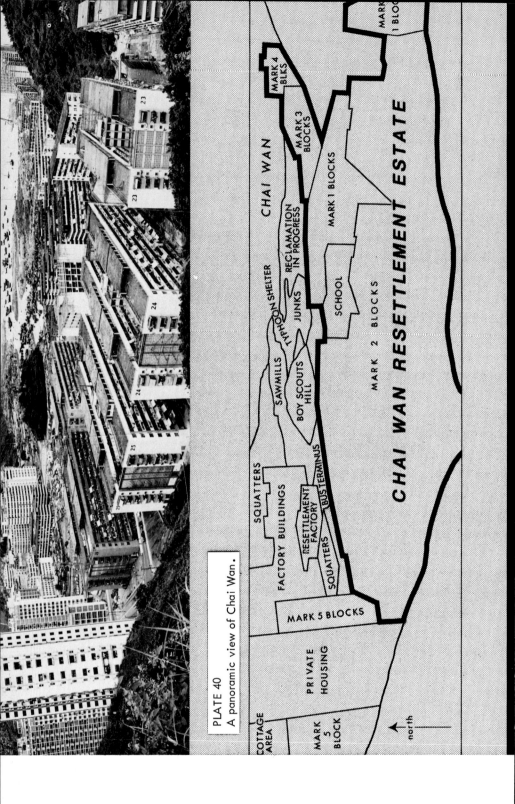

PLATE 40
A panoramic view of Chai Wan.

CHAI WAN

MARK 4 BLKS
MARK 3 BLOCKS
MARK 1 BLOCKS
RECLAMATION IN PROGRESS
TYPHOON SHELTER
JUNKS
SCHOOL
SAWMILLS
BOY SCOUTS HILL
MARK 2 BLOCKS
SQUATTERS
FACTORY BUILDINGS
BUS TERMINUS
RESETTLEMENT FACTORY
SQUATTERS
MARK 5 BLOCKS
PRIVATE HOUSING
COTTAGE AREA
MARK 5 BLOCK

CHAI WAN RESETTLEMENT ESTATE

MARK 1 BLOCK

north

TABLE 3,4

NUMBERS OF FAMILIES AND PERSONS LIVING BELOW THE STANDARD SPACE ALLOCATION IN CHAI WAN ESTATE, MAY, 1973

Living Space Sq. ft. per 'adult'	No. of Families	No. of Persons
12 and below	6	33
12.1 - 14	11	104
14.1 - 16	113	831
16.1 - 18	406	3,059
18.1 - 20	1,083	7,702
20.1 - 22	1,103	6,522
22.1 - 23.9	809	5,892
Total	3,531	24,143

Source: Monthly Density and Decantation Returns for the month of May, 1973, Chai Wan Estate.

a living space of 16 square feet per 'adult' they were eligible to apply for larger rooms.[29] If this figure were regarded as the limit of unacceptable overcrowding, 130 families consisting of nearly 1,000 persons in Chai Wan Estate would be qualified to apply for more space. However, their chance of obtaining larger rooms is very slim because there are so many people in other estates living well below the 16 square feet per 'adult' limit. For example, in March 1973, there was a total of 513 families, nearly 3,400 persons, in all of the resettlement estates in Hong Kong who had a living space less than 12 square feet per 'adult'.[30] This is the equivalent to the area of a grave of 2 feet by 6 feet. These families would therefore have the priority for relocation should there be available rooms to relieve their overcrowded conditions.

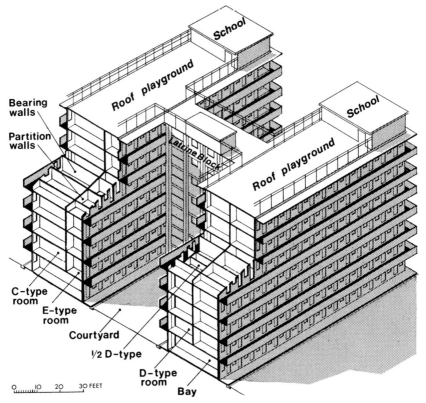

Bearing walls

Partition walls

Roof playground

School

School

Roof playground

Latrine Block

C-type room

E-type room

Courtyard

½ D-type

D-type room

Bay

0   10   20   30 FEET

FIGURE 4,4   A cut-away diagram of Block 18 in Chai Wan estate.

FLOOR USES AND FACILITIES

One of the most crowded resettlement blocks in Chai Wan Estate is Block 18 (Figure 4,4). It is a standard H-shaped seven-storey Mark I block which covers a ground area of about 16,000 square feet. In March, 1973, the block accommodated 462 families which consisted of 2,594 persons. Of these 1,148 were male, 1,131 female and 315 children.[31] The population density of the Block was therefore about 16 persons per 100 square feet of ground area. This approximates a density of over 4.5 million persons per square mile! The long wing of the H-shaped block is structurally divided into twenty-four elongated bays, each measuring ten feet wide and twenty-

TABLE 4,4

TYPES AND NUMBER OF ROOMS IN BLOCK 18

Type of Room	Approximate Size	No. of Rooms	No. of 'adults' per room	Monthly Rent($HK)
D	9' 6" x 12' 6"	196	4 - 5	18.00
Half-D	4' 9" x 10' 0"	358	2 - 2.5	9.00
E	9' 6" x 9' 0"	152	3 - 3.5	12.50
C	9' 6" x 16' 0"	152	5.5 - 6.5	23.00

Source: Chai Wan Estate Office, Unpublished data. The D- and Half-D type rooms are on the third and sixth floors and E- and C- type rooms are on all other levels but the ground floor.

five feet deep. On the ground floor, each bay houses a shop or workshop. On the upper six floors, the bays are partitioned into 858 domestic units or rooms which can be classified into four types according to their sizes (Table 4,4). The standard type is made up of D-type rooms formed by partitions running along the centre line of the bays. Each room has a floor area of about 120 square feet, but when it is sub-divided for the use of two families, each half-D-type room will have a floor area of only 48 square feet because an open space of about 24 square feet (2'6" x 9'6") is used as a small corridor inside the room. On some floors, the partition walls are built closer to the inner sides of the wings in order to provide larger C-type rooms of 152 square feet for larger families and smaller E-type rooms of 86 square feet for smaller families. Sometimes, the partitions may be removed so that a family of eight to ten 'adults' can occupy the entire bay of about 240 square feet. Ventilation in each room is provided by the door, a window, and a built-in grille in the upper part of the partition wall. Communal facilities on each floor include two separate latrines and bathrooms for men and women, two washing places and four water taps. Since electricity is not provided in the rooms, such installations are the responsibility of the tenants themselves. It was not until 1972 that the government began to replace the hazardous outside wiring that had been installed by tenants with proper cables in conduits (Plate 41).

The roof of the block is strengthened, fenced and used by a primary school run by a church. Four penthouses built at the ends of two wings provide a total of eight classrooms, and the open space between the penthouses is used as a playground. The school conducts separate morning and afternoon sessions, and in 1973 had a total enrolment of 548 pupils in sixteen classes.

OVERCROWDING AND THE USE OF SPACE

Many rooms in Block 18 have been occupied for so many years that the number of occupants per room now far exceeds the standard maximum of five 'adults' in a room of 120 square feet. The extent of overcrowding is revealed by a random sample of the amount of living space per person available to 148 families in the block. In June 1973, half of them were living below the standard space allocation (Table 5,4). Their overcrowding situation is attributed to four main causes. First is the rapid natural increase in the family. Second, as children reach ten years of age or above, they qualify as 'adults' and need more space. Third, many persons continue to live in the same abode after marriage, and now have children of their own. For example, a D-type room was formerly shared by four bachelors. Later two of them moved out but the other two got married. The room was therefore partitioned into two half-D-type rooms. Each family later had two children and continued to live in a room of 48 square feet, that is 16 square feet per 'adult' or 12 square feet per person. The fourth common reason for overcrowding results from the accommodation of tenants' relatives.

160

TABLE 5.4

THE DEGREE OF OVERCROWDING IN 148 FAMILIES, JUNE 1973

Living Space square feet per person	No. of Families	No. of Persons
Below 17	10	71
17 - 18.9	17	107
19 - 20.9	22	149
21 - 23.9	17	95
24 - 34.9	62	271
35 and over	20	43
Total	148	736

Source: Field Survey, June 1973.

After 1967 a stricter policy was adopted to curtail such increases. For example, if a tenant's daughter were to marry, his son-in-law would not be eligible to live in the same unit.[32]

The limited space available to each family has taxed human ingenuity to the maximum. Of the 92 families responding to the interview, 85 of them used at least one bunk bed, 26 families had built 'cocklofts' (attics built inside their rooms), and 31 families used at least one canvas folding bed. All the 92 families had at least one bed which was shared by two to three persons in the winter, 27 families had people sleeping at over four to a bed and only 23 families had a bed used solely by one person. Ventilation in winter is poor partly because too many people sleep inside and partly because the doors and windows are closed. Furthermore, even the ventilation holes on the rear walls are usually blocked by all sorts of household articles. In the summer, the rooms are so hot and stuffy that about half of the people in the 92 families sleep on floors, balcony corridors and

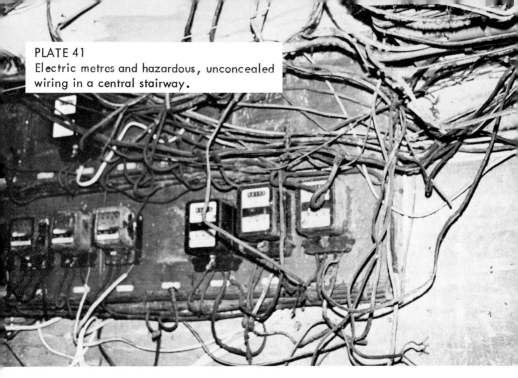

PLATE 41
Electric metres and hazardous, unconcealed wiring in a central stairway.

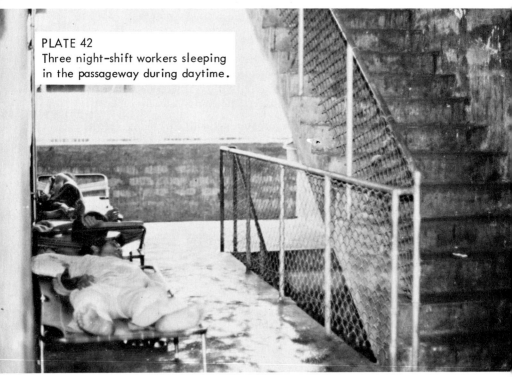

PLATE 42
Three night-shift workers sleeping in the passageway during daytime.

TABLE 6,4

SUMMER SLEEPING PLACES

Location	No. of Persons
Inside Places:	
Bedspace	176
'Cockloft'	69
Floor	188
Outside Places:	
Passageway next to stairs	34
Balcony corridor	21
Street	5
Elsewhere	4
Total	497

Source: Field Survey, June 1973.

passageways in order to get away from the steamy and claustrophobic atmosphere inside their rooms and to obtain better ventilation (Table 6,4 and
Plate 42).

The living conditions of three families were chosen for a closer exam-
ination. Families X and Y shared a D-type room, with each family thereby occupying a half-D-type room.[33] Mr. X. had built a 'cockloft' so that
he could make room for his cupboard, refrigerator, wardrobe and a small
table on the floor (Figure 5,4). In the summer his wife and young daughter
slept on the floor, and he and his son in the balcony corridor. In the winter
the whole family slept in the 'cockloft'. Since the room was so cramped,
this particular family had to do its cooking and dining in the balcony corri-

163

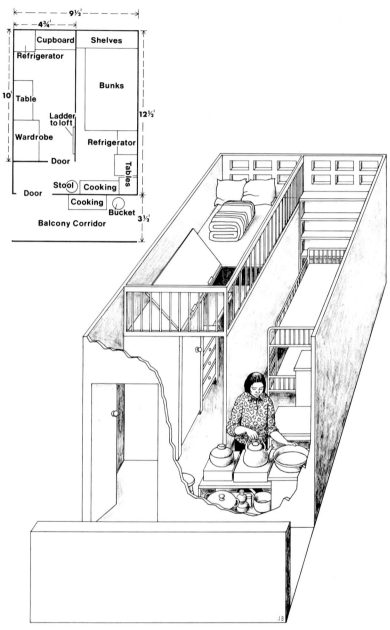

FIGURE 5,4   A drawing showing space utilization in two half-D-type rooms.

PLATE 43
An example illustrating the maximum use of the vertical space above, between and beneath the beds.

PLATE 44
A balcony corridor.

PLATE 45
Washing lines on balconies.

dor. Mr. Y. did not have a proper room. Instead he used a bunk bed
(4' 0" x 6' 0"), around which a curtain could be drawn to provide a little
privacy. He and his wife slept on the bottom deck and his two children
above. A cupboard, refrigerator and cooking box were placed in the narrow
corridor inside the room, where the family had its meals. The third family
consisting of nine members occupied a L-type room. Here, Mr. Z. and
his wife slept on a moderately large bed. His mother and sister occupied
a smaller bed, while his children slept in the 'cockloft'. As his mother and
sister were 'outworkers' employed by a factory manufacturing plastic toys,
they brought home parts for assembling and thus used up nearly all of the
available open space inside the room.

The above three families, like other families in the block, used folding
tables and chairs which could be packed up easily in order to save space.
Shelves were set up above the cupboard and wardrobe in order to use space
up to the ceiling. Household articles were crammed beneath the beds
Plate 43). In lieu of proper kitchens, cooking was done on the balcony
corridor. The cooking boxes that are used are wooden boxes consisting of
two shelves, the upper one holding two kerosene stoves and the lower one
storing cooking utensils (Plate 44). Cooking in the corridor was formerly forbidden but the regulation lapsed gradually in the face of extreme
overcrowding. Clothing is dried on wires or bamboo poles projecting from
the balcony (Plate 45).

Most of the ninety-two families responding to the interview declined
to reveal their incomes. The ten families who were willing to disclose their
approximate incomes, averaged about six persons per family and had an
average monthly income of about $HK1,800. With this income a family
of six persons may be able to live a simple, comfortable life in the estate
because rents are extremely low in comparison with those of private housing.[34] Other families in the resettlement block are not too poor either be-

cause they possess the symbols of 'affluent' life – refrigerators, radios, private telephones, television sets and other 'luxury' items. The interview also revealed that over one-third of the ninety-two families were on the payroll of factories, but most of their work was undertaken inside rooms and in balcony corridors. The work included painting plastic toys, assembly of plastic flowers, making rattan ware, embroidery, tailoring and many other home industries. Many families therefore used their rooms and balcony corridors not only for sleeping, dining, studying, recreation, and social entertainment, but also for the manufacturing and storing of raw materials and finished products (Plate 46). A poor residential environment is caused by the penetration of manufacturing activities into living areas and aggravated by inadequate washing, bathing and sanitary facilities and other amenities such as electricity supply.

SOCIAL AND ENVIRONMENTAL CONFLICTS

Over ninety percent of the ninety-two families responding to the interview indicated that they did not mind living in high density resettlement buildings and accepted it as the inevitable in Hong Kong because of its large population and lack of space. However, they desired very much to have more space per person, and complained that overcrowding had affected their health and led to an increase in illness in the hot, steamy summer. Most of the people attributed the causes of social and environmental conflicts to substandard provisions, namely, the lack of decent toilet facilities, inefficient systems of garbage and waste water disposal, inadequate water supply and washing places, and lack of recreation space for children. On the third floor of the block, for example, there were over 200 men and boys who had to share a latrine which consisted of two open horizontal trenches, one being partitioned into six cubicles and the other into five (Plate 47). This gave a ratio of one cubicle being used by about eighteen

PLATE 47
A latrine cubicle.

PLATE 46
Two workers in a D-type room.

persons. The trenches are flushed automatically every fifteen minutes. However, the cubicles nearest the latrine entrance cannot be used partly because they are too open to view and partly because flush-water splashes down onto the occupants there. The far cubicles in the rows are located at the point where the discharge from the trenches is ostensibly drained away. These cubicles are not always usable because a pool of foul water is invariably backed-up and the opening is usually blocked by paper and excrement. It is also common to find that other cubicles cannot be used because the footholds are in a filthy state. Sometimes, when the flush system is not working, the entire trench will be unusable. On July 9, 1973, a survey of seven "male" latrines with seventy-seven cubicles revealed that only fifty-one cubicles were suitable for use and these were shared by over 1,200 male residents in the block. This number of possible users does not include street hawkers who use the latrines on the ground and first floors, and pupils on the roof top who use the latrine on the seventh floor. Brawls among the residents are often caused by disputes over the improper use of latrine cubicles; impatient children are among the worst culprits. The floors of latrines are perpetually wet, slippery, and in a highly unsanitary state. As they are cleaned only once a day, they are always filthy and unhygenic.

Complaints in respect of poor bathing facilities are frequent by female residents in the block. The bathroom is partitioned into seven doorless cubicles which contain no fixtures apart from a drain. They are but empty, two-feet-square shelters, where users have to carry their cold or hot water in buckets. The bathroom not only lacks basic privacy but is also subject to intrusions by drug addicts and vandals who frequently break down doors leading to bathrooms used by women. Therefore, most of the female residents are wary of entering the bathroom during the late hours of the day, and wary of taking a bath unaccompanied by another woman. Most mothers stated that they had to stand guard by the entrance of the bathroom if their daughters were using it.

The lack of proper garbage disposal has also caused many conflicts among residents and between residents and resettlement officers. As refuse chutes are not provided in the block, each family is required to hang a small dustbin outside its room. This is emptied once a day. The residents however find it easier to throw their garbage into the street, especially when their dustbins are full or when they do not wish to keep the odorous rubbish right in front of their room. The open courtyards and the covers of hawkers stalls in the streets are therefore littered with garbage (Plate 48). Another place commonly used as a garbage dump is the washing area where housewives leave their rubbish after preparing their meals. Garbage is also found discarded in corridors, stairs, and streets (Plate 49). By their inconsiderate methods of waste disposal the residents have not only spoiled their own living environment but also created untold problems with garbage collectors and resettlement officers.

The facilities of disposing of waste water in the block are provided by sixteen drains which run vertically from the top floor to the ground floor. The spacing allows for two such drains for about ten families. Those whose rooms are further away from the drains sometimes do not bother to make the trip to the outlet; the dirty water is simply heaved into the streets. Those whose rooms are closer to the drains do not see this as an advantage because they complain that people are careless in pouring waste water into the drain and constantly wet the floor in front of their doors (Plate 50). Moreover, many people use spittoons as containers for urine and faeces in the evening. Instead of emptying these spittoons in the latrine, some people just poor the human waste into the drain. This has led to many a violent argument among tenants.

In each washing place there are only two taps which supply cold water to over forty families. Here people line up for their water and also undertake all kinds of washing and cleaning. Such places are packed with people late in the afternoon when housewives are preparing their meals and people returning from work come to collect water for bathing. Disputes are not un-common when someone splashes another during washing or when people fight for their turn at the tap.

Brawls are also frequently occasioned by noisy children, radios and television sets. Children are confined at home partly because there are insufficient facilities in playgrounds (Plate 51), and partly because their parents do not permit them to go away to the public playing ground. Thirty-five housewives stated that they did not allow their small children to go to the playgrounds outside the block, fearing that they might be bullied or badly influenced by undesirable persons. The playgrounds are usually mono-polised by thugs who frighten off most children and force others to join youth gangs. This was also the view shared by many people in other resettlement estates.[35] Children therefore are compelled to spend most of their time watching television or listening to radios inside their rooms or playing along the balcony corridors or passageways next to staircases. However, there is not much open space on the floor for the children to play and their fights and quarrels often lead to brawls among parents.

Vandalism and crimes are common in the estate. Residents complained that lighting fixtures in the stairways were frequently broken and that it took a long time to have them replaced by government agencies. As a result, residents have to grope their way up and down the staircases. Indecent assaults or robbery are therefore common. However, most of the cases are not reported to the police partly because of the fear of vengeance but main-ly because ot the 'red tape' involved in reporting such cases to the police. Girls in their teens were, for their own protection, constantly advised not to return home too late in the evening.

CONCLUSION

The study reveals in miniature the enormous problems of space avail-

PLATE 48
Garbage thrown onto the covers of hawker stalls in the street.

PLATE 49
A garbage dump at a street corner adjacent to the block.

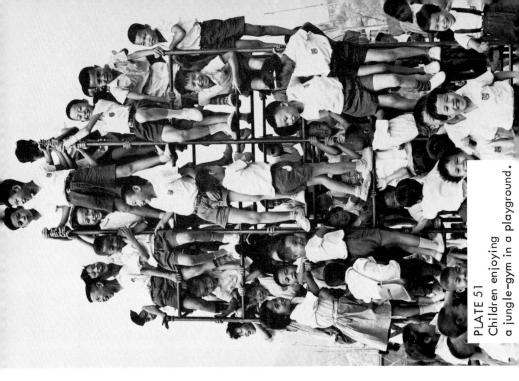

PLATE 51
Children enjoying
a jungle-gym in a playground.

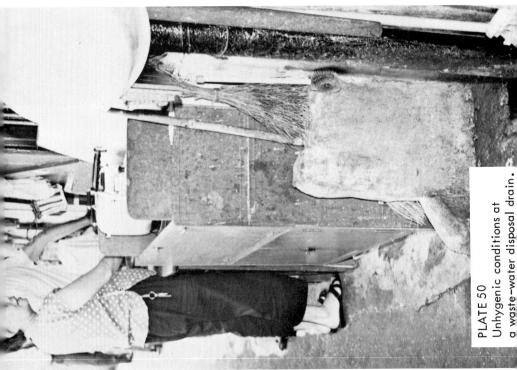

PLATE 50
Unhygenic conditions at
a waste-water disposal drain.

ability in relation to basic human needs, and the continuous struggle to utilize available space to its fullest advantage. The very restricted nature of the spatial environment has prompted much ingenuity in devising space-saving methods, comparable to the work of 'space-control' specialists of department stores.

It is observed from the study that Asian people, particularly, the Chinese, have a capacity to endure poor housing and afflictions of over-crowding unequalled by western people, who, if they were to live in a similar environment, might very well be driven to social and mental break-down by stresses and pressures arising in their lives. Therefore, without appropriate modifications, the criteria for population density, low cost housing quality, and planning approaches developed in western countries cannot be applied to Asian nations.

The study also reveals that except for those living in conditions below the standard space allocation, most residents in the old resettlement build-ing were not extremely vexed at the crowding problem. The majority of resi-dents attributed their unhappiness, irritation, social conflicts and poor living environment to sub-standard provisions and housing conditions. Disorderly conduct and anti-social behaviour were also major factors for the environ-mental and aesthetic degradation in resettlement buildings.

The government of Hong Kong became aware of the poor designs of the Mark I and Mark II blocks and since 1970 has been building the new Mark VI blocks in which each domestic unit is self-contained, and the minimum living space has been raised from 24 to 35 square feet per person instead of per 'adult'. In addition, the government has also carried out the 'de-cantation' programme to thin out the population in old resettlement blocks and convert their domestic units into self-contained flats, though at higher rentals. In spite of all these efforts, over half a million people in Hong Kong are still living in the earliest type of public housing described in this

175

paper. Many of these residents are now more affluent than when they were first resettled, but being unable to pay the high rents of private housing, they have to rely on public low-cost housing. From the preliminary results of the 1971 census it was estimated that only about eleven percent of all households in the Colony could afford to rent private self-contained accommodation without having to 'double-up' with other families.[36] Therefore, the government has to shoulder the responsibility of providing more public cheap housing and improving the living environment of the existing ones. The lessons learned from the experience gained in Hong Kong are that the early public housing programme should be considered only as emergency housing, and that squatters could be resettled cheaply at high densities but they should be provided with private sanitary facilities and other amenities such as piped water and electricity supply. Standards of public housing should be raised gradually and with them, rents should be increased in line with the capacity of tenants to pay. The squatter clearance and rehousing programmes in Hong Kong which, on the whole, are very successful, may be adopted by other developing countries confronted with similar problems of squatters, shortage of housing and rapid increase in urban population.

REFERENCES

1. The author wishes to thank the staff of the Housing Department and Chai Wan Estate for providing data and information. The author is also indebted to the residents of Block 18 who responded to questioning. Photographs (Figures 2,4, 3,4, 5,4, 7,4 14,4 19,4 and 21,4) are courtesy of Hong Kong Government Information Services.

2. Unpublished data, the Housing Department, Hong Kong Government, June 1973. Squatters are people living in all kinds of temporary housing such as roof-top structures, derelict boats, and wooden shacks which have been erected on government or private land without a right or title.

3. MITCHELL, R.E. Levels of Emotional Strain in Southeast Asian Cities. Taipei: The Orient Cultural Service, 1972, p. 405.

4. Hereafter, 'adult' in quotation marks implies that it includes children under ten years of age.

5. CALHOUN, J.B. "Population Density and Social Pathology," Scientific American, 206 (February, 1962), pp. 139-148. "The Role of Space in Animal Sociology," The Journal of Social Issues, 22, No. 4 (1966), pp. 46-59. MARSDEN, H. "Crowding and Animal Behavior," paper presented at American Psychological Association 1970 annual convention.

6. CHRISTIAN, J., FLYGER, V., and DAVIS, D. "Factors in the Mass Mortality of a Herd of Sika Deer Cervus nippon," Chesapeake Science, 1 (1960), pp. 79-95.

7. GAD, G. " "Crowding" and "Pathologies": Some Critical Remarks," The Canadian Geographer, 17, No. 4 (1973), pp. 373-390.

8. JACOBS, J. The Death and Life of Great American Cities. New York: Random House, 1961.

9. WINSBOROUGH, H.H. "The Social Consequences of High Population Density," Land and Contemporary Problems, 30, No. 1 (1965), pp. 120-126.

177

10. NEWMAN, O. Defensible Space. New York: The MacMillan Co., 1972, p. 72.

11. SCHMITT, R.C. "Density, Delinquency and Crime in Honolulu," Sociology and Social Research, 41 (1957), pp. 274-276. "Population Densities and Mental Disorders in Honolulu," Hawaii Medical Journal, 16 (1957), pp. 396-397. "Density, Health and Social Disorganization," Journal of the American Institute of Planners, 32, No. 1 (1966), pp. 38-40.

12. SCHMITT, R.C. "Implications of Density in Hong Kong," Journal of the American Institute of Planners, 29, No. 3 (1963), pp. 210-217.

13. MITCHELL, R.E., op.cit., pp. 465-466.

14. Ibid.

15. Ibid., p. 23.

16. Ibid., pp. 36-37.

17. Census and Statistics Department of Hong Kong, Hong Kong Population and Housing Census, 1971 Main Report. Hong Kong Government Printer (1973), Table 4, p. 28.

18. MITCHELL, J.S. Guide to Canadian Universities. Richmond Hill: Simon and Schuster, 1970, p. 137.

19. MITCHELL, R.E., op.cit., p. 407.

20. The total floor area of a residential building is called the gross residential floor area but the actual living space or the net residential floor area is the gross floor area minus the area of kitchens, toilets, bathrooms, corridors, staircases and landings. The net floor area is usually taken as fifty percent of the gross floor area. (See Census and Statistic Department of Hong Kong: "Overcrowding and Sharing of Housing Accommodation in Hong Kong as revealed by the 1971 census," Hong Kong Monthly Digest of Statistics, January 1973, p. 64-65).

21. Compiled from unpublished "Monthly Density and Decantation Returns for the month of March, 1973," Resettlement Department, Hong Kong, 1973.

22. Personal Communication, Mr. William A. Gray, General Manager of the Empress Hotel. The total inside space of the Empress Hotel is 335,000 square feet which includes over 450 sleeping rooms, hallways, passages and other living facilities. In 1971, Oak Bay Municipality had 18,430 persons or 17,555 'adults' with two children under ten years of age being equivalent to an 'adult'. At a density of 24 square feet per 'adult', the Empress Hotel will be able to accomodate about 14,000 'adults'.

23. After 1970 the standard and finish for new resettlement estates are the same as those for government low cost housing estates. Therefore in April, 1973 the Resettlement Department, Government Low Cost Housing and Hong Kong Housing Authority were abolished and replaced by one body, the Housing Department, which is now in charge of all kinds of public housing. The Hong Kong Housing Society remains as a government-aided housing agency.

24. Unpublished data, the Housing Department, Hong Kong Government, March, 1973. Other people who are eligible for resettlement include victims of fires and natural disasters, ex-tenants of buildings which are declared to be dangerous and have to be demolished, and others. See, Housing Board Report, Hong Kong Government, 1972, p. 7.

25. Annual Departmental Report, Commissioner for Resettlement, Hong Kong Government, 1971-1972, pp. 14-15.

26. Mark I and Mark II blocks which are basically similar in design, differ in that the two long wings of Mark II are connected by screens of perforated bricks within which are placed the end staircases. Mark II blocks also have large rooms of 310 square feet with private balcony at their ends.

27. Unpublished data, the Housing Department, Hong Kong Government, March, 1973.

28. Unpublished data, Chai Wan Estate Office, March, 1973.

29. Annual Departmental Report, Commissioner for Resettlement, Hong Kong Government, 1966-1967, p. 8.

30. Compiled from unpublished "Monthly Density and Decantation Returns for the month of March, 1973" Resettlement Department, Hong Kong, 1973.

31. Unpublished data, Chai Wan Estate Office, March, 1973.

32. Annual Departmental Report, Commissioner for Resettlement, Hong Kong Government, 1968-1969, p. 28.

33. Real names of the three respondents are not used in order to comply with their request for anonymity.

34. A friend of the author who lives in Causeway Bay pays a monthly rent of $HK320 for a room of 9' 0" x 9' 0" whereas the rent for a E-type room of 9' 6" x 9' 0" in a resettlement estate is only $HK12.50 per month.

35. CHEUNG, A. "Summer in the Ghetto," South China Morning Post, Hong Kong. July 22, 1973, p. 4.

36. PRYOR, E.G. "Private Housing in Hong Kong," The Planner. Journal of Planning Institute, 59, No. 10 (1973), p. 458.

CHAPTER 5

THE TOURIST GHETTOS OF HAWAII

Bryan H. Farrell

University of California, Santa Cruz

Hawaii has a number of characteristics stemming from the land, but more important by far than the direct products of Hawaiian land which have traditionally furnished income, are newly appreciated conceptual resources which economically, are now more valuable.[1] Collectively these may be called the ambient resource, a combination of such elements as a warm sensuous, and not debilitating climate; exciting coastal and mountain scenery; warm, clear, ocean water; uncluttered open spaces of crop land, forest and park and one of the most interesting cosmopolitan populations in the world, set in surroundings both exciting and peacefully tranquil. These are the amenities of Hawaii, which contribute to what Clawson would call a resource-based recreation area.[2] In the Mediterranean the increasing use made of the ambient resource is called by Svendsen the sunshine revolution.[3] This is equally appropriate for Hawaii.

The cynic may see polluted waters, grimy air, a ravished landscape and a population bereft of land,[4] yet it seems clear that almost 3,000,000 visitors a year must see the island group in a very favourable light.[5] To accommodate such a transient population, about three times the permanent population, construction and land development has continued uninterrupted and at a staggering pace, since World War II.

To understand exactly the character of Hawaii's ambient resource, it is necessary, very briefly, to go back to the nineteenth century.[6] All subsequent developments have had a profound bearing on the visitor industry which is not only a reflection of present day mores but also a logical extension of economic evolution and changing perceptions towards

181

land and ultimately leisure in Hawaii.

Nineteenth century Hawaiian society was highly centralized and socially stratified. A chiefly elite controlled the land at the will of the King, and at the base of the pyramid were the bulk of the people, toilers and labourers by the thousand. European merchants, missionaries and their families, and others quickly understood the system, or perhaps more correctly, saw the possible advantages of working to become an integral part of a changed Hawaiian society. This they did, some even to the extent of ingratiating themselves with Hawaiian Royalty and acting as advisers attempting to steer the course of Hawaii along a pre-determined white-oriented path.

The Royal Family made grants of land for services rendered, and the aliens who perceived the immense agricultural potential of vast acreages of land finally saw possibilities almost within their grasp. Powerful interest groups pressured the King in 1848 to redistribute nearly all his land and to allow both its lease and ultimately its outright purchase. To shorten and over-simplify a long and complicated story, the bulk of the land fell into the hands of a relatively few powerful haoles or whites, sometimes the sons or grandsons of missionaries, aided and abetted by Hawaiian Royalty and the chiefly elite, some of whom were learning to live in elegant splendour.

Sugar estates, both small and large were developed, and ultimately almost all privately-owned land fell into the control of relatively few individuals and companies. To operate the estates tens of thousands of Chinese, Japanese, Korean, Filipinos, Portuguese and other groups were brought to Hawaii, and their children and children's children stayed to form the bulk of the population. Only in the 1970s did the Caucasian element outnumber the formerly dominant non-Western group.

A feudal economy in time changed to a plantation economy. The indigenous Hawaiian actors were replaced, but not entirely by Americans and Asians. Basic elements of the situation remained the same - a land-owning elite and a landless majority. Today, on the island of Maui, eleven owners control half the total area of seven hundred and fifty square miles; thirteen owners have ninety-seven percent of the land. Essential environment attractions have been part of Hawaii since pre-human times. First settlement brought Polynesian Hawaiians, and developments in post-contact agriculture brought an ethnic mix, provided large acreages of open cane land and placed the bulk of the land in a relatively few white hands. The stage had now been set for the entry of the visitor industry.

THE TOURIST BOOM

At World War II tourism in Hawaii was minimal. Today the 500 acres of Waikiki, the size of the University of Victoria campus, support 22,000 hotel rooms. The reasons for this and other dramatic increases are numerous and interesting; in many ways they make sense, although this conclusion, in such a contentious area, depends largely on personal outlook.

During World War II, the Korean War and the conflict in Vietnam, hundreds of thousands of military personnel trained in Hawaii or arrived in Honolulu, en route to their final destination. To these people the myth of the South Seas, passed on from father to son, became something of a reality, and many were anxious to return with their families. In almost three decades since World War II, North Americans (and now Japanese) have become more affluent, their disposable income greater, and considerable mobility, at least on the home continent, is second nature. With increased affluence came vacations of a month or six weeks rather than two weeks, and for growing numbers vacations twice a year. To stimulate movement to Hawaii advertising has been essential. The intensity of advertising has increased and its potential as far as the adver-

tisers are concerned never seems to diminish. Where once there were minimal connections, eight major airlines now carry visitors from more than
thirty mainland metropolitan areas and two major and several minor airlines move people from island to island.[7]

In the 1960s the $99.00 fare (now only a memory) appeared along
with the box lunch, and package tours brought the secretary and the pen-
sioner where once Honolulu had been the preserve of the dowager and the
financier. By the end of the sixties the greatest volume of trade by far
was provided by prearranged group travel, which kept a large number of
hotels in business.

Immediately before the early seventies R and R servicemen and
families made up a significiant portion of visitors. Now this is over but
the momentum continues. A 1971 survey showed that thirty-five percent
of visitors are returnees who have enjoyed the islands at least once before.[8]
Another development of the seventies is the substantial increase of the
Japanese tourists who found Hawaii after the Japanese Government lib-
eralised the amount of foreign exchange which could be taken out of the
country. As a result of reevaluation of the yen the Japanese tourist found
that in 1973 he could buy forty-two percent more than he could in 1971,
and consequently Hawaii was economically very attractive. The devaluation
of the dollar encouraged more mainlanders to travel to Hawaii rather than
spend a summer in Europe. Travellers had the benefit of being able in 1974,
on the average, to rent the most reasonable hotel room of any major resort
area in the United States. Patriotism was thus reinforced by economic at-
traction. A final major consideration in boosting the visitor industry has
been the rapid growth of the convention trade and the provision of expensive convention facilities in Waikiki and on every island. Nor has an energy crisis had the expected negative impact on tourism. Although movement in Hawaii has been restricted, the restriction to travel on the mainland
resulted in extra persons deciding to travel to the islands rather than risk

TABLE 1,5

HOTEL INVENTORY BY COUNTY OR AREA 1974

County	Number	Percent
Honolulu	24,969	67
(Incl Waikiki)	(21,417)	(58)
Maui (Incl Molokai)	4,553	12
Hawaii	4,781	13
Kauai	2,926	8
County Totals	37,229	100

unpredictable conditions at home.

Despite the fact that Waikiki has unbelievable hotel density, and middle-class intellectuals affect to despise the area, construction continues uninterrupted, and in 1971 sixty percent of Hawaii's 5000 new rooms were built there. So far permissible construction has reached only forty percent of saturation. Honolulu zoning laws would allow a staggering 68,000 rooms, but it is interesting to note that hotel interests themselves recognise 26,000 as a practical upper limit.[9] Perhaps fifty rooms per acre in any 300 to 500 acre tract would be a useful formula indicating a level above which a city develops at its peril. It is usual to attribute anything offensive in the tourist industry to rapacious developers. However, it should be remembered that enthusiastic sellers, a city and county taxing system, and an apathetic public all contributed to today's situation.

Until the 1960s Neighbor Islands (as the outer islands are now called) Maui, Kauai and Hawaii were virtually overlooked by visitors. Even today the length of stay is relatively limited compared with Oahu, the major island. But Oahu has Waikiki which is exciting to many but anathema to a growing number of more discerning tourists who can go to a "Neighbor

185

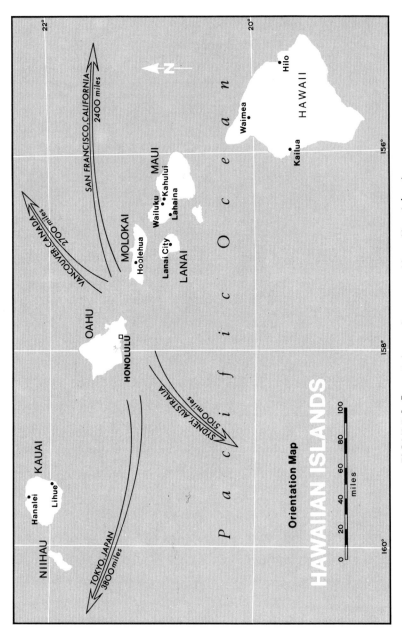

FIGURE 1,5 Orientation map, Hawaiian Islands

186

Island" of their choice for only $9 more than the regular round trip ticket to Oahu (common fare rate).

The most interesting development of the entire group is taking place in these islands (Figure 1,5), and Waikiki stands as a model of what not to do in the future for planners, citizens, developers and hotel operators alike. (Plates 52 and 53). Unlike past activity on Oahu, a characteristic development, but certainly not all development, on Neighbor Islands is large scale and well-planned. A significant proportion of such development is controlled by well-known locally-founded companies who since the end of last century have owned the land on which projects are being constructed. This type of development away from Honolulu is welcomed and encouraged by the State, who see in it a means of decentralization and an economic hedge against a not-too-buoyant sugar industry and a floundering pineapple business.

On the Neighbor Islands development is concentrated on the east coast of Kauai, the dry western coast of Maui, and a roughly corresponding strip of the Big Island, Hawaii, from Kohala to Kona (Figures 2,5 and 3,5). Extensive programmes are even in the planning stage for the small islands of Molokai and Lanai. Ultimately no part of the islands will be free of the signs of a growing leisure industry. So important is this development that in 1985 it is estimated that fifty percent of accommodation in Hawaii will be on the Neighbor Islands. This estimate probably excludes a large number of non-rental condominium units which are not usually listed with the Hawaiian Visitors Bureau, the source of most statistical information for the industry.

DEVELOPMENT ON THE VALLEY ISLE

The island of Maui has all the attributes of Hawaii listed in the introduction; in many respects it is a microcosm of the situation in the group as a whole. Its major resource is a dry, fifty-mile west coast with twenty-

187

PLATE 52
Waikiki: the results
of virtually unrestricted growth.

PLATE 53
Waikiki: the results of
uncritical attitudes towards
development.

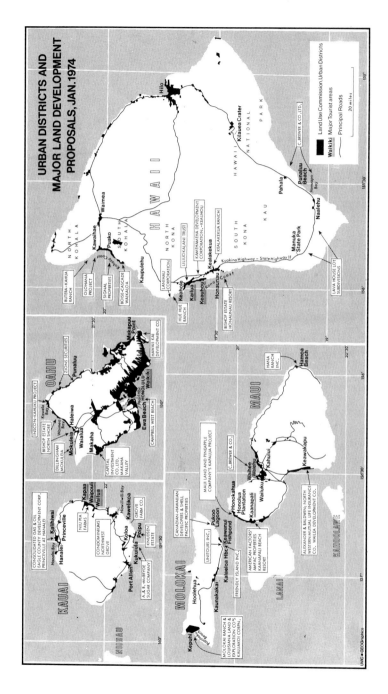

FIGURE 2,5   Urban districts and major land development proposals,   January 1974.

189

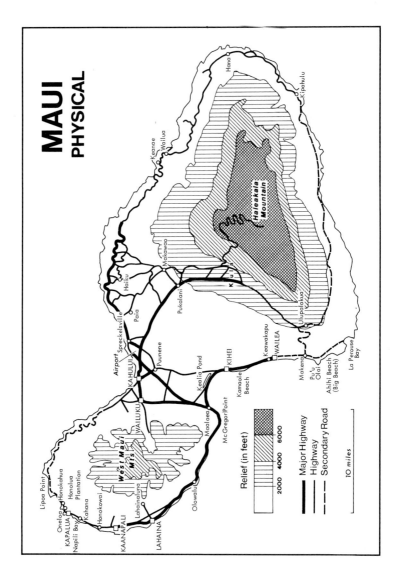

MAUI
PHYSICAL

Lipoa Point
Oneloa Honokohua
KAPALUA
Napili Bay Honolua Plantation
Kahana
Honokowai
KAANAPALI
Lahainaluna
LAHAINA
West Maui Mts.
WAILUKU
Olowalu
Maalaea
McGregor Point
KAHULUI
Airport
Spreckelsville
Paia
Puunene
Keolia Pond
Kamaole Beach
KIHEI
Haiku
Pukalani
Makawao
Kula
Keanae
Wailua
Ulupalakua
Keawakapu
WAILEA
Makena
Pu'u Olai
Ahihi Beach
(Big Beach)
La Perouse Bay
Hana
Kipahulu
Haleakala Mountain

Relief (in feet)
2000 4000 6000

Major Highway
Highway
Secondary Road

10 miles

FIGURE 3,5   Maui, physical

190

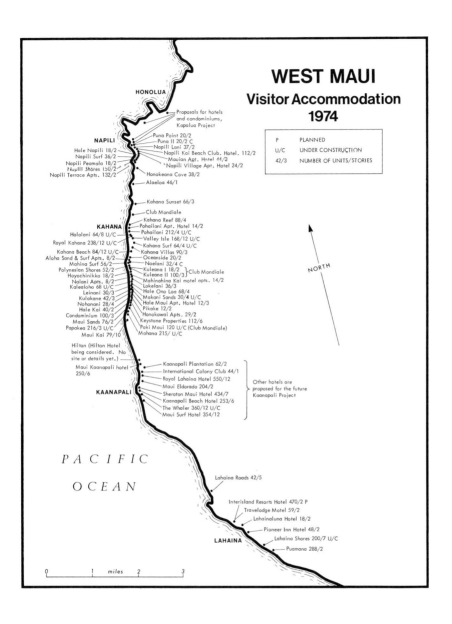

FIGURE 4,5   West Maui, visitor accommodation 1974.

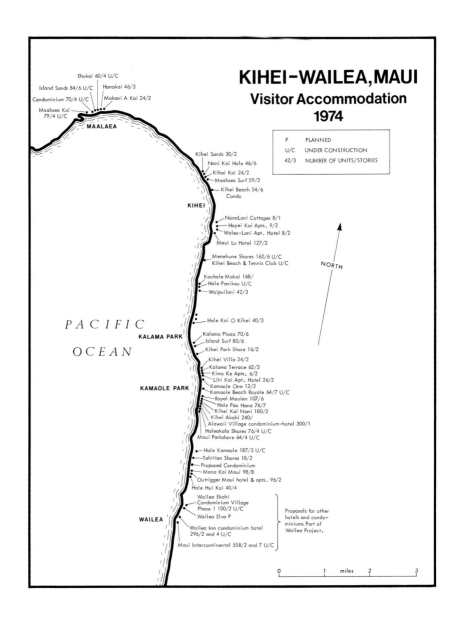

KIHEI-WAILEA, MAUI

Visitor Accommodation

1974

Ehukai 60/4 U/C
Island Sands 84/6 U/C   Honokai 46/3
Condominium 70/4 U/C   Makani A Kai 24/2
Maalaea Kai
79/4 U/C
MAALAEA

P	PLANNED
U/C	UNDER CONSTRUCTION
42/3	NUMBER OF UNITS/STORIES

Kihei Sands 30/2
Nani Kai Hale 46/6
Kihei Kai 24/2
Maalaea Surf 59/2
Kihei Beach 54/6
Condo

KIHEI

NonaLani Cottages 8/1
Hoyei Kai Apts. 9/2
Waleo-Lani Apt. Hotel 8/2
Maui Lu Hotel 127/2

Menehune Shores 162/6 U/C
Kihei Beach & Tennis Club U/C

Kauhale Makai 168/
Hale Panikau U/C
Waipuilani 42/3

NORTH

PACIFIC

KALAMA PARK

OCEAN

Hale Kai O Kihei 40/3

Kalama Plaza 70/6
Island Surf 80/6
Kihei Park Shore 16/2

Kihei Villa 24/2
Kalama Terrace 62/3
Kimo Ke Apts. 6/2
Lihi Kai Apt. Hotel 26/2
KAMAOLE PARK   Kamaole One 12/2
Kamaole Beach Royale 64/7 U/C
Royal Mauian 107/6
Hale Pau Hana 74/7
Kihei Kai Nani 180/2
Kihei Akahi 240/
Alawaii Village condominium-hotel 300/1
Haleakala Shores 76/4 U/C
Maui Parkshore 64/4 U/C

Hale Kamaole 187/3 U/C
Tahitian Shores 18/2
Proposed Condominium
Mana Kai Maui 98/8
Outrigger Maui hotel & apts. 96/2
Hale Hui Kai 40/4

Wailea Ekahi
Condominium Village
Phase 1 100/2 U/C
WAILEA   Wailea Elva P

Wailea Inn condominium hotel
296/2 and 4 U/C

Maui Intercontinental 558/2 and 7 U/C

Proposals for other
hotels and condo-
miniums Part of
Wailea Project.

0   1   miles   2   3

FIGURE 5,5   Kihei - Wailea, Maui, visitor accommodation 1974

192

TABLE 2,5
ETHNIC BACKGROUND, MAUI

Group	Percent
Hawaiian & Part Hawaiian	28
Japanese	25
Filipino	23
Portuguese[1]	10
Caucasian	9
Chinese	2
Puerto Rican	2

[1] Historically in Hawaiian statistics Portuguese have been separated from Caucasian.

Source: Maui Community Profile in State Planning System-Community Action Program, Honolulu, 1970, p. 42.

two miles of beautiful coral sand beaches. Population density is low (54 persons per square mile), if only the 40,000 permanent residences are counted, and because of a limited number of large land owners, open spaces devoted to sugar, pineapples, grazing and parks have until now been preserved. Above all Maui has a most cosmopolitan population in which a Caucasian finds himself part of a minority group (Table 2,5).

The bulk of development has taken place on the western coast of Maui in two distinct regions: Kapalua-Lahaina in the north and Kihei-Wailea in the south (Figures 4,5 and 5,5). In the north are two major resort developments, Kapalua just begun, and Kaanapali partially developed after a decade of use. The remaining portions contain the historic whaling town of Lahaina and scattered but nevertheless relatively intensive, small scale developments. Kihei has considerable, and growing, small-scale ribbon development paralleling the coast. To the south is the major 1,500 acre planned unit development of Wailea.[10] This is representative of large-scale resort development which will always dwarf "small-scale" although the visual and emotional impact of the latter may be much greater than the former (Figures 6,5 and 7,5).

The development philosophy in large-scale resorts varies from Wailea where an attempt will be made to develop a major community as a micro-cosm of Hawaiian society, to Kapalua which will be low-density, high-class and exclusive. Kaanapali is a little older and through experience relatively realistic. In comparison with Waikiki it tends to be elegant, beautiful and open. It finds it must now more than ever depend on high-volume package tours and high powered advertising. Many initial dreams have been shelved by developers in coming to grips with the realities of trying to control hotel operators, maintain profits and still have relatively beautiful surroundings. Initially in a number of cases, buildings, golf courses, and landscapes have been designed by some of North America's leading architects and planners. All have maintained or, without a doubt, will try to maintain openness, beautiful vistas and environmental control. (Plates 54 and 55). It is in their interest to do so. The degree of exclusive-ness varies considerably and is psychological, architectural and economic.

The attitudes of hotel operators with some remarkable exceptions, tend to be the same the world over. Unlike developers of large-scale projects, many of whom are on-the-scene in Hawaii, the head office of hotel chains is usually outside Hawaii, looks at the operation in the ab-stract, apart from the state and community in which it is found, and in-structs managers to maintain occupancy, increase profits and keep the cash flowing. The developers of course, reap rewards from the activities of lease or concession holders even if they do not condone every aspect of their behaviour and consequently frequently find themselves in an ambivalent position profiting from activities they know, over the long

PLATE 54
The new Wailea resort area
golf course clubhouse.

PLATE 55
The clubhouse of the Puamana
condominium development near Lahaina.

haul may lead to the eventual destruction of the project.

Whereas in Kaanapali in 1972 only about a quarter of the 2,212 units were condominiums, since the beginning of the 1970s other parts of Maui's west and south shores have been undergoing a condominium boom.[11] (Plate 56 and 57). Kaanapali too is reflecting this change with its latest development, a condominium hotel. Ultimately the bulk of accommodation will be condominiums which have advantages over vacation homes and problems quite different from hotels. Of the thirty establishments built or under construction in Kihei in 1973, only two were purely hotel, the remainder represented condominiums, apartments or places where the clientele will be less transient than at a hotel. For the first ten years the Kapalua Project plans 1,100 hotel rooms and 1,900 residential units, an indication of the growing importance of non-hotel type accommodation.[12]

The resident of, or visitors to, these developments in many ways display similar characteristics. Those living in condominiums are more homogeneous than those in hotels. By and large they are white, affluent, mobile, relatively well-educated, have similar social values, and are able to live equally well in second-home or retirement developments in Florida, Arizona or Mexico. Whereas the average income of visitors to Hawaii is $10,000 a year, owners of condominiums are generally earning well over $20,000, live in western United States or Honolulu and probably hope eventually to retire to Maui. They then will occupy their unit eighty to a hundred percent of the time rather than for only ten to fifteen percent of the year. If the unit is part of a rental pool it may be rented forty or fifty percent of the time depending on the type of management or the strategy of the manager. Possibly no more than sixty percent of owners have their units available for rent during that portion of the year when they are absent. The more expensive or exclusive the development, the fewer the units offered for rent.

Supporting the new wave of contemporary leisure seeking colonizers

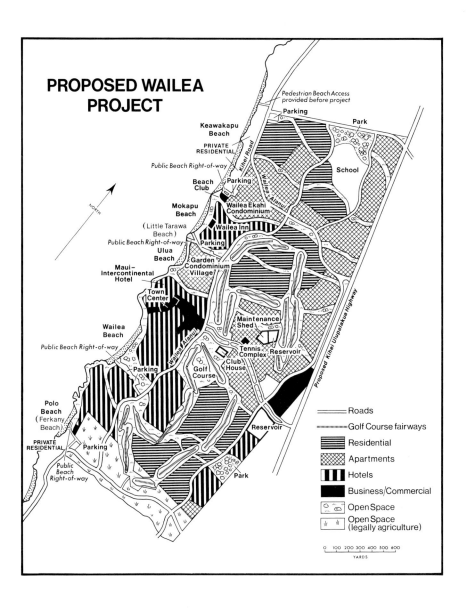

FIGURE 6,5   Proposed Wailea project

197

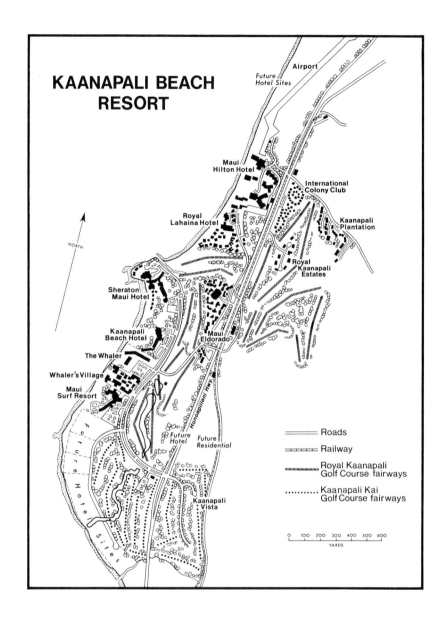

FIGURE 7,5   Kaanapali Beach resort

PLATE 56
A Kihei condominium; close to the highway
unscreened and unsightly.

PLATE 57
The Royal Mauian condominium,
a monolithic barrier between
observer and sea.

are construction workers, hotel employees, shop assistant, gardeners and a hundred and one different other occupations and professions. Direct employment is about 0.8 workers to one room or unit, more for hotels, less for condominiums. The multiplier effect brings the total of direct and indirect employment closer to two workers per unit. Service workers, are residents of Hawaii possessing something of a locally developed culture, and in comparision to out-of-state settlers, represent every ethnic group of the islands in varying percentages. Compared with the 'colonizers' they are not generally mobile, are more inward-looking, are family-oriented, and live on incomes perhaps half that of the condominium visitors. Ironically because of their attractive presence, local people provide not only a service function, but also a not insignificant part of the total conceptual resource being used by the visitors.

THE MAUI COMMUNITY

The community as a whole is apathetic concerning development or quietly prepared to tolerate the good with bad. There is a realization that tourism has lifted the island out of the economic doldrums and provided numerous jobs. Although parents see in development a means of keeping sons and daughters in Hawaii, this has not stopped young people leaving the island for occupations with greater prestige than those of hotels. There is a justifiable realization that plantations cannot sustain the economy and employment (Figure 8,5) for ever. For this reason the union membership of ILWU 142 which covers agriculture workers and many other individual groups is wholehearted in support of further tourist development in the interests of job security.[13]

If the majority of local residents are quiet, and this has been attributed to residues left over from a plantation background or employment in big companies themselves interested in Maui development, the island does not lack spokesmen.[14] The present Mayor of Maui County is articu-

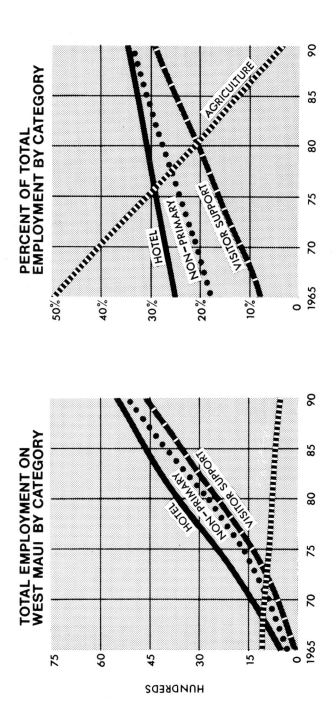

FIGURE 8,5   Total employment on West Maui by category and percent
of total employment by category

201

late and benevolently powerful. He can give the nod to developers, can provide water ahead of time, can decide which development will receive his blessing, and also can hold up or speed development. Working through the Planning Commission and the Department he can, and does persuade or cajole companies concerned with planned unit development into making extra concessions; such as providing roads, green belts, parks, extra set backs and sewage schemes.

With the Mayor acting as a catalyst, developments are increasingly reflecting the growing importance of the local society in visitor planning. The Maui County Planning Commission approves all plans and provides for public hearings. It names the rules and will give bonuses for the maintenance of vistas, for providing extra open spaces and so on. Development can only take place in those areas designated by the State Land Use Commission as being urban, and the County defines which will be hotel, apartment or residential. The islands have a number of community and interest groups of which "Life of the Land" is the most vocal community watchdog. Although many of its aims appear admirable when observed in the early seventies it seemed poorly organized, had inadequate information-gathering techniques, and prefered confrontations and court cases to effective cooperation. Although borne of conflict its methods may also create conflict. Its members and those of similar organizations are composed largely of liberals interested in civil rights as much as the environment. Middle class teachers and professionals appear most active, and energy is devoted towards the prevention of special priviledge, landscape change, the high cost of land, and the invasion of attractive beach front sites by outsiders.

IMPACTS, POSITIVE AND NEGATIVE

Large areas are being developed to low-density levels using the best planning consultants available, at a time when agriculture weakens and landowners modify their former perception of land use to ensure a satisfactory level of income. Not only is the economic base widening but also much is being attempted to improve the quality of life and to provide a pleasant milieu for settlers. An austere dry landscape at Wailea is being transformed into what the developers used to call a 'City of Flowers'.

Mainland residents are being provided with expensive attractive house-sites and units, and from time to time one hears the argument that these "intruders" should be kept out. This is partially stimulated by envy but there is no way that those who have paid much of the agricultural bill in the past, provided excellent national parks, and the major component of the Hawaiian income, should be prevented from using a resource that legal-ly belongs to them as well as to residents of Hawaii.

For many local citizens propinquity to development and appropriate County zoning have brought windfall gains. Homesteaders at Kihei have found their land increased in value from a few cents to five dollars a square foot. Many local citizens buy condominium units with the minimum of de-posits and sell out to mainlanders even before completion of construction, making $5,000 to $50,000 profit in the process.[15] Early resales, which unnecessarily escalate prices, are frequently negotiated by local sellers wishing to 'make a packet' quickly. The philosophy seems to be - "if we must have development why not have part of the action". Not only is the increasing value of land an asset to the small local landowner or investor but it is also a godsend to the large developer. His development land increases in price spectacularly after public plans are announced and so too do thousand of acres of nearby agricultural land. If owned by the same developer so much the better. This is, or will likely be the case at Kapalua. Development also brought fantastic gains to the real value of nearby Amfac's Pioneer Mill sugar lands as the result of Amfac's recreat-ional development at Kaanapali. (Plate 58).

In many ways the second home market is the most satisfying for the

PLATE 58
Construction of the Kaanapali Beach resort in the late 1960's.

Am Fac Properties Pho

developer. The initial risk is reduced to the minimum; each purchaser
is a secondary developer; by closing date the financial burden is substantially lifted from the primary developer; and he then knows, if not sooner,
that he can now contemplate his next project. For the community, the
second house concept is interesting. It brings into the area persons whose
stay in Hawaii is not just eight or nine days, but several months or in-
definite. It also introduces a psychological threat. The usual traditional
tourist is a transient phenomenon which, if one so wishes, can be ignored –
at least an offensive individual may be gone tomorrow. The condominium
owner is a problem of another dimension. He will use local parks and
recreational facilities, learn where the uncrowded beaches are, intrude
into local shopping places and above all, in his rapidly growing numbers,
will wish to participate in community affairs.

Adequate land has been zoned for apartment-condominium use, but
so far no real criterion regarding "need for accommodation" has ever been
applied at the time of approval. Speculators, a great many of whom are
local expecting a quick return, may snap-up all units from a desirable
project before construction. This will be used by those who benefit from
construction or the sale of units to demonstrate insatiable demand. In
really large projects, sales offices will be opened and prospective custo-
mers will be flown from Honolulu or the west coast. There are plans to
tap Chicago and further east the same way. Inevitably, after a period of
time, most owners will be mainlanders. In relatively few years Wailea,
it is estimated, will be a community of 35,000 persons, with a large number living in second homes or second homes converted to primary residences.
The question which comes to mind immediately is "Do a few persons in
corporate board rooms have the right to engineer major migrations from the
mainland when 'need beyond providing reasonable growth and shoring up
agriculture' cannot be established?" Development already planned more than
offsets the worst possible losses which would be sustained by the final demise

of agriculture.

Although resort areas are meticulously planned and every aspect of planning and design is approved by local authorities on-site resort planning is of limited use without accompanying meticulous infrastructure planning, which should, at least, be partly a responsibility of the project developer. Has provision been made for automobile repair shops, laundries, rental agencies, the supply of extra water, power, bulk fuel facilities, adequate public transport, low-cost worker housing and a host of other things usually located away from these peripheral places in an established urban centre? The Planning Commission of Maui has recently insisted that some worker-housing be incorporated in the building of major projects, but this can only hope to accommodate a small part of the total service personnel. In other words, the degree of planning going into actual resort developments exceeds by far the energy invested in extra-mural physical planning.

GOLDEN GHETTOS - SHADOW GHETTOS?

On Maui's west side and south side, land prices have soared as the result of great demand and the limited availability of Hawaiian land, for public purchase. Other contributory factors have been the relatively restricted area designated urban by the State (Figure 2,5), and zoned apartment and hotel by the county, speculation, extremely high taxation encouraging disposal of land for development, and the goals of a number of small local landowners. Some are either aspiring developers themselves or wish to hold land indefinitely as a reaction to the present conditions of flux. Others keep land from the market in the hope that even greater increases can be expected in the future. All, in their way, contribute to rising land values.

The result of this situation is that despite efforts at Lahaina, Kihei

206

and Kapalua (Napilihau) to provide moderate-cost housing, this has proved to be exceedingly difficult. Traditionally the major concentration of population has been from Wailuku through Kahului to Makawhao and the developing leisure industry in the beginning drew large amounts of labour from this area and Lahaina. With more and more development, young married people from the western dry side, even if they have formerly lived there all their lives, find that rents and the price of land so beyond their means that they must seek housing in the east, perhaps in new residential subdivisions in Kahului, Pukulani and elsewhere, where prices are still high but nevertheless lower than in the golden ghettos of the west.

This situation is unlikely to improve. If development maintains its present momentum, labour will be in extremely short supply. New, and for the State, expensive, immigrants will have to be imported to serve the contrivedly-introduced settlers. An obvious place to look for labour may be the Philippines and at least this would help balance the growing Caucasian population component. The ultimate and worst possible situation one might conceive of, would be a movement of Hawaiian-Asians to the east where the main centres of Wailuku and Kahului have always been non-Caucasian, while wealthy Caucasians filled every available gap in the west.

This could create a "golden" and a "shadow" ghetto, the west and the non-west, homogeneous and heterogeneous, and perhaps the beginning of a new colonial era fraught with possible conflicts (Figure 9,5). It is hoped that this will not happen, but the distinctive regional differentiation that could facilitate such a trend is already present.

A psychological line will never consciously be drawn by local people between the two sides because it is not in their nature to do so. But nevertheless the line is there, the inevitable result of past history and current development. The visitor did not cause the distinctive region in

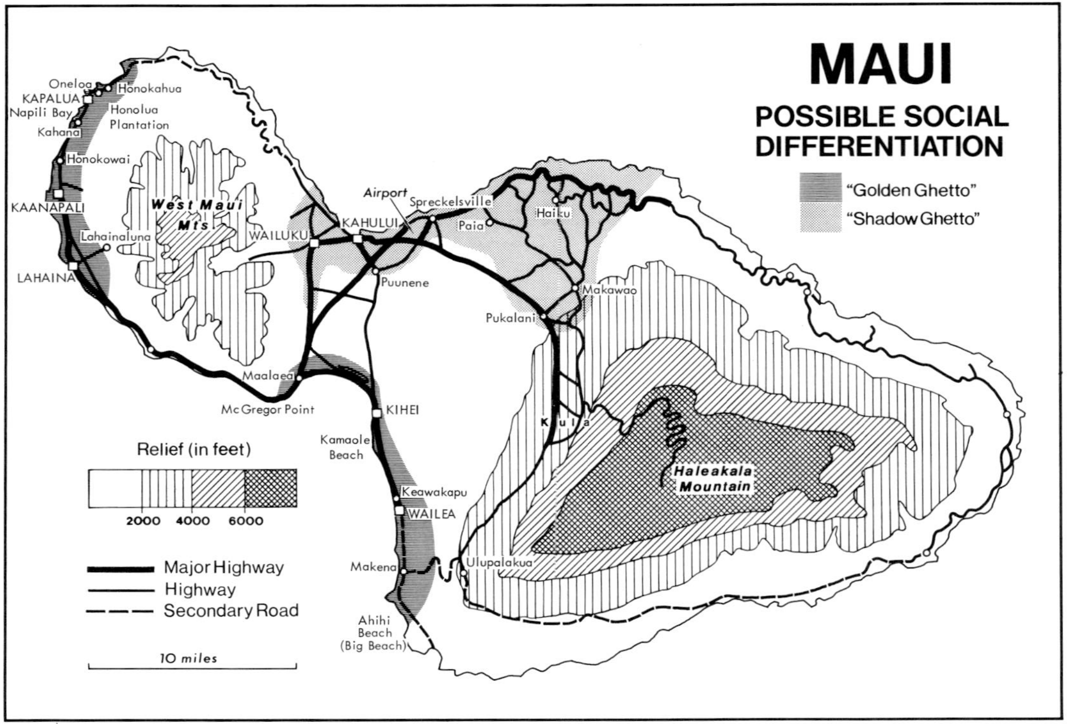

FIGURE 9,5   Maui, possible social differentiation

208

the east in its initial form - later development aggravated the situation
of ethnic differentiation and caused the white region in the west. The
processes of differentiation will continue. Wealthier local non-Caucasians
will continue to occupy houses in the west and will strive to buy attractive
sites for a reasonable sum. A number may settle for a condominium unit
as the only type of affordable dwelling. The County and State will make
efforts to ameliorate the growing distinction, but present trends suggest a
loosing battle . To what extent ethnic, social, and economic separation
of the type discussed indicates a lowering of the quality of life and an
erosion of the ambient resource is unknown. It may be conjectured that
it does represent ambient damage, real enough, but probably difficult
to measure or evaluate. The question merits considerable future investigation.

There will always be new Hawaiians living in the west as there
are Caucasian individuals and enclaves in the east. For a time the distinction may grow more marked only to be eventually clouded by the
growing group of Caucasians who unable to afford the expense of buying
on the dry side will seek sites on which to live in the wetter but very
pleasant east. In the next century, the distinction that is very real now
and in the immediate future, may be only academic . This socio-economic
separation is not confined to Maui. It occurs to some degree on every island, and ultimately will do so to some extent everywhere in the Pacific
where intensive leisure development is attempted .

THE SECOND HOME SYNDROME

The bulk of development hinges on the building and purchase of a
second home. There is a small but still inadequate body of theory regarding vacation homes in geographical and cognate literature but very little
on the second generation second homes of which the Hawaii condominium

is a good example. The burgeoning condominium-second home in a
Hawaiian resort area is a vacation home with a distinct difference.

The second home community of any variety, as Seigel states, was
"almost undetected two decades ago."[16] Now it appears in many areas,
although upon completion it may be, as in Hawaii, an instant ghost-
town because of low annual or short-term seasonal occupancy. Ultimately
however, it will become the core of a new permanent community, as present owners retire and live in the area full time. This is more probable
in Hawaii than in Wisconsin, Madison, New York, and Ontario where
most of the present studies have been done.[17]

As in many other areas the Hawaiian second home is sited on waterfront property or close to water which Wolfe and others call the premier
outdoor resource. All water front recreation land values have skyrocketed
over the past decade.[18] This is typical of most similar land elsewhere
but does not accord with Dulhunty's view that prices in recreational areas
are lower than those in cities.[19]

In talking about vacation homes Ragatz feels that they must be located 100-150 miles from a major city; Tombaugh puts the maximum distance at about 300 miles.[20] One can only surmise that the occupants of
Hawaii's second homes find the friction of distance relatively unimportant
and that these settlements, rather than drawing from one nearby city,
skim the cream of adventurous travellers from dozen of cities mainly, but
not exclusively, on the west coast of North America. These are what
Wolfe calls people of high momentum - well educated, with interesting
jobs, high incomes, and few children; in other words, the affluent and
mobile elite.[21]

Elsewhere in the United States, in Canada and in Australia the
quality of vacation homes is frequently much lower than that of the primary home in the metropolitan areas. This is understandable when a
building is to be occupied for a limited amount of time during the year,

210

is liable to damage from vandals and is to serve a purpose far less formal than houses in towns. Marsden, citing conditions on the Gold Coast in Queenland, Australia talks of "a socially and economically wasteful combination of a high grade resource and generally lower grade plant, in terms of building materials and styles, structures and functional coherence, and infrastructure standards."[22]

In Hawaii and especially in Maui where this study focusses, the lowest priced condominium unit in 1974 was approximately $32,000 while a significant percentage of units ranged from $100,000 to $150,000. It is estimated that the median age for buyers was 50 to 55 years. In comparison with the seasonally-occupied vacation house, the architecture of the Hawaiian second home is elegant and tasteful though leaving something still to be desired. Surroundings are maintained at a high level throughout the year and accomodation is "urban" rather than "rural". Although in comparison with the quality of the owner's primary home the second may fall short, it nevertheless is exceptionally high. Like vacation homes, many condominium units lie empty, but this is not a necessary characteristic. Rental pools are organised in most projects, and whereas in the usual vacation home lack of security is a problem, here in Hawaii as in similar modern development elsewhere, the block or project is under constant supervision by a management staff employed by the owners.[23]

The Architectural Record of November 1965, contains one of the best statements written about the new generation of vacation homes communities, of which Hawaii has a number of examples.[24] "The best of those big new developments outside the commuting ranges of cities are establishing standards of environment and house design virtually unknown in the suburbs." In the four developments described, environment was always uppermost in planners' minds, and in each case areas of greatest natural beauty were left undisturbed. It is suggested that the houses in these and other good vacation communities are better than most suburban houses, "not because interested architects designed them, but because budget limitations...and the use of inexpensive and simply finished materials imposed a useful design discipline." In all areas communities had strong covenants, environmental controls, and committees with wide powers concerning upkeep, environmental changes and aesthetics.

At present the concept of a condominium - second home is new and few projects show signs of marked deterioration. The demand by buyers for further units never seems to abate and from this point of view, with a rapid price appreciation, the investment-resale area of activity is as bouyant as in the most attractive suburbs of a metropolian area. Unlike vacation homes in some areas finance for purchase is easily available. The type of accommodation discussed above therefore displays many of the characteristics of the vacation home, but its other distinctions warrant viewing it in a separate category.

CONCLUSION

After several years of close observation a number of conclusions may be drawn. Some development embodying man-made change is inevitable, and it can be argued that large-scale projects which are controllable and manipulatible are better than small haphazard subdivision-type ventures. Hawaii has both.

The State and County could control the speed of development by freeing only meagre amounts of land for leisure development every five years, holding much already designated "urban" in reserve, and allowing its allocation only when needs of Hawaii or an individual island for such development could be conclusively demonstrated.

Reactions to tourists and visitors is largely a matter of psychological attitude. Old timers have probably a better attitude than newcomers who having achieved their ends, frequently display great possessiveness and a sense of territoriality difficult to justify. In general the aloha spirit brings a very healthy approach to tourism; nevertheless, throughout the world there is a degree of hostility brought about by cultural threat, and the possibility of change or territorial invasion. Mass education and broad community participation is necessary to overcome hostility and to bring understanding as to how a "one resource" country has limited options which must be nurtured carefully so that the present quality of life may be sustained or improved. Development will bring degrees of social distance and socio-economic separation which in themselves are offensive, but the impact can be tempered perhaps even removed by changed attitudes. If attitudes do not change various types of conflict seem probable. Further efforts should be made by State and County to create a more balanced social mix than seems to be developing by ensuring that both low and moderate cost housing is provided in those areas which are becoming economically and socially exclusive.

Change resulting from resource use is inevitable, and is not synonomous with deterioration. Much change in the past has been damaging, but changes imposed by man to either enhance or to maintain quality may be expected and should be considered beneficial. The enhancement of quality in one area may offset deterioration in another and may either improve quality or maintain the overall level. The State must now decide upon the degree of use it feels ambient resources can stand without deterioration.

In theory, the quality of the ambient resource is extremely high initially, when there is little or no human interference. This implies a largely unaffected natural landscape. One could postulate that with each increment of human use, the resource deteriorates correspondingly. This is true only to a point and is not so at the outset. It can be argued that a certain number of human beings are essential to the creation of a degree of human excitement in an appealing natural landscape. Thus in Hawaii the presence of a number of imported ethnic groups together with Caucasians and original Hawaiians contributes considerably to acceptable ambience, even if, in theory, their occupation may have caused slight upset to the physical and biological environment. If "balance" in nature is a goal and if man may be conceived as part of nature, "balance" must then be extended to a reasonable number of human beings occupying a habitat which is for them to enjoy as much as it is for any other organism.

When tourism is being developed in contrast, it can be argued that extra population can have nothing but a deleterious effect on landscape and the quality of life. But again, on the other hand, well-planned development by the creation of landscaped vistas, gardens, and beautiful golf-courses for a time, most certainly delays the diminution of quality. Purists would avow that any change in the natural habitat is a detrimental event; a greater number however, would agree with the student of aesthetics who cites the temple garden of Japan as an example of human enrichment by no means inferior to the neighbouring forest. In Hawaii the change is not usually as dramatic nor as delicately conceived as in the Japanese garden. What is thought to be 'natural' is usually only an older cultural landscape, and this is replaced by another which is newer. Some landscape changes, although often not to the liking of individuals or particular groups may be shown not to impair either life or humanly perceived landscape in more than a trivial way. But some landscape transformation is actually, or potentially harmful and for those who care the signs are there to read.

Discussions concerning limitations to use, preliminary action and necessary planning must be taken now to establish upper-level, critical carrying capacity values. Carrying capacity, Wagar states, "is not an end in itself but a means to an end. The final objective is to produce a

214

high and sustained social value in the form of quality recreation for people....<u>Carrying capacity</u> is the level of recreation use an area can with-
stand while providing a sustained quality of recreation."[25]

Ceilings must be established now in various areas. The more hard-
pressed the ambient resource is, the more its initial energy, with exceptions noted above, is dispelled. Its potency virtually diminishes before
one's eyes, but in an area of great population growth this can only be
perceived by a minority who have observed the area over a long period
of time and have established in their minds an early baseline, the <u>initial
threshold of change</u>. This is the first image of a place we all have, and
one which allows comparison, subjective though it may be, with the present scene. Over long periods there is a tendency for the <u>initial thres-
hold</u> to change and to be reestablished as a <u>secondary threshold</u> at a later
date, in a new context of contemporaneous values both general and personal. For a much larger number of persons the <u>initial threshold of change</u>
is more recent. As most of these people will be from crowded urban centres, contact with Hawaii may bring immediate spiritual renewal together
with a tolerance of crowding (indeed Hawaii may seem relatively empty)
and environmental deterioration considerably higher than for persons with
an earlier perceived <u>threshold of change</u>. The process may be never-end-
ing; while some are equipped to perceive the change and deterioration,
others, in contrast to the crowded conditions they have left, see only a
dramatic improvement in the quality of life and environment in their new
surroundings. Because of this, support for any use limitation may be less
than one would expect.

But quality does deteriorate, and it is a dubious advantage to have
significant numbers who are not able to see it. Fortunately in both State
and County government, there are decision-makers whose memories are
long and who seem increasingly prepared to recognise a problem despite
the fact that many of its facets are not within grasp. Already work has

215

been done in tentatively defining areas of overload. The report of the Temporary Commission on Statewide Environmental Planning is a bold step in the right direction.[26] But the question can be taken further as the Commission would wish. A small representative body, with knowledge of changes that have taken place, and an assumption that future change, if nothing is done, will be even greater, can make subjective decisions now, on densities, intensities, and crowding. Questions such as "what degree of crowding on beaches would be considered the upper limit of acceptablity by the committee now, for twenty years hence?" should be asked. The same could be done for hotel density, numbers of shopping centres, inter-island aircraft landings and takeoff, visitor arrivals, transport flow on certain categories of highways, and so on. Once upper limits are established ways of implementing appropriate recommendations should be sought. Some would be practicably, others would not. Already such basic concerns as the delimitation of urban areas and the location of major visitor destinations have been dealt with, but these and a host of other issues need refinement.

It would be completely unrealistic in the face of world developments to say that the show must not go on. There is nothing to suggest that the community would generally be in favour of this. There is every indication however, that many would like the momentum slowed to give greater time to reassess the situation and to take stock. A committee to assess critical limits could do just this, and implemented recommendations could be reviewed from time to time. A very long period between reviews would likely slow the pace quite effectively.

The picture painted may be grim. It is meant to be realistic. Hawaii is a beautiful place and its resources have been generally developed with taste. In many ways it is a model for the world. But for everything worthwhile there are frequently harsh realities. It has been the aim of this paper to point these out as sympathetically as possible.

MAUI NO KA OI

REFERENCES

1. ARMSTRONG, W. "Our Ecology in the Pacific." Paper presented to conference, Ecology, the Law and Public Policy, Honolulu: May 25, 1971. The term conceptual resources, as used by Armstrong implies a dominance of the mind over the perceived stimuli which can themselves change independently of the perceptions based upon them. The term ambient resource, attempts to embrace the interaction between the mind, thoughts and behaviour of the perceiver and those things about him - people, air, water, rocks, life styles, activities, perfumes, colour, lighting, warmth, sounds, sky, clouds, landscapes, seascapes, moonlight, underwater gardens, buildings and a host of other elements which create the ambience on which leisure experience is built.

2. CLAWSON, M. Land and Water from Recreation. Chicago: Rand McNally, 1963, p. 15.

3. PARSONS, J.J. "Southward to the Sun: The Impact of Mass Tourism on the Coast of Spain," Yearbook of the Association of Pacific Coast Geographers. 1973, pp. 129-146. PEARSON, R. "The Geography of Recreation on a Tropical Island: Jamaica," Journal of Geography, 56 (1957), pp. 12-22. SVENDSEN, A.S. "Det Moderne Reiseliv og det private masse konsum av reiser og rekreasjon," Ad Novas, 8 (1969), p. 124.

4. WEHRHEIM, J. "Paradise Lost," Ecology, 1, No. 10, (1971), pp. 4-8.

5. The Hawaiian islands provide much more than the "primary elements" of tourism emphasised by Christaller - "remoteness and distance". CHRISTALLER, W. "Some Considerations of Tourism Location in Europe," Regional Science Association Papers, 12 (1963), p. 105.

6. For histories of Hawaiian land see the following works: KUYKENDALL, R.S. The Hawaiian Kingdom. Honolulu: University of Hawaii Press, 1938; DAWS, G. Shoal of Time. Toronto: The Macmillan Co., 1968; HOBBS, J. Hawaii, a Pageant of the Soil. Palo Alto: Stanford University Press, 1935.

7.   Western Management Consultants, Honolua Project Economic Evaluation, Phoenix 1970, p. 3.

8.   Economic Indicators, October 1971, p. 1.

9.   Honolulu Visitors Bureau. A Report of the Committee on Statewide Goals for the Visitor Industry of Hawaii. Honolulu: 1969, pp. 63-64.

10.   'Small-scale' here refers to developments on lots ranging from several thousand square feet to 50 acres or so. 'Large-scale' refers to development on sites of more than a hundred acres and ranges on Maui from 300 to 1500 acres. Large-scale operations are planned unit developments. See, SIEGEL, R. "Vacation Homes," House and Home. February 1964, p. 110. And MOSES, S. "The Revolution in the Land Game," Real Estate Reveiw. Spring 1971, p. 17 and 19.

11.   "Condominuim Activity Paces Maui Action," Hawaii Business, 18, No. 2 (1972), pp. 21-32. "The Condominuim Comes to Kihei," Hawaii Business, 19, No. 2 (1973), pp. 37-39.

12.   Belt Collins and Associates Ltd., and Charles Luckman Associates, Proposed Kapalua Master Plan, Maui, Hawaii. Kahului: 1973.

13.   Personal Communication, Joe Franco, Chairman Political Action Group, Maui Division, Local 142, ILWU, July 13, 1972. Also, ILWU, Local 142, Resolution No. 5, 8th Biennial Convention September 1967.

14.   Eckbo, Dean, Austin and Williams, and Muroda, Tanaka and Hagaki Inc. for County of Kauai and the State of Hawaii, A General Plan for the Island of Kauai, Lihue (1970), p. 15.

15.   "The Condominium Comes to Kihei," op.cit., p. 38 and Personal communication Walter Witte, Developer, Kihei.

16.   SIEGEL, R. op.cit.

17.   FINE, I.V. and TUTTLE, R.E. Private Seasonal Housing in Wisconsin. State of Wisconsin Department of Resource Development, Madison 1966, pp. 42. TOMBAUGH, L.W. "Factors Influencing Vacation Home Locations," Journal of Leisure

Research, 1, (1969), pp. 54-63. Chautauqua County
Planning Board and Department of Planning. Second
Homes: Report on Their Use and Occupant Character-
istics, Mayville, 1973, pp. 43. WOLFE, R.I. "Summer
Cottages in Ontario," University of Toronto, Depart-
ment of Geography, Unpublished Thesis, 1950. RAGATZ,
R.L. "Vacation Homes in the Northeastern United States:
Seasonabily of Distributive," Annals of the Association
of American Geographers, 60, No. 3 (Sept. 1970), pp.
447-455.

18.   WOLFE, R. "Perspective on Outdoor Recreation: A Bibliographical
        Survey," Geographical Review, 54 (1964), pp. 207.
        TOMBAUGH, L.W. op.cit., p. 56. DAVID, E.J.L.
        "The Exploding Demand for Recreational Property,"
        Land Economics, 45, No. 2 (1969), pp. 206, 209-210.

19.   DULHUNTY, R. "Some Aspects of Land Subdivision in Resort Areas,"
        The Valuer, 21, No. 4 (1970), p. 264.

20.   RAGATZ, R.L. op.cit., p. 453 and TOMBAUGH, L.W., op.cit.,
        p. 57.

21.   WOLFE, R. "Discussion of Vacation Homes, Environmental Pre-
        ferences and Spatial Behaviour," Journal of Leisure Re-
        search, 2, No. 1 (1970), p. 87. For incomes of second
        home owners and other characteristics see, U.S. Bureau
        of Outdoor Recreation Selected Outdoor Recreation
        Statistics, Washington (1971), pp. 129 and 133, and
        Chatauqua Country Planning Board, op.cit., p. 17 and
        18.

22.   MARSDEN, B.S. "Holiday Homescapes of Queensland," Australian
        Geographical Studies, 7 (1969), pp. 71-72. RYAN, B.
        "The Dynamics of Recreational Development on the South
        Coast of New South Wales," The Australian Geographer,
        9, No. 6 (1965), pp. 331-348.

23.   "A Fresh Look at the Second Home Market," American Builder,
        July (1968), p. 22.

24.   "Second-Home Communities," Architectural Record, November (1965),
        pp. 143-158.

25.   WAGAR, A.J. The Carrying Capacity of Wild Lands For Recreation. Society of American Foresters, Forest Science Monograph No. 7, Washington 1964, p. 3 and 21; See also, STANKEY, G.H. and LIME, D.W. "Recreation Carrying Capacity: An Annotated Bibliography," U.S.D.A. Forest Service, General Technical Report INT-3, 1973, 45 pp.

26.   State of Hawaii: Temporary Commission on Statewide Environmental Planning. A Plan For Hawaii's Environment. Honolulu: 1973, 63 pp.

CHAPTER 6

SOCIAL DEMANDS ON THE FOREST ENVIRONMENTS
OF VICTORIA, AUSTRALIA:
SOME COMPARISONS WITH COASTAL BRITISH COLUMBIA

Michael C.R. Edgell

University of Victoria

Southeastern Australia and western Canada contain productive forests
which are situated in close proximity to large, mobile and affluent urban
populations. Whilst these antipodean forest environments are not identical
in terms of resource characteristics, utilization and national economic
roles, some parallels emanate from ecological, silvicultural and timber
harvesting considerations. Other analogies lie in management problems
associated with increasing and widening social demands placed upon the
forest resources of the two areas.

THE TWO ENVIRONMENTS CONTRASTED

Eighty percent of Canada's merchantable timber resource is coniferous,
but Australia's native commercial softwood resources are meagre. Species
of the broadleafed hardwood sclerophyll genus Eucalyptus dominate ninety
percent of Australia's forest area. The only indigenous conifers of any importance are members of the genus Callitris (Cypress pines) which occupy a
mere five percent of the forest area in semi-arid regions; and Hoop pine
(Araucaria cunninghamii) in the rain-forests of southern Queensland and
northern New South Wales.

Australia's forest area is small indeed in comparison with that of Canada
which contains eight percent of the world's forest resources (Table 1,6). [1]
Unfavourable climatic and edaphic conditions, and the prevalence of fire-
requiring and fire-promoting eucalypts, result in vast areas of treed or semi-

223

TABLE 1,6
AUSTRALIAN AND CANADIAN FOREST AREAS (SQUARE MILES)

	Australia	(%)	Canada	(%)
Total land area	2,941,526	100	3,851,809	100
Forested area	531,828	18	1,244,292	32
Area of commercial forests	132,000	4	919,209	24

Sources: National Forest Inventory, Canada, 1968; Year Book Australia, 1971.

TABLE 2,6
NET VALUE OF PRODUCTION OF PRIMARY INDUSTRIES (EXCLUDING MINING) 1969-1970 ($'000)

	Victoria	(%)	N.S.W.	(%)	Tasmania	(%)	Australia	(%)
Total primary industry	789,509	100	889,259	100	93,355	100	2,907,565	100
Forestry	27,939	3.5	36,832	4.0	15,572	16.7	117,235	4.0

Source: Year Book Australia, 1971 (figures for other States and Territories not included).

treed vegetation of very low productivity.[2] Only two percent of the
Australian continent (57,000 square miles, or half of the potentially productive forest) is currently regarded as economically exploitable forest.[3]
Most of this is coastal or upland wet and dry sclerophyll forest concentrated in the densely populated southeast, with an outlier in southwestern
West Australia (Figure 1,6). The few commercially valuable eucalypts
that occur in these forests supply the bulk of Australia's sawlog production.[4]
New South Wales, Victoria and Tasmania contain approximately fifty-six
percent (only 28,000 square miles) of all 'productive forest reserves' permanently dedicated to timber production. Whilst these reserves generally
contain the highest quality indigenous timber, some of them are occupied
by inferior stands degraded by wildfire. Others contain species that currently have little commercial value, and a number are economically inaccessible.[5]

Timber-based industries and associated government agencies form a
dominant and interlinked resource-use complex in Canada, a position often
enhanced by long historical precedent. In Australia, commercial forestry
and the logging industry generally are not given such a high status in the
overall management of forest lands. Even in the relatively well-timbered
southeastern States, the economic value of forest-based industry is minimal
(Table 2,6). Locally, it may be an important part of rural economies, especially in Tasmania, but in the State of Victoria, for instance, it employs
only eight percent of the work force engaged in primary industry, and less
than one percent of the total work force. This is small beer indeed compared with British Columbia, where over half of each dollar of Provincial
income almost literally grows on trees, and the timber industry is the largest
single employer of labour. Australian State Forest Services are also small
in scale of operations compared with their Canadian Provincial counter-
parts. The 1971-1972 expenditure of the Forest Commission of Victoria
was $11.5 million dollars,[6] but in the same period the British Columbia

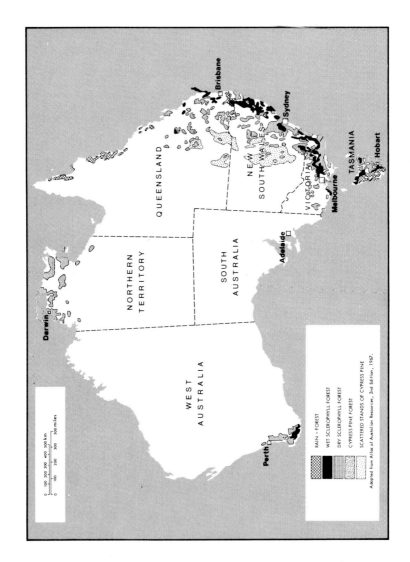

FIGURE 1,6   Commercial forests of Australia

226

Forest Service spent \$45.6 million dollars.[7] Such a difference is hardly surprising considering the resources at hand. The annual average allowable cut for all Crown Forests in Australia for the period 1960-1965 was 286 million cubic feet,[8] and this compares with a total scale of almost two billion cubic feet in British Columbia in 1972.[9] The Vancouver Forest District alone scaled 713 million cubic feet in that year, but in 1970, total log output from all forests in the State of Victoria was only 93 million cubic feet.[10]

Notwithstanding their limited commercial value, the forest environments of southeastern Australia are a significant resource, influencing a broad spectrum of social and economic activities, and subject to a wide range of demands. Whilst productive forests occupy relatively small portions of each State, 'protective' forests cover much larger areas. Management of these forests to maintain soil stability and regulate stream flow is a matter of some concern in a basically agricultural State such as Victoria, where the greater proportion of forest land occupies large water catchments providing both irrigation and domestic supplies. Of equal concern is the fact that the forests of southeastern Australia generally, and Victoria especially, are the most fire-prone in the world, rivalled only by those of California. Measures to reduce bush-fire frequency, intensity and damage are intensively applied to all forests, commercial or non-commercial.[11]

Protective forests provide important wildlife habitats, and a number of minor traditional products ranging from honey and railroad ties to eucalyptus oils and charcoal. Demands upon recreational, aesthetic and amenity values of these and productive forests are increasing rapidly in scope and intensity, compounding the problems, and yet also quickening the application, of multiple-use management.

THE TWO ENVIRONMENTS COMPARED -
SOCIAL DEMANDS AND MANAGEMENT PROBLEMS

General Analogies

Increasing and conflicting demands for a complex array of recreational experiences and facilities can impose a tremendous strain on a limited forest resource base, and on the many planning and management agencies that are directly or indirectly concerned with the general field of outdoor recreation. The single most important influence precipitating the development of multi-ple-use as a distinct guiding concept of forest management in North America over the last thirty years has been the phenomenal rise in outdoor recreation. A comprehensive, idealistic and socially-oriented view of resources, multi-ple-use aims to improve or maintain, for the benefit of society, the quality, quantity, availability and durability of tangible and intangible values associated with the forest.[12]

Multiply-use of forest lands in Canada is of more recent origin than it is in the United States,[13] but the traditional concept that the forests are for timber is now being reassessed in the light of changing social needs and demands. As a consciously-applied management philosophy or system, re-creation-oriented multiple-use is of even more recent origin in Australian forests, although integrated management for environmental protection is of long standing. Multiple use may mean little more to the Canadian public than the right to hunt, fish, camp and sightsee on forest land, but there is in association, a popular idea that previously accepted land use management priorities should be questioned. In Australia, a popular idea of multiple-use probably as yet does not exist,[14] but the last decade has witnessed the beginnings of a marked increase in the scope and intensity of recreational demands upon forest environments. It is these demands and responses to them that provide the most striking parallels between southeastern Australia and western Canada.

Forest policy concerning recreation in the two areas exhibits marked similarities. In the State of Victoria, the Forest Commission feels that:

> ...notwithstanding an acknowledged primary aim of management, it is the duty of the forester to realise any other benefits obtainable without prejudice to the main objective. [15]

These other benefits are becoming more important as:

> The extent to which forests, as one of the community's most valuable resources, can contribute towards improving the quality of the environment, is becoming ever more widely recognised...the indirect values of soil conservation, aesthetics, protection of water catchments, provision of habitat for native fauna and ideal conditions for public recreation and relief from modern-day tensions are becoming more and more appreciated. ...Management, protection and utilization of the State forests so as to preserve and develop all of these resources is multiple purpose management, the Commission's general policy for the State's forest resources. [16]

To accommodate demands for these values and resources, the Forest Commission of Victoria in 1970 established a Recreational Forestry Branch, and instituted a programme for the identification of visitor use, desires, and needs in the most popular multiple-use forest areas.

Similar views to the Australian are stated by the British Columbia Forest Service as follows:

> If the forest industry wishes to continue its success as the prime user of British Columbia's forest resources, it must accept the need for maintaining an environment satisfactory and suitable to the needs of all British Columbians. [17]

229

> The solution is to manage the forests for the
> optimum economic and social benefit of all.
> ...Maximum public use of the forests con-
> sistent with a minimum of interference with
> industry is the general guideline. [18]

> On the one hand the Forest Service is admin-
> istering the forest for consumptive use by a
> logging industry which is technocentric, and
> on the other hand, moving towards adminis-
> tration of the same forest for largely appreciative
> uses by a general public which is democentric.
> The success achieved...will depend upon how
> well we practice integrated use management. [19]

As an aid to this broader management, the Forest Service has instituted a recreation section in its Management Division, which had its first operational year in 1972. Activities have included collation of recreation data in public sustained-yield units and areas of high recreational potential, but the major emphasis so far has centred on improvement or extension of existing forest and water access and camping or picnicking facilities.

The Lower Mainland and Vancouver Island forests of British Columbia and the forested uplands or 'Alps' of northeastern Victoria provide opportunities for a wide range of outdoor activities such as camping, picnicking, fishing, bushwalking, mountain climbing, snow-skiing and pleasure driving or sightseeing. But the relative importance and intensity of these and other recreational activities differ between the two areas.

There is, for example, some indication that in British Columbia, 'traditional' or extensive recreational uses of forest environments such as hunting, hiking, pleasure driving and picnicking are either decreasing or only slowly increasing (Table 3,6). A marked trend towards more sophisticated equipment and activities has resulted in a dramatic increase in facility or environment – intensive activities such as highly motorised camping, snow-mobiling and trail-bike riding. This more intensive use is exerting heavy pressure on pre-

PERCENTAGE CHANGES IN INCIDENCE OF PARTICIPATION IN
OUTDOOR RECREATION ACTIVITIES IN CANADA, FROM 1969 to 1972

Activities	Canada	British Columbia	Metro Vancouver
Tent camping	+ 58	+ 71	+ 80
Trailer camping	+ 67	+ 57	+ 50
Pick-up camper	+100	+150	- 12
Walking-hiking	+ 5	+ 2	+ 2
Picnicking	0	- 5	- 9
Hunting	- 15	- 6	- 30
Power boating	+ 21	+ 29	+ 4
Canoeing	+ 25	+140	+ 44
Sailing	+ 33	+250	+300
Visiting historic parks/sites	- 3	- 8	- 21
Driving for pleasure	- 3	- 6	- 15
Sightseeing from a private vehicle	- 12	+ 2	- 18
Snow-skiing	0	+160	+114
Snowmobiling	+ 28	+150	+400
Bicycling	+ 46	+167	+238

Source: Outdoor Recreation Research Section, National and Historic Parks
Branch, Parks Canada. Trends in Participation in Outdoor Recreation
Activities. Cord Technical Note No. 22. Ottawa, August 1973.

viously unused or little-used recreation resources; changing use patterns
associated with technological innovations or changing social mores are therefore more significant in British Columbia than is an increasing volume of

use.[20] Whilst general trends suggest that demands for intensive water-based recreation facilities and attractions are paramount, increasing demands on forest environments are almost equally significant.

Recreation use patterns are also changing in Australia, but the boom in recreation technology and equipment has not yet influenced the 'quantitative participation rates and qualitative values of today's recreationsts'[21] to the degree that it has in British Columbia. Much recreation activity is still traditional; most Australian campers use a tent rather than a trailer, and sightseeing or motor-touring is the most popular form of recreation for much of the urban population. Water-based recreation, in which the technology boom is most noticeable, is probably at least as important in the total outdoor recreation spectrum as it is in British Columbia, but it has been suggested that most Australians have no strong urge to use forest lands as a whole for recreational purposes.[22] Certainly, recreation pressures on the forest environment are lower than they are in British Columbia, but they are growing. Conflicts are emerging between use of forest lands for commodity resources or environmental protection on the one hand, and social amenities on the other. As the diversity of recreational uses expand, conflicts are also becoming apparent between different recreation demands.

Due to the mobility of urban populations, many of the forest areas of coastal British Columbia and to a lesser extent, southeastern Australia, must now be considered an inseparable adjunct to the urban environment (Plate 59). Forests of the two areas lie largely within the recreational hinterlands of the major population centers, and in Victoria, demand is coming from:

> ...a population which is becoming increasingly urbanised and which travels by car, using the forests for a brief time on each visit.[23]

The spatial and functional distinctions between 'wildland' and 'urban'

PLATE 60
Mountain ash forest, Victoria, reserved for recreation.

PLATE 59
Family escape from suburbia: weekend picnicking near Melbourne.

forests are becoming less clear, and social aspirations for recreation, amenity and general environment or landscape quality involve a broad set of parameters in forest land management. The factors that have to be considered in deciding whether a forest area should be utilized for single-use forestry, compromise multiple-use, or at the other end of the spectrum, single-use recreation, are complex. Demands for outdoor recreation in particular can be prodigal in their use of land, and can create serious problems when incorporated into multiple-use systems where they compete with more 'basic' uses such as timber production, water supply, fire control or residential development.[24] Yet, whilst the needs of urban populations are difficult to assess and accommodate, and while they may change rapidly, they are more and more influencing the nature of forest land management in Victoria and British Columbia.

Some Specific Management and Demand Comparisons

Two of the major commercial eucalypts in Victoria, mountain and alpine ash, have ecologies similar to that of Douglas fir in the coastal forest of British Columbia. All three are essentially 'catastrophe climax' species, in that stands of them are maintained or replaced by windthrow, disease, and especially fire. Whilst these natural events kill the mature or over-mature timber, they simultaneously create the open conditions, expose mineral soil or provide ash-beds that are necessary for the regeneration and rapid growth of these light-demanding species. The result is a stand mosaic of relatively even-aged and even-sized trees, and some of the most valuable timber stands in both areas have followed such natural catastrophies (Plates 60 and 61).

Clear cut logging, the dominant felling technique in both the ash-type Victorian forests and the coastal British Columbian forests, in its sudden and complete or near-complete removal of trees, closely follows the pattern of these catastrophies. When followed by site preparations such as scarification, slash burning, seeding or planting, clear cut logging can also be an efficient

234

PLATE 62
Replanted clear cut, Vancouver Island: visual degradation or sound forest use?

PLATE 61
Cathedral Grove in MacMillan Park, Vancouver Island.

method for the rapid establishment of a fast-growing, even-aged crop. The technique therefore has advantages beyond that of efficient timber removal, but in spite of these silvicultural, economic and management advantages, public opposition to the supposed or real ecological and aesthetic impacts of clear cutting has gathered such momentum in North America, that recently the U.S. Senate held hearings on the issue.[25]

Rigidly laid out, rectangular clear cut blocks, reminiscent of 'diapers on a line',[26] marching across hillsides with apparent disregard for any natural form, are clearly visible over large areas in British Columbia and in the ash forest areas of the Victorian Alps. To many people, the apparent intensity of impact on the forest environment brands clear cutting as the antithesis of sustained-yield or multiple use forestry,[27] and arguments to the contrary by professional foresters often fall on deaf ears (Plate 62). As more people take to the woods, using logging roads for access, the visual and ecological 'degradation' associated with residual and burnt slash or bare soils and stream banks in recently logged areas is exposed to the motor-born public and not only to anglers, hunters and bushwalkers. Ellefson has suggested that in North America the clear cutting controversy is symptomatic of a general environmental concern about the alleged indifference of land managers towards public questioning of the environmental impact of timber management. Further, the attack on clear cutting may be a springboard for criticisms, by the general public or special-interest groups, of a broad sprectrum of forest management issues such as overcutting, monoculture, forest road building and wilderness preservation.[28]

The impact of these criticisms and concerns upon forest management is difficult to guage with any accuracy, but certainly the adoption of an 'environmental' or 'socio-ecological' forestry by professional foresters and some segments of the forest industry in Canada and the United States in the past decade has been accelerated, if not triggered, by them.[29] As already noted, such concerns are not confined to the clearcutting issue, although this has been the focus of much discussion. Rather concern covers the whole range of previously accepted management techniques and attitudes affecting a forest environment that is now increasingly viewed as a public commodity rather than an industrial woodlot.

The ash-type forests of Victoria that are clearcut are small in comparison to the State's total forest area, and generally occur at higher elevations or in more inaccessible places where they are less visible to the recreating public (Plate 63). Criticism of clearcutting per se, and of the relating practice of slash burning to promote a good seed bed, is therefore not the public concern that it is in British Columbia, where clearcuts are everywhere and slash burning for fire control causes periodic air pollution. The major source of criticism is a small, vociferous bush-walking fraternity, but the rapid regrowth of these eucalypts (on a moderate site, mountain ash can reach a height of 50 feet ten years after seeding) and the small area of forest (three to four percent) that is logged or in early stages of regrowth at any one time, blunts much of this criticism.

But the real or imagined effects of ubiquitous fire-control measures upon Australian forest environments do cause growing public concern and criticism from conservation organisations. Whereas in British Columbia's forests, many problems of multiple use and recreation planning are inherent in a 'single-use and single-minded'[30] system of commercial timber production in which secondary uses do not receive an unbiased consideration in resource allocation, similar problems in Victoria are sparked by the necessity of managing forests for fire hazard reduction.

Forest fires are, of course, a major concern in British Columbia; during 1972 fire suppression cost the B.C. Forest Service $11 million dollars, the largest single item of expenditure after general forest administration, protection and management.[31] In that year, fires burned 64,400 acres, and although only 14,700 of these contained commercial timber, stumpage losses[32] to the Crown were over $600,000 dollars; loss to the Provincial economy may be estimated at approximately ten times this figure.[33] Loss of stumpage revenue over the period 1963 to 1972 has averaged $3.5 million dollars per year, ranging from a low of $25,000 dollars in 1964 to a high of $12.9 million in 1971.[34] But in relation to the total forest area of just over 134 million acres, fires in British Columbia inflict less damage than they do in Victoria which contains only 15 million acres of forests under the protection of the Forests Commission (Table 4,6). In only eight years since 1900 have less than 75,000 acres of this forest land been burned. Whilst the cost of fires to the timber industry (and thus to the total economy) is high in British Columbia, it is the 'social' costs that are perhaps of more significance in southeastern Australia,[35] as fires are more likely to sweep through areas of high residential, recreational, or amenity value than they are to destroy valuable commercial timber. In the Tasmanian fires of 7 February 1967, 1,446 major buildings, valued at $6.3 million dollars, were destroyed; 1,085 homes were lost, and 2,000 people were left homeless. Over 60 people were killed by fires in Victoria during 1924, 72 in 1939, 49 in 1944 and 21 in 1969.

Fire is as integral to Australia as is drought; most Australians live in a fire environment. The probability of extensive fires is highest in the densely populated southeastern States, due to combinations of fuel availability, erratic summer rainfall and periodic drought.[36] Highest danger levels and damage potential occur in Victoria, and in no other fire-prone area is there so great a need for human activities to adapt to fire over such long periods and such large contiguous areas (Plate 64).

Adding to the severity of the ecological and climatic conditions are:

1. increased demands for recreational outlets adjacent to large population centres;

2. demands for desirable bushland residential sites and a proliferation of

PLATE 63
Natural regrowth of alpine ash following logging, Victoria.

PLATE 64
Suburban sprawl meets flammable forest at Ferntree Gully, Victoria.

TABLE 4,6

ACREAGE BURNED BY FOREST FIRES IN
VICTORIA AND BRITISH COLUMBIA 1961-1970 (1,000 acres)

	Victoria	British Columbia
1961	144.9	1,227.1
1962	167.3	45.6
1963	79.8	43.3
1964	291.4	7.7
1965	807.6	307.1
1966	71.0	54.7
1967	39.5	244.5
1968	547.0	33.4
1969	71.5	406.7
1970	12.6	206.9

Sources: Annual Reports of Forests Commission of Victoria and British Columbia
Forest Service.

low density unplanned developments;

3.   speculative subdivision encroachment of suburban areas into high hazard
zones; and

4.   the general inefficiency of planning attempts to separate residential areas
from surrounding bushland.

All of these factors have brought more people into contact with high-risk fire
environments and have compounded the problems of adjusting fire-control measures to changing social demands from, and expectations of, forest management.
Eucalypts create conditions in which fires will start and spread rapidly.
Burning pieces of bark from some species exhibit remarkable aerodynamic pro-

240

perties; when airborne in the violent convectional updrafts of a fire, they can cause 'spotting' of fires eighteen miles ahead of the main fire-front.[37] Eucalypt oils and combustible waxes are distilled into explosive gases at high temperatures, and can enhance fire movement and intensity. The spread of crown fires[38] in Australian forests can be appalling; it took only five hours for a series of fires to sweep over 653,000 acres in southeastern Tasmania in February 1967. The Campbell River fires of the late 1930's on Vancouver Island pale in comparison. Even the frequent fires of interior British Columbia, such as the 1973 Shushwap Lake fire, never reach such devastating intensities.

But it is the ability of eucalypts to produce abundant fuel that is the major link in the chain reaction of fire. Dead bark, branches and leaves can accumulate at the rate of 2.5 tons per acre per year, and total fuel levels may reach 150 tons per acre in extreme conditions. The view dominating fire prevention is that:

> ...The only alternative to preventing the huge
> monetary damage and loss of lives and deteriora-
> ation of our environment...is to make a deter-
> mined and systematic effort to control the quantity
> of fuel available for combustion.[39]

This control is exercised through the deliberate use of low-intensity control fires that reduce fuel accumulations to a level incapable of supporting destructive wildfires. Incendiaries dropped from low-flying aircraft and sup- plemental ignition by ground crews are used to burn between 500,000 and 750,000 acres each year in Victoria and New South Wales. Burning rotations average four to six years in Victoria, and provide protection to about three million acres.[40]

Although the lowered incidence and intensity of wildfires in areas sub- ject to control burning is incontrovertible, widespread objections are raised to the aesthetic and little-known long-term ecological effects. In particular, the deliberate use of fire on public lands such as national parks, ecological reserves, water catchments and recreation areas, where management object-ives are validated in terms other than protection of timber resources, has been strongly criticised.[41]

Problems of reaching effective compromises between fire control and social demands are highlighted in 'urban forest playgrounds' close to the large population centres. Twenty-two miles east of Melbourne lie the forested Dandenong Ranges, a readily accessible and increasingly popular recreation and low density subdivision outlet for the adjacent urban con-centration of 2.3 million people. High real estate, recreational and aes-thetic values are associated with the maintenance of, and ready access to, the varied forest setting, and there is opposition to legislation or manage-ment that might decrease these values. Even the use of increased fire-prevention publicity is opposed on the grounds that it might adversely effect land sales and tourism; and this in an area where eight people were killed and 453 buildings lost in 1962, and where six years later, fire covered an-other 2,600 acres and destroyed a further 53 buildings. Still, in the face of such damage, control burning is considered by many residents and visitors alike to be at variance with the maintenance of aesthetic and recreational values, and the effects of this control method are regarded as being equally detrimental to environmental quality as bushfires themselves. Protection plans therefore have to accommodate these values in addition to the needs of fuel reduction to safeguard life and property, and it is difficult to success-fully employ any single type of fire strategy.

To counteract public questioning of the ecological and aesthetic impacts of control burning, foresters in southeastern Australia use rebuttals similar to those used by defenders of clear cut logging in British Columbia. It is often argued that frequent low-intensity control burns approximate the fire environment of aboriginal, pre-European Australia, and are closer to the

242

'natural' fire environment than are the less frequent but devastating conflagrations that originate in massive fuel accumulations resulting from complete fire protection. Whether this is so, and if such a supposition has any
direct relevance to widening social aspirations towards the forest environment, is debatable. Clear cut logging also, in British Columbia, is seen
as being the equivalent of natural processes, and to be ecologically compatible with the maintenance of a sustained-yield forest cover: "much of
the Canadian forest occurs naturally as the result of catastrophic distur-
bances - insects, wind, fire and latterly, logging."[42] Again, the ecological
soundness of clearcut logging is not proven in all cases, and depends upon
the manner in which it is applied. Also, the relevance of a method, that
may be sound ecologically, to demands that are increasingly of a social
nature, cannot be implicitly assumed. Although it is argued by some that
clearcut logging is potentially or actually compatible with wildlife and
aesthetic management,[43] others argue with equal conviction that it should
not be employed in areas with high recreational and amenity value where
its aesthetic and environmental impacts are incompatible with the objectives
of the key users.[44]

Whilst climate and fuel combinations set the basic parameters for forest
fire outbreaks, the direct cause of many fires lies more in human activity.
The degree to which the public, through general use of and increased recreational activities in forest areas, is involved in this activity, thereby
creating particular problems in forest management, differs markedly between
southeastern Australia and British Columbia.

Increased public use of forest areas in coastal British Columbia is partly
a result of 'open-gate' policies that, in many cases, now allow twenty-four
hour access on non-operational logging roads. Although some logging operators are also providing recreational facilities and information, thus encouraging even greater use, there is widespread concern by the industry

that existing conflicts will intensify and particularly that fire incidence will rise due to public carelessness.[45] Such fears do not seem justified; it has been shown by Telfer that an increase in outdoor recreation does not necessarily mean an increase in fires caused by recreationists.[46] Lightning has always been the major cause of fires in British Columbia, on average accounting for 33 percent of all fires in the period 1963-1972. Recreational activities have accounted for only 9.5 percent, barely more than the 9 percent that is attributable to industrial (logging) operations, and this percentage shows no sign of increasing. Significantly, the damage caused by industrial fires has been constantly higher than damage from recreational fires.[47] Widening public demands on the forest environments in British Columbia therefore do not appear to threaten an intensification of the fire hazard. Rather, they pose problems of reorientation and reorganisation for an industry and a government agency which, until recently, have been somewhat myopic in their view of meaningful concessions to recreation and amenity values on public land.

In Victoria, however, forest recreationists, along with residents of bushland or semi-bushland suburban fringe areas, are an integral part of the fire environment. Fires are overwhelmingly a man-induced hazard; more than ninety percent of them are caused by inadvertent, negligent or deliberate acts, and only six to ten percent by lightning. Man-caused fires may be smaller than lightning fires, but the social impact of many is often greater simply because of their location in the forested suburban/ rural fringe areas that are so extensive around the larger cities of southeastern Australia. They can also develop into conflagrations such as the 1967 Tasmanian fires, when 88 out of 110 known fire origins were not only man-made, but were deliberately lit.[48] In the dominance of human activity as a cause of fire, as well as in environmental parameters, Victoria is closer to California than to coastal British Columbia.[49]

As in British Columbia, increasing public use of road access in the forested areas of Victoria is a major focus of recreational planning, and in addition has an important bearing on fire incidence. Few areas in the Victoria Alps are more than three miles distant from part of a dense network of fire-access and logging roads. Whilst allowing rapid access for fire-fighting crews and general forest management, this network simultaneously allows easy access by one of the main instigators of fire — the re-creationing general public. And with a sharp increase in general forest-based recreation there is, unlike in western Canada, an increase in fire outbreaks. Although an impressive array of restrictions and regulations concerning the use of fires in forests is brought into effect during the fire season, access restrictions to forest areas are less comprehensive and more difficult to enforce than in coastal British Columbia. Minimization of fire incidence in recreational areas therefore necessitates raising both recreationists' levels of awareness and willingness to change behaviour within a high-hazard environment. And as more logging, fire-access and public roads are opened or improved; as the Forests Commission accelerates its recently started programme of providing recreational facilities, and as the public increasingly uses its right to enjoy the forest as it sees fit, the necessity to change attitudes and behaviour will intensify.

Increasing public use of forest access roads highlights many other aspects of recreation planning in Victoria's forests. The scope for general pleasure driving and touring, a major activity, has been expanded, and more 'specialised' recreationists, such as skiers, anglers, climbers and bushwalkers now have easy access to large areas. Adventure driving with four wheel drive vehicles or trail bikes is another rapidly growing pastime. The bushwalker and 'wilderness buff', however, although he may use roads to get to his starting point usually regards them as anathema once he is in the bush, especially if he happens to meet a Land Rover or a Honda. Theoretically, the careful design of a forest road system can provide a sense of remoteness for the motorised recreationist, without reducing wilderness values for the bushwalker. But the logging road systems in both Victoria and British Columbia, from which many of the public roads have developed, were usually not designed for recreation. Although on Vancouver Island, wilderness seekers can escape to Strathcona Park, the NitiNat Triangle, or, before publicity ended its isolation, the West Coast Trail, the amount of forest land in Victoria that can provide a similar wilderness experience is small and dwindling.

It has been argued by one Australian worker that:

> ...People are more likely to support preservation of large natural areas if they are given the opportunity to see them, albeit from the comfort of a motor car. This treatment acts to protect the wilderness by increasing the number who visit it in a visual rather than a physical sense.[50]

Whilst the first statement may be true, the second would seem, from planning experience in Pacific Coast recreation areas of Canada and the United States, to be naive and over-hopeful. But the growing demands of motorised and/or family group recreationists certainly influence much forest management in Victoria. Forest parks, with walking trails, picnic facilities and amenities designed to meet the needs of campers, are increasing; scenic reserves have been established to preserve worthy environmental, aesthetic, historical or recreational forest values in locations accessible to the public. In the management of 'popular wilderness' forest recreation areas such as the Grampians in western Victoria and the national parks around Melbourne, the Forests Commission is also attempting to blend intensive with extensive recreation.

Forest management in southeastern Australia is becoming more complex. Increasingly it has to accommodate possible conflicts between production of commodity resources or environmental protection on the one hand, and satisfaction of broader socially-oriented goals on the other. Conflicts between different recreational uses are also intensifying. Yet multiple use generally

246

does not have to compete with the economic interests of a powerful single-use oriented timber industry, and recreation, amenity and aesthetic values are not relegated to the residual use status that they are in much of coastal British Columbia. The greatest future conflicts of recreation may well be with domestic water catchment managers rather than with forest managers per se. Large forested areas of high recreational potential are controlled by the Melbourne Metropolitan Board of Works in their water catchments. The Board adheres to a strict closed-catchment policy, only recently even considering the possibility of logging operations. In view of the increasing need for day-trip family recreational facilities in the immediate hinterland of large cities, this policy is questionable, and may well come under attack in the future, as it has recently in various catchments in the State of Washington and British Columbia.

CONCLUSION

The management of forest land in British Columbia is largely conditioned by the economic dominance of the logging industry and the almost exclusive management control exerted by the Forest Service. In spite of recent significant changes in legislation and managerial priorities, responsibilities and attitudes, the traditional position of recreation and amenity as residual uses, having a last claim on resources, tends to be perpetuated. There remain many barriers to the establishment of a 'socially relevant' system of forest management, which would adequately meet the needs of today's society and maintain enough flexibility for relocation of resouces as conditions change.[51]

The provision of recreation-oriented forest management in Victoria would appear superficially to face fewer problems. Due to the lack of a powerful logging industry, there is less economic opposition to the accommodation of changing social demands upon forest environments.[52] But the ecological dictates of fire control in some ways make up for the absence of economic constraints on multiply use. The Forests Commission of Victoria does not exercise the degree of control over forest management that the B.C. Forest Service does, but this lack of a single dominant agency can pose serious problems. The responsibility for forest management is shared by nine State government or public agencies, often working separately for different objectives; co-ordination of effort, so crucial to a comprehensive multiple use programme, is difficult to attain under such a system. The difficulty has been recognised and met by the establishment of a Land Conservation Council, similar in com-position and aims to the recently formed Secretariat for the Land Use Envir-onmental Committee in British Columbia.

In both Victoria and coastal British Columbia, forest environments are capable of providing a wider range of social benefits than they do now. This inherent capability can be diminished or enhanced by the types of management employed. To what extent should public demands and needs dictate forest management policies if these needs conflict with the aims of professional man-agers? Who is to be the arbiter of 'minimum interference' to single-use in-terests, and who is to decide actual use combinations and the 'optimum social benefit' for which these combinations are chosen? These are the questions that now dictate management priorities in the increasingly urbanised forest envir-onments of southeastern Australia and coastal British Columbia.

REFERENCES

1. There is some uncertainty about what constitutes 'forest land' in Australia,
    especially in the vast semi-arid and sub-humid regions support-
    ing open woodlands, mallee and scrub forests. A survey for the
    Food and Agricultural Organisation in 1965 showed the forest
    area to be 937,000 square miles, or 31 percent of the continent.
    This area contained "lands bearing vegetative associations dom-
    inated by trees of any size, exploitable or not, capable of pro-
    ducing wood or other forest products, of exerting an influence
    on the climate or on the water regime, or providing shelter for
    livestock and wildlife" (FAO World Forest Inventory 1958,
    p. 123). The estimate was subsequently reduced to 532,000
    square miles in the 1970 FAO Inventory, but even this reduced
    area is mostly occupied by non-commercial vegetation. Only
    25 percent of these 532,000 square miles contains vegetation
    dominated by trees with a more or less continuous canopy con-
    taining useful timber. It is this area of potentially commercial
    timber (approximately 132,000 square miles or 4.5 percent of
    the continent) that is summarised in Figure 1,6.

2. According to McARTHUR, A.G. "The Influence of Fires on the Product-
    ivity of Hardwood Forests in Australia," Australian Forestry
    Research, 3 No. 1 (1968), pp. 24-35, the present cut of
    broadleafed (mainly Eucalyptus) species in Australia is 0.9
    m^3/ha. But YOUNG, H.E. "Five Hundred Million Potenti-
    ally Useful Forest Acres in Australia," Australian Forestry, 33,
    No. 2 (1969), pp. 129-134, states that annual production of
    semi-arid scrub forests is comparable to that of northern temp-
    erate forests commercially exploited under extensive forms of
    management.

3. Of this economically exploitable forest, perhaps 50,000 square miles
    are in use, including 38,000 square miles of State owned,
    and 12,000 square miles of privately owned forest.

4. The most important species are: blackbutt (Eucalyptus pilularis), tallow-
    wood (E. microcorys), flooded gum (E. grandis) and red maho-
    gany (E. resinifera) in New South Wales and Queensland;
    alpine ash (E. delegatensis) in New South Wales and Victoria;
    mountain ash (E. regnans), messmate (E. obliqua) and blue
    gum (E. bicostata, E. globulos) in Victoria and Tasmania;
    jarrah (E. marginata) and karri (E. diversicolor) in West

Australia. These are concentrated and most productive in areas receiving at least 40 or 50 inches annual precipitation.

5. This discussion is centred on the more productive upland and coastal forests, especially in the recreational hinterlands of urban centres. Less productive dry sclerophyll and box-ironwood or stringy-bark woodlands and forests are more extensive than commercial forests. This second group of forests provides timber that may be extremely durable but of limited utility, and large areas are being replanted to exotic Pinus radiata at the rate of 75,000 acres per year. Recently, however, many of these low productivity forests, especially in eastern Victoria and New South Wales, have assumed commercial value due to technological breakthroughs in the use of short-fibred Eucalyptus pulps and the rapidly growing demand for paper pulp in Australia.

6. Forests Commission, Victoria, Australia, Annual Report, No. 50 (1971-1972), p. 48.

7. British Columbia Forest Service, Annual Report 1972, p. 117.

8. Canberra, Forestry and Timber Bureau, Leaflet No. 105, 1968. (Progress Report 1961-1965 for the Ninth Commonwealth Forestry Conference). According to JACOBS, M.R. "Forecasts for the Future." Australian Timber Industry Stabilisation Conference, Hobart, April 1966, the total output from all State and private forests in Australia is 347 million cubic feet. McARTHUR, A.G. (op.cit.) suggests that with improved management, this figure may be doubled by the year 2000. Such an increase would bring the total Australian timber output, by the end of the century, to a level comparable with that of the Vancouver Forest District in British Columbia.

9. British Columbia Forest Service, op.cit., p. 93.

10. Commonwealth Bureau of Census and Statistics, Victorian Office, Victorian Year Book 1972, (Number 86), p. 355.

11. For a discussion of bushfires in these forests, see: EDGELL, M.C.R. Nature and Perception of the Bushfire Hazard in Southeastern Australia. Monash Publications in Geography, No. 5 (1973), 51 pp.

12. Useful general discussions of multiple-use in North America are contained in: BEHAN, R.W. "The Succotash Syndrome, or Multiple Use: A Heartfelt Approach to Forest Land Management." Natural Resources Journal, 4 (1967), pp. 473-484; HALL, G.R. "The Myth and Reality of Multiple-Use Forestry." Natural Resources Journal, 3 (1963), pp. 276-290, and SHANKLIN, J. Multiple Use of Land and Water Areas. ORRRC Study Report No. 17, (196?), Washington, D.C. 41 pp.

13. BICKERSTAFF, A. (ed.) Multiple Use of Forest Land in Canada: A Collection of Summary Statements Provided by Provincial and Federal Agencies. Forest Management Institute, Ottawa. Information Report FMR-X-20, 1969. For further discussions of Canadian multiple-use, see: Canadian Institute of Forestry, Position Papers prepared by Institute members for the Man and Resources Conference (1973), 28 pp.; GILES, W. "Forest Land Policy Statement of the Canadian Institute of Forestry, 1971." Forestry Chronicle, 48, No. 4 (1971), pp. 201-206; National Committee on Forest Land. Towards Integrated Resource Management. Report of the Sub-Committee on Multiple Use, Quebec. NCFL, Misc. No. 4 (1969), 34 pp., and PEARSE, P.H. "Conflicting Objectives in Forest Policy: The Case of British Columbia." Forestry Chronicle, 46 (1970), pp. 281-287.

14. LUCAS, A.E. and SINDEN, J.A. "The Concept of Multiple Purpose Land Use: Myth or Management System?" Australian Forestry, 34 (1970), pp. 73-83.

15. Forests Commission, Victoria, Australia. Annual Report, No. 51 (1969-1970), p. 6.

16. Forests Commission, Victoria, Australia. Annual Report, No. 52 (1970-1971), p. 7.

17. CAMERON, I.T. (Chief Forester, British Columbia Forest Service). Preamble to Planning Guidelines for Coast Logging Operations. B.C. Forest Service, Victoria, B.C. (1972), 5 pp.

18. British Columbia Forest Service. Management of British Columbia's Forest Lands. B.C. Forest Service, Publication B. 57 (1972), 24 pp.

19. Contained in a report by MARSHALL, H.N. (Forester, Recreation, Management Division, B.C. Forest Service), entitled: Forest Recreation Review: A Report Dealing with the British Columbia Forest Service Role in Forest Recreation. B.C. Forest Service, Victoria, B.C. (1970).

20. See, for example: De VOS, A. "Outdoor Recreation on Forest Land." Paper presented at the National Forestry Conference, Montebello, Quebec, 1966; also SCHAFER, E.L. and MOELLER, G. "Predicting Quantitative and Qualitative Values of Recreation Participation" in: Forest Service, USDA. Recreation Symposium Proceedings, Northeastern Forest Experimental Station, Upper Darby, Pa. (1971), pp. 5-22.

21. Ibid., p. 19.

22. LUCAS, A.E. and SINDEN, J.A. op.cit.

23. Forests Commission, Victoria (1970-1971), op.cit., p. 7.

24. See RODGERS, H.B. "Leisure and Recreation," Urban Studies, 6, No. 3 (1969), pp. 368-384.

25. These hearings created heated discussions on the pros and cons of clear-cutting. See, for example: DAVIS, K.P. and DUFFIELD, J.W "SAF Testimony at Senate Clearcutting Hearings," Journal of Forestry, 69, No. 6 (1971), pp. 338-343, MONTGOMERY, K. and WALKER, C.M. "The Clearcutting Controversy: a Forum on Clearcutting," Journal of Forestry, 71, No. 1 (1973), pp. 10-13, et.seq.

26. This description was used by SMITH, Z.G. "Modifying Clearcutting and Related Practices," Proceedings, Society of American Foresters, (1971), pp. 67-73.

27. DAVIS, K.P. and DUFFIELD, J.W. op.cit.

28. ELLEFSON, P.V. "The Attack on Clearcutting," Proceedings, Society of American Foresters, (1971), pp. 57-59.

29. "Environmental" forestry, now much discussed by professional foresters and the forest industry, is seen by these interests as the means by which they can satisfy increasing social demands on the forest environment and simultaneously retain control over

forest lands; see the statement by CAMERON, I.T. op.cit. General discussions of environmental forestry are provided by, among others: GOULD, E.M. "Forestry and the Urban Realm," Forestry Chronicle, 42, No. 3 (1966), pp. 285-293; HOPKINS, W.S. "Are Foresters Adequately Contributing to the Solution of America's Critical Social Problems?" Journal of Forestry, 68, No. 1 (1970), pp. 17-21; RUCKELSHAUS, W.D. "Forestry in an Urbanised Society," Journal of Forestry, 69, No. 10 (1971), pp. 712-714, and SPURR, S.H. and ARNOLD, R.K. "The Forester's Role in Today's Social and Economic Changes," paper presented to the World Consultation on Forestry Education and Training, Stockholm, Sept. 1971.

30. See PEARSE, P.H. op.cit. for a discussion of forest resource allocation problems in British Columbia.

31. British Columbia Forest Service, Annual Report, 1972, p. 117.

32. Companies harvesting timber from Crown land pay to the Provincial Forest Service, and thus to the Crown, stumpage charges on all timber removed. Stumpage value is simply the value of the standing crop as established by the Forest Service. Whilst stumpage appraisal is a complicated procedure, basically in the Coastal Forest Region, stumpage is calculated by determining the current market value of logs in Vancouver, and subtracting from this value the cost of getting the logs to market together with a profit margin.

33. Ibid., p. 109.

34. Ibid., p. 112.

35. Direct monetary costs of Australian bushfires are also high, although because of the dearth of statistics, no one really knows how much of Australian GNP goes up in smoke. The costs to the forest industry of fires that burnt four million acres of forests in Victoria during 1939 have been put at $200 million dollars, and the Tasmanian fires of 1967 caused $40 million dollars of damage in one day.

36. Large areas of southeastern Australia face major fire problems on average every other year. Bad fire seasons, with between 200,000 and 500,000 acres of reserved forest burned, occur every six or seven years in Victoria, and potentially catastrophic

seasons burning in excess of 500,000 acres, every 13 years.
See VINES, R.G. "A Survey of Forest Fire Danger in
Victoria (1937-1969)," Australian Forestry Research, 4
(1969), pp. 39-44. Catastrophic outbreaks occurred in
1851, 1878, 1886, 1898, 1912, 1925, 1939, 1951 and
1964. Although the most extensive of these holocausts was
the 1851 outbreak, the most notorious occurred on "Black
Friday", January 13, 1939, when over four million acres
were razed in Victoria, and 72 people were killed. More
recently in 1967, 62 people died in one day in southeastern
Tasmania.

37. HODGSON, A. "Control Burning in Eucalypt Forests in Victoria,
Australia," Journal of Forestry, 32 (1968), pp. 601-605.

38. Crown fires burn in the forest canopy, and although less common than
ground fires which are confined to the forest floor, are much
more devastating. They are of two types: dependent crown
fires are sustained by the heat and flame of an original
ground fire, but do not move ahead of it and are relatively
easy to contain; running crown fires are characterised by
the fact that the fire in the tree canopy progresses independently from, and ahead of, the original surface fire. These
are the so called 'blow-up' fires, as their geometry is three-
dimensional, and their energy output may be comparable
with that of a thunderstorm.

39. McARTHUR, A.G. "The Historical Place of Fire in the Australian Environment," paper presented to the Fire Ecology Symposium,
No. 2, Monash University, Melbourne, 1970.

40. HODGSON, A. op.cit., p. 604.

41. See Australian Conservation Foundation, Bushfire Control in Australia,
Viewpoint Series No. 5 (1970).

42. PLACE, I.C.M. in Canadian Institute of Forestry, op.cit., p. 4.

43. DAVIS, K.P. op.cit., and HOOVEN, E.F. "A Wildlife Brief for the
Clearcut Logging of Douglas Fir," Journal of Forestry, 71,
No. 4 (1973), pp. 211-214.

44. ALEXANDER, R.R. Partial Cutting in Old Growth Spruce Fir, U.S.D.A.
Forest Service, Research Paper RM 110 (1973); Rocky

Mountain Forest and Range Experimental Station, Fort Collins, Colo., and CRAFT, E.C. discussion in MONTGOMERY, K. and WALKER, C.M. op.cit.

45. Recent well publicised policy implementations by MacMillan Bloedel in British Columbia are noteworthy, as are the less well known, but equally effective implementations of British Columbia Forest Products.

46. TELFER, E.S. "Outdoor Recreation and Forest Fires," Forestry Chronicle, 45, No. 2 (1969), pp. 96-99.

47. Information on fire causes from various Annual Reports of the B.C. Forest Service.

48. McARTHUR, A.G. "The Tasmanian Bushfires of 7 February, 1967, and Associated Fire Behaviour Characteristics," Second Australian National Conference on Fire; Australian Fire Protection Association and the University of Sydney, 1968, pp. 17-48.

49. For a discussion of the human role in Pacific Coast forest fires, see CHRISTIANSEN, et.al. "Forest Fire Prevention Knowledge and Attitudes of Residents of Utah Country, Utah, with Comparisons to Butte County California," Social Science Research Bulletin, 5 (1969), pp. 1-26, and FOLKMAN, W.S. "Forest Fires as Accidents; an Epidemiological Approach to Fire Protection Research," paper presented to Western Forestry and Conservation Association, 56th Western Forestry Conference Vancouver, B.C., 1965.

50. BODEN, R.W. "The Role of Ecology and the Provision of Rural Recreation," Proceedings, Ecological Society of Australia, No. 4 (1969), pp. 8-16.

51. PEARCE, P.H. op.cit., and JEFFREY, W.W. et.al. "Foresters and the Challenge of Integrated Resource Management," Forestry Chronicle, 46 (1970), pp. 196-202.

52. LUCAS, A.E. and SINDEN, J.A. op.cit., however, argue strongly for a rigidly applied economic approach to evolving resource management problems in Australia, and criticise the often vague and emotive application of multiple use concepts in North America.

CHAPTER 7

PROBLEMS IN CANADIAN WEST COAST FISHERIES: GOVERNMENT POLICY AND INTERVENTION

M.A. Micklewright

University of Victoria

The maritime fishing industry of Western Canada, as elsewhere in the world, is facing problems of both a biologic and economic nature, which the market economy in which it operates has failed to correct. Low and often violently fluctuating incomes, physical depletion of the resource and low returns on capital investment have resulted in government intervention in the free operation of the market; legislation designed to mitigate the social effects of economic and biological changes have been initiated not only by Canada, but by most fishing nations.

As with all common property resources, the free operation of the market works against the most efficient allocation of resources. The principal of "free entry"[1] results in overcapitalisation of the fishing fleet and overfishing of the stock. In the absence of catch quotas and limitations to entry, the stock of fish will inevitably decline and the value of the marginal physical product labour will diminish, resulting in lower returns to fishermen.

The physical volume of fish available for exploitation in any given fishing ground varies over time, depending partially on changing water temperatures, food availability, and the population of predators including man. However, this paper is mainly concerned with the interaction between the availibility of fish, the impact of this scarcity or abundance on economic returns, and the Canadian government's reaction to these conditions. The changing quantity of fish stocks in an established fishery is only one complicating variable in an array of factors which have induced governments to intervene in the market mechanism in an attempt to improve the economic status of that part of the population involved, and to improve the net contribution of the industry to the aggregate welfare of the nation.

The problem of allocating labour and capital inputs in the exploitation of a common property resource are well known.[2] The problems of maximising net economic yield, and of reconciling economic efficiency with social welfare, have made implementation of rational policies difficult, in many cases resulting in legislated inefficiency. The social costs[3] of limiting free entry into the industry, and the political incentives to subsidize non-economic fishing units are a world-wide problem which no nation has so far satisfactorily solved.

The rational exploitation of a fishery is made even more complex when it is open to international use. The division of fishing effort and allocation of catch limits amongst nations with differing goals and value systems is an even more difficult problem than the allocation of these inputs within countries.[4] The incentives for one country to conserve fish stocks in an international fishery are directly analagous to the incentives for a single fisherman to conserve the resource in an intra-national situation, and while the principal of "free entry" may be being slowly eroded within a nation, the difficulty, and perhaps the equity of this solution in an international context is open to serious question. All these classical problems are in evidence in the operation of Canada's west coast fishery.

A discussion of the effects of government intervention in the fisheries may be approached from a number of viewpoints, each of which has advantages depending on the purpose of the study. Thus an analysis based on the dominant fish stock in a particular fishery would study the salmon fishery, the halibut fishery or the herring fishery. Normally this approach would be primarily applicable to biological and micro-economic studies. Alternatively, the effects of intervention may be classified according to the purposes of the intervention, and further classified on the basis of whether the intervention

impinges on the inshore, mid water or high-seas international fisheries.
On a more abstract level a procedure which highlights the problems common
to all fisheries may be more suitable when discussing government actions
related to fisheries in general. This approach does not deny that particular
stocks of fish require specific and sometimes unique investigation and regulation; rather, that the level of abstraction is higher. Indeed mention
will be made in this paper of specific programmes related to the salmon
fishery.

THE PACIFIC FISHERY

The Canadian Pacific fishery, based in the province of British Columbia,
is a relatively small employer of labour. In the period 1960-1971 the number of fishermen varied between 17,000 and 11,000 (Table 1,7). There has
been a consistant downward trend which appears to have stabilized in the
latter part of this period.

During the same period however, despite a significant decline in the
numbers of vessels engaged in the west coast fishery, the value of the fleet
increased by more than one hundred percent (Figure 1,7), and returns per
fisherman increased from approximately $2000.00 per year in 1960 to over
$5000.00 per year in 1970 (Table 1,7). At the same time the volume of
fish caught per fisherman shows a more complex pattern, steadily increasing
from 1960 to 1964 but decreasing from 1965 to 1972 (Table 1,7).

Federal government involvement in the fishery may be seen as an
attempt to resolve problems in three specific areas:

1. Low and fluctuating income;

2. Protection and enhancement of fish stocks;

3. Protection of Canadian fishermen from foreign competition.

TABLE 1,7

PARTICIPANTS, VALUE OF LANDINGS, VOLUME OF LANDINGS 1960-1972

Year	A No. of fishermen	B val. of landing 000000's $	B/A val. per fishermen	C val. of landing 0000's lbs	C/A vol. per fisherman
1960	15159	29.0	1913	340.5	22462
1961	16805	39.7	2362	638.5	37995
1962	16437	49.1	2987	686.7	41778
1963	16624	40.5	2436	772.7	44075
1964	13300	48.4	3639	712.3	53556
1965	13000	47.5	3654	626.1	48162
1966	12000	60.7	5058	574.7	47892
1967	12117	49.6	4093	332.6	27449
1968	12133	37.4	4731	267.2	22023
1969	10924	47.4	4339	174.0	15928
1970	11647	60.7	5177	238.5	20477
1971	11015	58.2	3284	227.6	20663
1972	11154	72.9	6536	322.8	28940

Source: Annual Statistical Report of Canadian Fisheries Economic Branch, Fisheries Service, Department of Fisheries, 1954-1969 - updated to 1972.

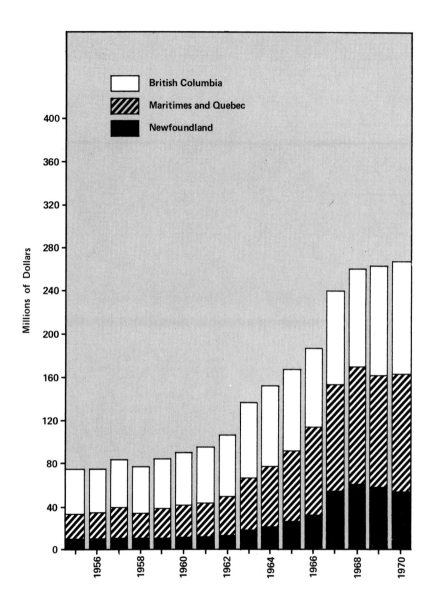

FIGURE 1,7   Value of fishing craft, sea fisheries 1955-70.

Low and fluctuating income (Figure 2,7) has been characteristic of the fishery throughout its history, due primarily to: the common property nature of the resource which has permitted free entry and prevented conservation measures being adopted in the absence of regulation;[5] the lack of alternative employment opportunities for fishermen, and the social and institutional character of isolated fishing settlements which has made both lateral and vertical mobility low.

The inclusion of fishermen in the national social insurance programme since 1957 has, to some extent, alleviated problems of low and fluctuating incomes in the primary sector. While this problem manifests itself in economic terms in the short run, the main difficulties of designing measures to increase income are social and structural. Government programmes for minimum price guarantees,[6] the establishment of the Salt Fish Marketing Board[7] for the east coast salt cod industry, and a number of provincial subsidy nostrums may be viewed as palliatives rather than as measures designed to correct the basic problem of too many fishermen exploiting a declining resource base.

The first international agreement which had a potential impact on the fisheries was the Boundary Waters Treaty between Canada and the U.S.A. signed in 1909. This established the International Joint Commission which has jurisdiction over problems involving the obstruction or diversion of waters along the Canada-U.S. boundary. While the Treaty does not specifically mention pollution, the I.J.C. does investigate, report and made recommendations on pollution problems to the two governments concerned. So far, however it has taken no action of the pollution of the marine environment and has been wholly concerned with inland waters.

Later, in 1923 the U.S.A. and Canada signed an agreement which provided for the establishment of the International Pacific Halibut Commission for the Preservation of the Halibut Fishery of the North Pacific Ocean

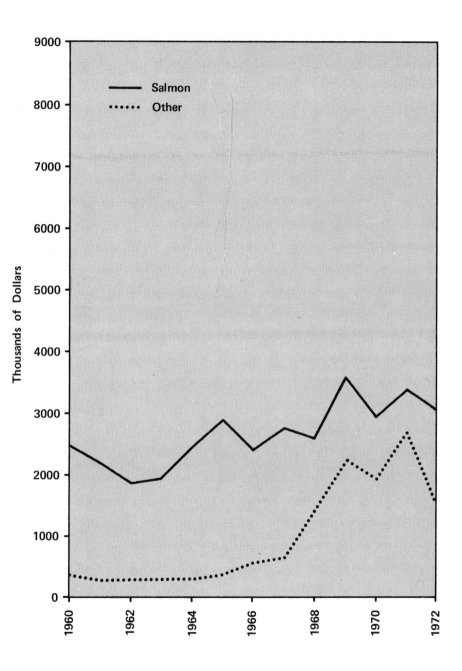

FIGURE 2,7   Price per unit of catch, 1960-1972.

and the Bering Sea. Halibut landings prior to this date had declined seriously despite ever-increasing intensity of fishing effort,[8] and it was recognised by both countries that to preserve and enhance the productivity of
this fishery some form of joint management to prevent overfishing and restore
the level of stocks was necessary. The powers vested in the Commission enable it to set yearly catch quotas for each sub-area and to limit the length
of the fishing season as well as to establish restrictions on permitted types
of gear. The goal of this regulation was to limit the annual catch to the
maximum sustainable yield.[9]

In 1930 the International Pacific Salmon Fisheries Commission was established under a Convention signed between Canada and the U.S.A. whose
objectives were primarily concerned with the conservation of the sockeye
salmon stocks of the Fraser river system and the provision of an equitable
distribution of the catch between the two countries. While the Convention
was signed in 1930, it was not until 1937 that it was ratified by the two
governments and became operative. In 1956 an ammendment to the Convention provided for the inclusion of the pink salmon fishery of the Fraser
within the jurisdiction of the Commission (Figure 3,7). The conservation
powers in the agreement provided not only for catch regulation and distribution, but also for the enhancement of the Fraser system through the construction of fishways, improvement of spawning grounds and the removal of
natural obstructions to the free movement of fish.[10]

Greatly increased fishing activity by Japan after World War II, and the
perceived threat of this unrestricted activity to the fish stocks (Figure 4,7),
of the North Pacific led to the signing in 1952 of an International Convention
the High Seas Fishery of the North Pacific Ocean by Canada, the U.S.A.
and Japan. Concern with the capture, by high seas fishing fleets, of anadromous fish which had spawned in the lakes and rivers of another country
was the initiating force in this agreement, and led to the ennunciation of
the principle of abstention. This principle refers to the proposition that when

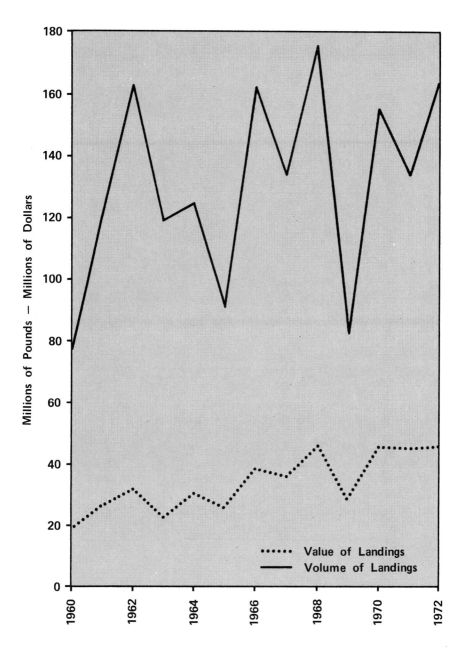

FIGURE 3,7   Volume and value of salmon landings, 1960-1972
(millions of dollars).

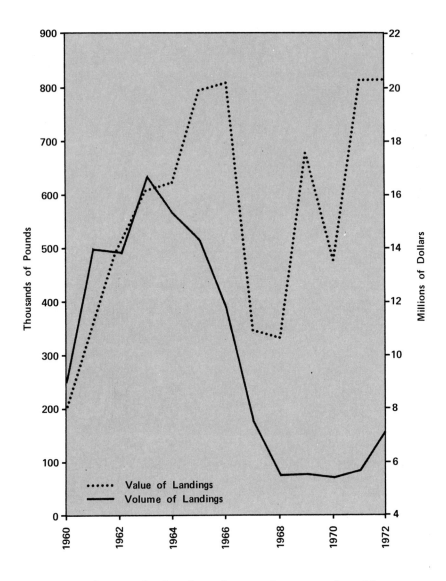

FIGURE 4,7   Fish other than salmon, volume and value of landings, 1960-1972.

a fish stock is being managed by a country, and is being fully utilised under regulation, those countries which have not recently participated in that fishery shall abstain from fishing. In this particular case Japan agreed to abstain from fishing for salmon east of 175° west longtitude.

An annual review by a commission composed of representatives from all governments involved examines the state of the fishery and makes appropriate recommendations to the contracting parties. The commission may also recommend joint conservation action for any stock of fish in the North Pacific and Bering Sea which it feels requires closer management. Under the terms of the Convention, provision is made for joint enforcement of the Commissions decisions.

The 1958 and 1960 Law of the Sea Conferences failed to reach agreement on the nature and limits of coastal states' jurisdiction over fisheries adjacent to their shores. Subsequently, Canada, in 1964, unilaterally declared a nine mile exclusive fishing zone beyond its three mile territorial sea,[11] and changed to a straight base line system of measurement, thus effectively gaining control for fishing purposes of a twelve mile zone contiguous to its coast line. This fishing zone was in 1970 declared to be the Territorial Sea, giving Canada exclusive jurisdiction for all purposes. At the same time, fisheries closure lines were created which effectively reserved for Canada larger bodies of water then would have been possible under the twelve mile straight line base system. On the west coast, the Queen Charlotte Sound, Hecate Strait and Dixon Entrance were subject to these new fisheries closure lines.

The phasing out of the traditional fishing rights of foreign nations was in the main accomplished during the period 1970-1972, and by 1978 the only countries fishing in the Canadian Territorial Sea and Exclusive Fishing Zone will be France and the U.S.A., both doing so under negotiated agreements.

Closely related to the operation of Canada's fisheries was the declaration in 1970 of the Arctic Waters Pollution Prevention Act. This Act unilaterally declared Canada to be responsible for enforcing pollution control measures to a distance of 100 miles seaward from Canada's Arctic coast, and subsequent legislation provided for Canadian control of anti-pollution measures for Queen Charlotte Sound, Hecate Strait and Dixon Entrance.

During 1970 Canada also negotiated two draft agreements with the U.S.S.R. which specified the privileges extended to Soviet fishing vessels in Canadian waters, and limited the permissible fishing areas for the Soviet fleet.

Virtually all the conventions, commissions and treaties related to the fishing industry in which Canada has participated have been concerned with the protection and extention of the rights of Canadian fishermen, the protection of specific fish stocks, or the protection of the marine environment. However, in recent years the government, fishermen and processors have become increasingly aware that even the exclusive fishing zones and control over landings, the fishing industry would still be subject to a very low rate of return on both capital and labour.[12]

In 1968 the Federal Department of the Environment initiated a programme designed to reationalise the salmon fishing industry of the west coast. The plan was to be introduced in four phases, each phase designed to increase the economic efficiency of the fishery and thereby increase per-capita income of participants and reduce the evident over-capitalisation of the fleet (Figure 1,7).

Phase I was intended to reduce the number of vessels fishing for salmon, through placing restrictions on the type of vessel elligible for license. Under the new regulations, no vessel could be granted an "A" category license for salmon if it had not fished for salmon in the previous eighteen months (these regulations were made effective from September 1968), unless it was under construction as of 6th September 1968, or it had replaced a vessel which had in the previous year had landings of more than 10,000 lbs of either pink or chum salmon (Table 2,7). In "special circumstances", provision was made for the establishment of an appeal board which could review decisions on licensing and rule on the validity of the license rejection. An adverse decision of the appeal board could then be subject to a direct appeal to the Minister of Fisheries.

Because of the mobility of vessels moving from one type of fishery to another, Phase I regulations were changed so that a vessel which had been engaged in <u>any</u> fishery in 1967 or 1968 could obtain either a "A" or "B" category licence. Category "B" licenses were reserved for those vessels which had had landings of less than 10,000 lbs of pink or chum salmon. These vessels could continue to obtain licenses, but could not be replaced, improved or lengthened.

Phase II of the scheme was introduced in January 1970, and consisted of an upward revision of license fees for all vessels, and a limit of ten years for the licensing of category "B" vessels. To prevent the salmon fleet from coming under too much direct control by the fish processing companies, the number of company owned vessels was limited to twelve and one half percent of the total fleet. In June of 1970 the "vessel for vessel" replacement provisions were changed to replacement on a ton-for-ton basis.

The increased revenues from the new licensing fees were to be used to finance a "buy-back" of category "A" vessels (Table 3,7). Through the buy-back programme, the federal government could buy category "A" vessels at appraised value and then conduct auctions of the vessels bought, stipulating that the new owner could not use the vessel in either the primary or secondary sectors of the fishing industry of British Columbia.

Phase III of the license control programme was put into effect in late 1970, and was concerned mainly with ensuring that vessels which did not conform to a minimum standard of quality would not be elligible for licensing. It had been found that on many vessels in the salmon fishery, fish storage facilities on board were such that the quality of the catch deteriorated un-

269

TABLE 2,7

TOTAL NUMBER OF LICENCED SALMON VESSELS BY CATEGORY 1967-1971

Year	# of Vessels Licenced For Salmon	'A' Category	'B' Category	# of Vessels Fishing Salmon
1967	7 639 *			6 639
1968	7 548 *			6 603
1969	6 931	5 869	1 062	6 136
1970	6 601	5 641	960	6 201
1970	6 285	5 322	963	5 806

a) All these vessles* were not licenced to fish for salmon in 1967 and 1968 but were eligible for salmon licence in 1969 because they had fished for other species.

b) In 1971, 178 vessels that qualified for 'A' category licences opted to 'B'.

c) A total of 97 'A' category vessels were retired and 84 new category 'A' vessels were built in 1971.

d) Forty-six vessels that were 'A' licences in 1970 did not renew in 1971.

e) A total of 401 vessels owned by Indians took out special licences in 1971.

Source: Limited Entry in the Salmon Fishery: The British Columbia Experience, Blake A. Campbell, Fisheries Programs Centre for Continuing Education, University of British Columbia, PASGAP6 - May 1972.

270

TABLE 3,7

REVENUE FROM 'A' CATEGORY LICENCE FEES TO BE USED FOR "BUY-BACK"

	Licence Fee $	Number *	Revenue **
1970			
Under 15 tons	100	5 123	461 070
15 tons & over	200	524	99 560
		5 647	560 630
1971			
Under 30 feet	100	477	42 930
30' - 15 tons	200	3 962	752 780
Over 15 tons	400	488	190 320
Special Indian	10	401	--- ---
		5 328	986 030

* Slight difference in number of 'A' category vessels licenced due to such factors as retirements, sinkings and cancellations during the year.

** Computed after deducting the $10 administrative fee.

Source: Campbell, B., Limited Entry with Salmon Fishery: The British Columbia Experience, Fisheries Programmes Centre for Continuing Education, University of British Columbia, PASGAP, May 1972.

acceptably in the period between catching and delivery to a processing plant.

The last part of the rationalisation programme, Phase IV, was announced in February 1973. It was intended to cover regulations related to types of gear permitted in the salmon fishery, and delimitation of fishing areas. Although this phase was scheduled for implementation in April of the same year, the advisory committee did not make its report until June. After the submission of the majority and a minority report, there was to be consultation between the participants to obtain a consensus on the points at issue before final publication of a report on recommendations. This report was made public in late September, after the main recommendations had been issued as guidelines one week earlier. It seems apparant that no consensus was achieved and that implementation of the whole of Phase IV is still in limbo.

The four phases of the license limitation programme – designed primarily to raise incomes of fishermen, to reduce capitalisation of the salmon fleet and bring fishing effort in line with available resources – is difficult to evaluate. It is true that gross returns to fishermen have increased over the period of the programme (Table 1,7). But whether this has been due to the scheme itself or is a result of inflationary pressures and increased product demand is difficult to assess at this time, and will require further research. Reduction of capitalisation of the salmon fleet has evidently not been accomplished for although the "buy-back" programme has resulted in three hundred and sixty-one vessels being taken out of use, the value of the remaining fleet has increased sixteen percent in constant dollars in the time the scheme has been in effect. The phasing out of the buy-back auctions in the spring of 1974 was apparently due to greatly increased vessel prices unrelated to catching ability, and the necessity to increase license fees to an unacceptably high level to finance further purchases.

Little has been done to save the halibut fishery which is in serious difficulties through over fishing. The future of this fishery seems dependent on international agreements restricting catch levels and involving all nations using the north Pacific stocks.

The introduction of a landings tax on the salmon and roe herring fishery advocated when Phase IV was introduced is being strongly opposed by the fishermen, who see this as a form of double taxation which throws the burden of fleet rationalisation directly on them rather than spreading the cost amongst all participants in the industry.

Canada is at present advocating a "functional approach"[13] to fisheries management. In essence this is management of individual species in such a manner that the annual catch of a particular kind of fish is limited to the maximum volume of fish that can be sustained over the years for the relevant size class. To achieve this "maximum sustained yield" Canada is proposing exclusive coastal state management responsibility for all fish stocks within a two hundred mile economic zone (Figure 5,7), or the limit of the continental shelf, slope and rise, whichever is the greater. Rights to catch within this economic zone would be vested in the coastal state, but catching privileges could be extended to other countries through bi-lateral agreements if a stock was not being fully utilized. Property rights in anadromous species would be vested in the coastal state which would have exclusive catching rights on the high seas as well as in the economic zone.

The establishment of management control in international fisheries may be accomplished through a variety of means:

1. Bilateral or multilateral treaties.

2. Regional groupings involving coastal states and prime users.

3. Unilateral actions.

4. Regulation through supranational bodies.

In the past Canada's participation in international fishery management has been mainly through formal treaties and regional commissions. Recently,

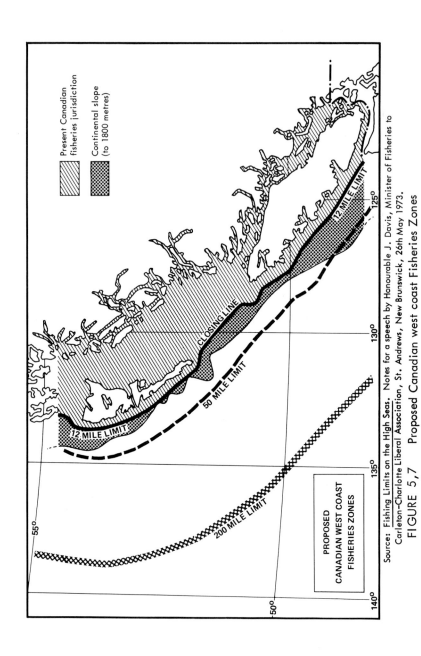

Present Canadian
fisheries jurisdiction

Continental slope
(to 1800 metres)

12 MILE LIMIT

CLOSING LINE

50 MILE LIMIT

12 MILE LIMIT

200 MILE LIMIT

55°

130°

125°

135°

140°

50°

PROPOSED
CANADIAN WEST COAST
FISHERIES ZONES

Source: Fishing Limits on the High Seas. Notes for a speech by Honourable J. Davis, Minister of Fisheries to Carleton-Charlotte Liberal Association, St. Andrews, New Brunswick, 26th May 1973.

FIGURE 5,7   Proposed Canadian west coast Fisheries Zones

however, Canadian policy appears to have changed in the direction of unilateral action, and seems to be predicated on the undermining of the powers of the international commissions just at a time when agreement was being reached by the participating countries on closer regulation of catch quotas and gear.

While this position may be justifiable in the short run for anadromous species, it is open to serious reservations on a number of points. There is no doubt that exclusive fishing rights would benefit the Canadian fisher- man in the short run. Yet protection of this nature is unlikely to benefit the nation as a whole unless it is coupled with long range planning to in- crease the economic efficiency of the Canadian fleets. Conservation measures would still be required to ensure that overfishing did not deplete stocks. If the nature of future conservation measures follow past trends of gear and boat restrictions and limitations on area and fishing time, little improvement can be expected. Methods to improve the economic efficiency of the catching units and the restrictions of particpation in every fishery to the point where net economic yield is maximised would be only marginally easier under exclusive rights than under commission reg- ulation. If the exclusive rights provisions are used as a shelter for in- efficiency, and this applies particularly to the large inshore fishery of the east coast, Canada would be a net loser.

If Canada's proposal for coastal state jurisdiction and exclusive catch- ing privileges are accepted by the Law of the Sea Conference currently taking place in Caracas, then it must be expected that it will be applied universally. If this becomes the case than a number of questions concerning economic efficiency and social welfare become apparant.

1. Under the proposed scheme, exclusive jurisdiction would be with the coastal state, but bi-lateral agreements would be possible, by which other nations could use the resource under the supervision of the coastal state. It seems possible that in this situation political pressure from

large nations and the threat of retaliation in areas unrelated to the
fishery could result in the principal of equity being violated.

2.   The terms under which new entrants to a fishery might have access
     might be predjudiced by political considerations, particularly in the
     case of developing nations trying to gain access to an established fish-
     ery. Some important fishing nations – and Canada is perhaps one of
     the best examples, are in fact fishing for foreign exchange dollars,
     rather than food. Provision would have to be made so that those nations
     whose nutritional needs are greatest receive preferential treatment.
     These are essentially political, not economic, decisions, although pre-
     ferential treatment would necessarily have economic efficiency con-
     straints, and the temptation under bilateral negotiation to extract a
     quid pro quo, either under pressure from the coastal state or third parties,
     might be difficult to reject.

The strengthening of the international commissions, by giving them en-

forcement powers as well as advisory powers, would no doubt in the short

run be a complicated, time-consuming and acrimonious process. However,

in the long run, international regulation of this type would appear to avoid

many of the political, efficiency, and equity problems associated with coastal

states assuming sole jurisdiction in management and sole property rights in the

fish stocks within their economic zone.

REFERENCES

1. For a discussion of "free entry", see for example, PEARSE, P.H.
    Rationalization of Canada's West Coast Salmon Fishery: An
    Economic Evaluation. University of British Columbia, p. 1,
    and SCOTT, A. "The Fishery: The objection of Sole Owner-
    ship," Journal of Political Economy. LXIII April 1955, p.
    116.

2. GORDON, H.S. "An Economic Approach to Optimum Utilization
    of Fishery Resources," Journal of Fisheries Research Board
    of Canada, 10, No. 7 (1953), p. 443.

3. SCOTT, A. Natural Resources: The Economies of Conservation.
    Toronto: The Carleton Library No. 68, McLelland and Stewart,
    1973, pp. 54-70.

4. Ibid., pp. 177.

5. CRUTCHFIELD, J.A. "Common Property Resources and Factor Allocation,"
    Canadian Journal of Economics and Political Science, XXII
    August 1956, pp. 292.

6. The Fishery Prices Support Board established in 1944 has the power to
    recommend government action to support fish prices when
    decline in prices adversly affect incomes of fishermen.

7. The Canadian Salt Fish Corporation established in 1970, operates to
    maintain and improve earnings of fishermen engaged in the
    production of salt fish by buying, curing and regulating inter-
    provincial and export trade in cured fish and cured fish by-
    products.

8. CRUTCHFIELD, J.A. op.cit., p. 293.

9. SCOTT, A. op.cit., p. 175.

10. OZERE, S.U. "Survey of Legislation Affecting Fisheries," Resources
    for Tomorrow Conference Background Papers. July 1961, p.
    800.

11. DAVIS, J. Fishing Limits and the High Seas: Notes for a Speech by

The Hon. Jack Davis, P.C., M.P., Minister of Fisheries, to the Carleton - Queen Charlotte Liberal Association Meeting, St. Andrews New Brunswick, 23rd May 1973.

12. PEARSE, P.H. op.cit., p. 6.

13. A thorough review of Canada's "functional approach" to fishery management is contained in the statement by Mr. J.A. Beesley, Canadian representation to the United Nations Sea Bed Committee, Sub-Committee II, New York, 15th March, 1972.

CHAPTER 8

VANCOUVER'S SHIPPING TRADE WITH WESTERN PACIFIC RIM COUNTRIES[1]

C.N. Forward

University of Victoria

Vancouver is the leading port of Canada in terms of commodity tonnage and the only major port on the nation's Pacific coast. Its port history extends little more than a century into the past, in contrast with that of the more venerable ports in eastern Canada (Plate 65). Its trans-Pacific trade, natural though it seems, did not materialize on the scale expected until recent years, partly owing to the traditional trading linkages connecting Canada with the United States and Europe. Though overshadowed at times by commodity exchanges with other parts of the world, the shipping trade with countries of the western Pacific rim has been important to Vancouver from the earliest lumber shipments in the 1860's.

It is the purpose of this study to trace the development of the Port of Vancouver in reference to the western Pacific rim from its beginning to the present, with emphasis on the recent patterns of trade. Commodity tonnages handled in specific calendar years of the past decade are examined in detail, in order to determine the type and scale of trade relationships and to define trends. On the basis of such evidence future prospects are discussed in general terms.

THE FIRST HALF CENTURY

Commercial shipments from Burrard Inlet, on which Vancouver is situated, were made in the mid-1860's from sawmills that had been established at Moodyville on the north side of the Inlet and Hastings on the south side. Luxuriant forests of Douglas fir, hemlock and cedar surrounded Burrard In-

PLATE 65
Metropolitan Vancouver on Burrard Inlet
has a population exceeding one million.

let, providing a rich resource at tidewater. The first foreign export of lumber was consigned on the "Ellen Lewis" for Adelaide, Australia on November
9, 1864.[2] In following years additional sawmills were built and many shipments of lumber, spars, pickets and shingles were made. A special order
was received in 1884, specifying huge beams for the Imperial Palace in
Peking, China: the trees were felled near English Bay in the present-day
highrise core area of Vancouver and the beams produced were 122 feet long,
28 inches square, and without a knot.[3] The export of lumber persisted as
the main activity of the port up to World War I.[4]

A new dimension was added to the port with the arrival at Burrard Inlet of the transcontinental Canadian Pacific Railway. Initially terminating
at Port Moody at the head of Burrard Inlet in 1885, the line was extended a
year later to a new dock built at Vancouver. The door was opened to new
imports destined to eastern Canada and to exports from the frontiers of the
British Columbia interior and the Prairies. The new route offered a direct
and fast link between the Orient and eastern Canada that was taken advantage of immediately. On July 17, 1886 the barque "W.D. Flint" tied up
at Port Moody with a cargo of more than one million pounds of tea from
Japan destined to Montreal.[5] The Canadian Pacific Railway Company
chartered three former Cunard Line vessels and placed them in service in
1887 between Vancouver and oriental ports.[6]

The silk trade was inaugurated in 1887 when a special train in Vancouver
loaded sixty-five bales of raw silk consigned to Montreal and New York by
rail, and to London, England by rail and trans-Atlantic ship.[7] This was the
first use of Canada as a "land bridge" in the movement of goods from the
Orient to Europe in far less time than would be required by an all-water
route. For a high value, perishable product, the time-saving advantage
of the route was a great asset. The dispatch of silk trains eastward from
Vancouver was a characteristic port activity for nearly half a century.

281

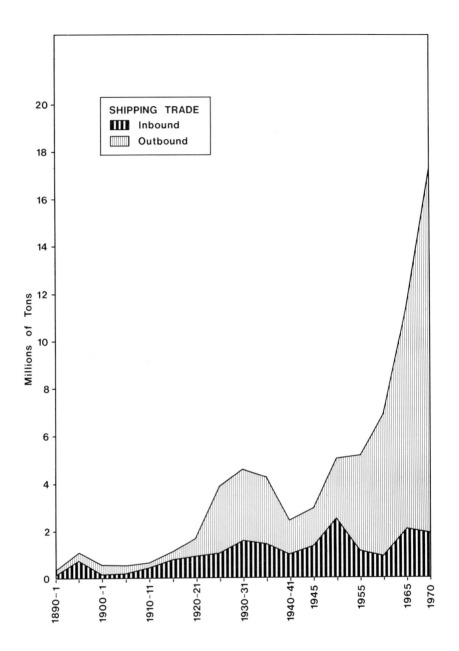

The establishment of liner service to the Orient added greatly to the value and variety of goods handled by the Port of Vancouver (Figure 1, 8). The liners specialized in carrying passengers and mail, and inbound cargoes of tea, silk, porcelain and matting. The value of imports greatly exceeded that of exports.[8] More sophisticated and faster ships were built for the Canadian Pacific Railway Company, the famous "Empresses" of "India", "Japan" and "China" (Plate 66). New records were set for express freight from the Orient: mail and cargo carried by the "Empress of Japan" in June 1881 reached London, England from Yokohama in twenty-two days.[9] The availability of the new transcontinental railway route attracted other shipping lines to Vancouver, such as the Canadian-Australian Line.

After the turn of the century Vancouver was well established as a trans-Pacific port. Direct steamship lines operated on regular schedules to the Orient, Australia, New Zealand, Hawaii, Fiji and other south Pacific islands. The lines included the Canadian Pacific, Canadian-Australian, China Mutual and British Columbia-New Zealand.[10] Besides the typical imports from the Orient of silk and tea, large quantities of raw sugar were unloaded from Fiji and a variety of other cargoes came from Australia and New Zealand.[11] Trans-Pacific exports were dominated by lumber, which was particularly important in the Australia trade. During the period 1906 to 1912 Vancouver shipped approximately 25,000,000 board feet a year, about half of the British Columbia total.[12] The first wheat shipments to the Orient were dispatched about 1907, but the movement was rather small.[13] The wheat was handled in bags until the first grain elevator was erected in Vancouver in 1914, the same year that saw the completion of the Panama Canal.[14] Small quantities of coal from the Kootenays in southeastern British Columbia were hauled by rail to Vancouver for shipment to Hong Kong, Japan and other western Pacific rim points, this trade beginning as early as 1890 and continuing sporadically.[15]

PLATE 66
Panoramic view of the City of Vancouver, B.C., 1898.
Hastings Saw Mill on the left and Canadian Pacific docks
on the right where the Empress of India appears in the drawing.

British Columbia Provincial Archives Photo

Owing to the high cost of the seven hundred-mile rail transport leg, however, another sixty years were to elapse before that trade assumed major proportions. Other exports included agricultural machinery and paper manufactured in eastern Canada and canned salmon produced in British Columbia.[16] Australia was a major destination of these goods.[17]

The pre-World War I decade was one of great optimism that nourished a real estate boom and fond thoughts of Vancouver becoming a great world port and vanguard of Canada's trading reach across the Pacific.

> Commanding as it does the key to trade on the Pacific, as well as being the outlet for the products of the vast interior districts, its position, both from the standpoints of commerical utility and beauty, is unique. Into the harbour of Vancouver, justly famed for its size, safety and beauty pours the ever-growing volume of Australasian, Oriental and northern goldfields trade.[18]

The vision of the future included the establishment of manufacturing in Vancouver for overseas markets, as well as the fostering of trans-shipment activities.

> Canadian agents in the Orient are already prompting the manufacturers of the Dominion as to the character of the goods that will be wanted, and all the products of the busy cities of the East will find their way to Vancouver to be shipped. There will be branch factories established in the Terminal City also when the volume of Canada's trade with China and Japan demands them.[19]

With the opening of the Panama Canal and the completion of bulk grain handling facilities, the stage was set for a tremendous growth of Vancouver's shipping trade. The occurrence of World War I postponed this expansion until the 1920's. The Panama Canal created a far shorter route to the east coast of North America and to Europe, suddenly rendering

285

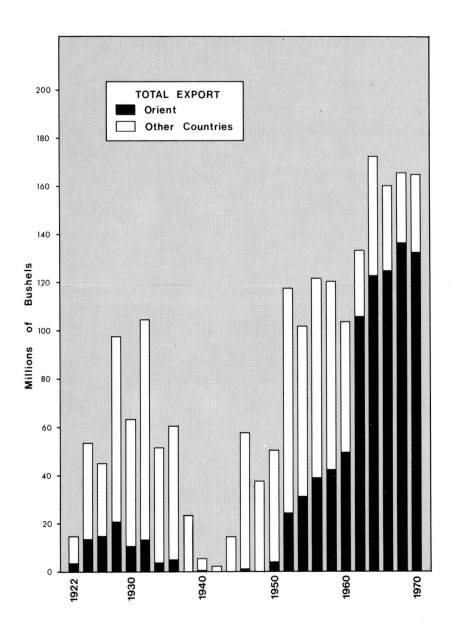

FIGURE 2,8   Grain exports from Vancouver, 1922-1970.

Vancouver a viable port for export commodities, such as grain, destined to European markets. The war caused a desperate shortage of vessels relative to the immense need for trans-Atlantic shipping, and vessels could not be spared for transport of goods from Vancouver.[20] As a result, the grain elevator was little used during its first few years of existence.[21]

THE SECOND HALF CENTURY

The decade of the 1920's witnessed a fourfold expansion of commodity tonnage handled by Vancouver, the major growth being in export trade, although imports doubled in tonnage (Figure 1,8). Much of the growth was occasioned by the new trading patterns made possible by the Panama route, but Pacific rim trade experienced a modest gain. Exports of grain to the Orient accounted for a significant part of this increase. Vancouver's grain shipments were minimal until the 1921-22 crop year and it was not until 1924 that shipments reached the 50,000,000 bushel level (Figure 2,8).[22] The grain movement to the Orient, mostly wheat to Japan and China, built up to a peak of 23,000,000 bushels in 1929, but it never amounted to more than one-third of the total grain exports from Vancouver. That trans-Pacific shipments were not greater has been attributed by Kerfoot to the Oriental cultural preference for rice and to shortages of capital for import financing.[23] The Orient, particularly Japan, was the main market for wheat flour, accounting for eighty percent, on the average, of the total shipped.[24] Paralleling the grain trade, flour shipments to the Orient escalated from 700,000 bushels in 1923 to 2,500,000 in 1929.[25] Lumber, of course, continued as a leading product shipped, with Japan accounting for a larger proportion than previously. The increase was especially great in 1923 in response to the enormous demand for building materials following the disastrous earthquake.[26] Other important lumber markets were Australia, New Zealand and China.[27] Lumber was replaced by grain during the 1920's as the number one commodity handled by

287

Vancouver and the proportion of Vancouver's expanding total trade directed across the Pacific declined.

The world-wide depression of the 1930's, followed by World War II, exerted a deflationary effect on Vancouver's shipping trade. Both exports and imports declined in tonnage terms, the total for 1940-41 being little more than half that of a decade earlier (Figure 1,8). Like a reflex action it was the formerly more buoyant export sector that suffered the more pronounced decline. The grain trade that had invested the Port of Vancouver with a new world role dwindled in the 1930's and almost disappeared during the war (Figure 2,8). Again, the war effort required a concentration on trans-Atlantic shipping activity and many commodities that normally moved west were diverted to eastern ports. In keeping with the overall decline, trade with the Orient, including grain, slumped badly during the 1930's and virtually ceased after the Asian war began in 1941 (Figure 1,8). On the other hand, trade with Australia and other Commonwealth countries benefited from the preferential tariffs negotiated in the early 1930's, and increased lumber shipments to Australia were recorded.[28]

Following World War II, Vancouver entered a period of steady growth of foreign water-borne trade that gained added momentum during the 1960's, thrusting Vancouver into the number one position among Canadian ports, above its rival, Montreal, and into the ranks of major world ports. The expansion of trade began toward the end of the war with the resumption of grain shipments on a significant scale to markets other than trans-Pacific. The flow of grain to the Orient remained insignificant until the 1950's when shipments in almost every year greatly exceeded those of the earlier 1929 peak (Figure 2,8). Even during the 1950's the proportion of total grain shipments moving to the Orient was seldom more than one-third. It was in the 1960's that the Orient became the main destination of grain exports and quantities involved set new records almost yearly (Figure 2,8 and Plate 67). Shipments

288

PLATE 67
Alberta Wheat Pool Elevator.

British Columbia Government Pho

of coking-quality bituminous coal to Japan for the iron and steel industry began in the late 1950's and increased rapidly during the following decade to join grain as a leading export commodity. The coal trade has been rendered viable by the lowering of rail freight charges on the seven hundred-mile haul from the Kootenays, through the use of unit trains and efficient handling systems. Lumber shipments also increased slowly after the war and more rapidly in the 1960's. The main destination was Japan, with its booming economy and insatiable demand for raw and semi-finished materials. It was exports of bulk commodities that accounted for most of the growth: while outbound cargo tonnage grew ten-fold from 1945 to 1970, inbound tonnage increased by less than half (Figure 1,8).

ANALYSIS OF RECENT SHIPPING TRADE

Detailed analysis of Vancouver's water-borne foreign trade has been facilitated by the inauguration in 1961 of an annual publication containing commodity tonnage figures by origin and destination for the eight leading ports.[29] Prior to that date the Shipping Reports did not provide such data for individual ports, but only in consolidated form for the Pacific coast region.

Vancouver's shipping trade became strongly Pacific-oriented during the 1960's. Western Pacific rim trade as a proportion of total foreign cargo tonnage increased from 55 percent in 1961 to 67 percent in 1970.[30] Both imports and exports registered gains in that period: imports rose from 26 percent of the total to 33 percent and exports from 58 to 71 percent.[31] Within the western Pacific rim the great bulk of Vancouver's trade is conducted with the Orient or East Asia (Table 1,8 and Figures 3,8 and 4,8). The shipping trade with the Southwest Pacific has at least kept pace with the substantial overall increase, but with Southeast Asia it has lagged. In 1970 Japan alone accounted for 70 percent of the total western Pacific

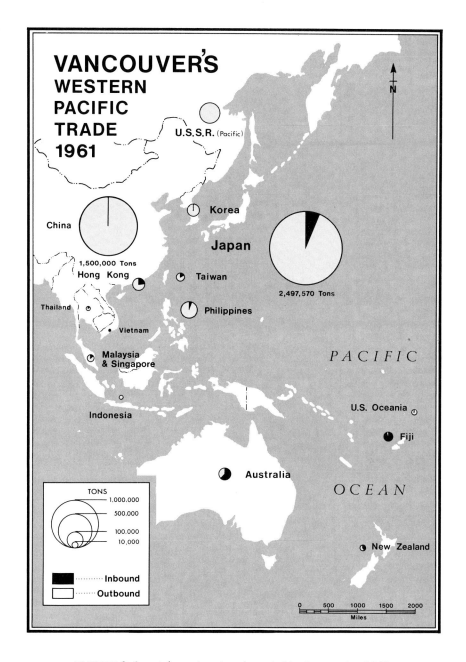

VANCOUVER'S WESTERN PACIFIC TRADE 1961

U.S.S.R. (Pacific)

China

1,500,000 Tons

Korea

Japan

Hong Kong

Taiwan

2,497,570 Tons

Thailand

Philippines

Vietnam

Malaysia & Singapore

PACIFIC

Indonesia

U.S. Oceania

Fiji

Australia

OCEAN

TONS
1,000,000
500,000
100,000
10,000

New Zealand

Inbound
Outbound

0   500   1000   1500   2000
Miles

FIGURE 3,8   Inbound and outbound shipping trade, 1961.

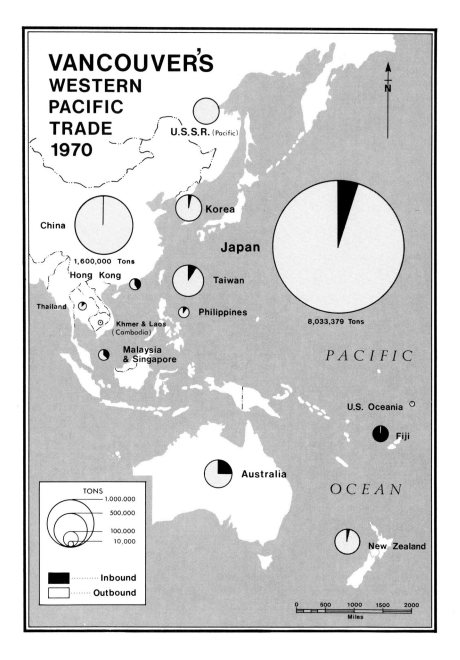

VANCOUVER'S
WESTERN
PACIFIC
TRADE
1970

U.S.S.R. (Pacific)

China

1,600,000 Tons

Hong Kong

Thailand

Khmer & Laos
(Cambodia)

Malaysia
& Singapore

Korea

Japan

Taiwan

Philippines

8,033,379 Tons

PACIFIC

U.S. Oceania

Fiji

Australia

OCEAN

New Zealand

TONS
1,000,000
500,000
100,000
10,000

Inbound
Outbound

0   500   1000   1500   2000
Miles

N

FIGURE 4,8   Inbound and outbound shipping trade, 1970.

292

TABLE 1,8

VANCOUVER'S SHIPPING TRADE WITH THE WESTERN
PACIFIC RIM IN TONS, 1961-1970

Region	1961	1965	1970
East Asia	4,363,093	5,063,108	10,725,544
%	94	89	93
Southeast Asia	158,790	260,563	121,269
%	3	4	1
Australia and			
Southwest Pacific	126,388	393,628	695,227
%	3	7	6
Total	4,648,271	5,717,299	11,542,040
%	100	100	100

Source: Shipping Report, Part IV, Dominion Bureau of Statistics, Ottawa,
1961, 1965, and 1970.

trade and China for 14 percent; no other nation accounted for more than 4
percent.

East Asia

Japan, which has become Vancouver's dominant trading partner, greatly overshadows the other countries in East Asia, both as the source of imports
to Vancouver and as the destination of exports (Table 2,8). It also has by
far the most varied trade, with more than one hundred product categories
handled in recent years. As a proportion of the regional totals, imports
from Japan have held firm at about 86 percent, while exports have increased
from 56 to 74 percent, (Table 2,8 and Figures 3,8 and 4,8). While grain

TABLE 2, 8   VANCOUVER'S SHIPPING TRADE WITH EAST ASIA IN TONS, 1961-1970

Country	1961 In	1961 Out	1961 Total	1965 In	1965 Out	1965 Total	1970 In	1970 Out	1970 Total
Japan %	145,689 89	2,351,881 56	2,497,570 57	313,361 86	3,070,831 65	3,384,192 67	380,073 86	7,653,306 74	8,033,379 75
China %	1,399 1	1,551,772 37	1,553,171 36	14,440 4	1,286,523 27	1,300,963 26	4,314 1	1,596,256 16	1,600,570 15
Taiwan %	4,786 3	23,649 1	28,435 1	15,263 4	125,471 3	140,734 3	32,805 7	395,960 4	428,765 4
U.S.S.R (Pacific) %	0 -	165,002 4	165,002 4	0 -	163,051 4	163,051 3	0 -	311,365 3	311,365 3
Korea %	1 -	61,942 1	61,943 1	1,145 -	2,935 -	4,080 -	4,826 1	291,108 3	295,934 3
Hong Kong %	12,417 7	44,555 1	56,972 1	22,325 6	47,763 1	70,088 1	21,974 5	33,557 -	55,531 -
Total %	164,292 100	4,198,801 100	4,363,093 100	366,534 100	4,696,574 100	5,063,108 100	443,992 100	10,281,552 100	10,725,544 100

Percentages are rounded to whole numbers and a dash indicates zero or less than one percent.

Source: *Shipping Report, Part IV*, Dominion Bureau of Statistics, Ottawa, 1961, 1965 and 1970.

and coal are the two most important commodities in the Japan trade, coal shipments have achieved dominance recently (Figures 5,8 and 6,8). Potash, fertilizers and other bulk commodities are of increasing importance. Although trade with China has remained stable in tonnages exchanged, it has dropped steadily in relative terms, but China retains the second rank. It consists almost entirely of grain exported from Vancouver, chiefly wheat in recent years. Trade with Taiwan and Korea has increased significantly, and a variety of products is involved, but trade with the Pacific area of the Union of Soviet Socialist Republics has grown more slowly. It consists largely of export wheat. The Union of Soviet Socialist Republics finds it convenient to supply the eastern Siberian market with foreign imports, rather than moving wheat long distances eastward via the Trans-Siberian Railway. Consistently small tonnages have been recorded in the trade with Hong Kong, but a high percentage is classed as general cargo and includes a wide variety of high value manufactured goods.

A more detailed consideration of the general cargo category, goods not suitable for mass mechanical handling or stockpiling, reveals several interesting aspects of the trade (Figures 7,8 and 8,8). Most obvious is the increasing dominance of Japan. The general cargo trade with Japan has achieved a virtual balance between imports and exports. Major changes among export commodities are the decreased shipments of wheat flour and increased shipments of milled grains, malt, oils, woodpulp and zinc. Noteworthy changes in imports are the strong increases in iron and steel, motor vehicles and machinery from Japan and plywood from Taiwan.

Southeast Asia

The lagging Southeast Asia trade is marked by considerable irregularity (Table 3,8). Only Malaysia and Singapore, the Philippines and Thailand have been regular trading partners of Vancouver throughout the decade. The

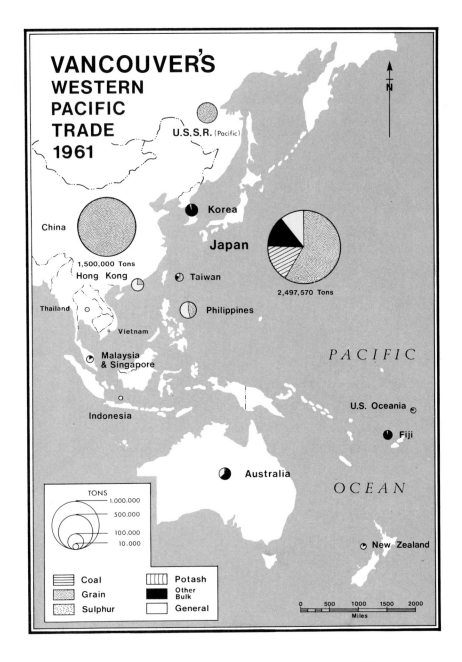

VANCOUVER'S
WESTERN
PACIFIC
TRADE
1961

U.S.S.R. (Pacific)

China

1,500,000 Tons

Hong Kong

Thailand

Vietnam

Malaysia & Singapore

Indonesia

Korea

Japan

Taiwan

Philippines

2,497,570 Tons

PACIFIC

U.S. Oceania

Fiji

Australia

OCEAN

New Zealand

TONS
1.000.000
500.000
100.000
10.000

Coal
Grain
Sulphur

Potash
Other Bulk
General

0   500   1000   1500   2000
Miles

FIGURE 5,8   Leading commodities by tonnage, 1961.

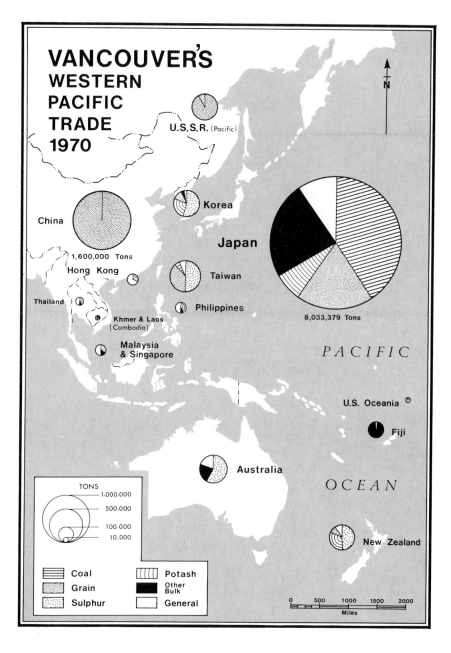

FIGURE 6,8   Leading commodities by tonnage, 1970.

297

TABLE 3,8   VANCOUVER'S SHIPPING TRADE WITH SOUTHEAST ASIA IN TONS, 1961-1970

Country	1961 In	1961 Out	1961 Total	1965 In	1965 Out	1965 Total	1970 In	1970 Out	1970 Total
Malaysia and Singapore	2,150	17,088	19,238	2,890	44,501	47,391	17,324	30,585	47,909
%	33	11	12	53	17	18	79	31	39
Philippines	2,524	123,096	125,620	2,552	202,795	205,347	2,039	37,754	39,793
%	38	81	79	47	80	79	9	38	33
Thailand	542	7,127	7,669	20	6,404	6,424	2,640	20,472	23,112
%	8	5	5	-	3	3	12	21	19
Khmer (Cambodia) and Laos	0	0	0	0	0	0	0	10,405	10,405
%	-	-	-	-	-	-	-	10	9
Vietnam	1,359	9	1,368	0	46	46	9	39	48
%	21	-	1	-	-	-	-	-	-
Indonesia	4	4,891	4,895	0	1,355	1,355	0	-	2
%	-	3	3	-	-	-	-	-	-
Total	6,579	152,211	158,790	5,462	255,101	260,563	22,012	99,257	121,269
%	100	100	100	100	100	100	100	100	100

Percentages are rounded to whole numbers and a dash indicates zero or less than one percent.

Source: Shipping Report, Part IV, Dominion Bureau of Statistics, Ottawa, 1961, 1965 and 1970.

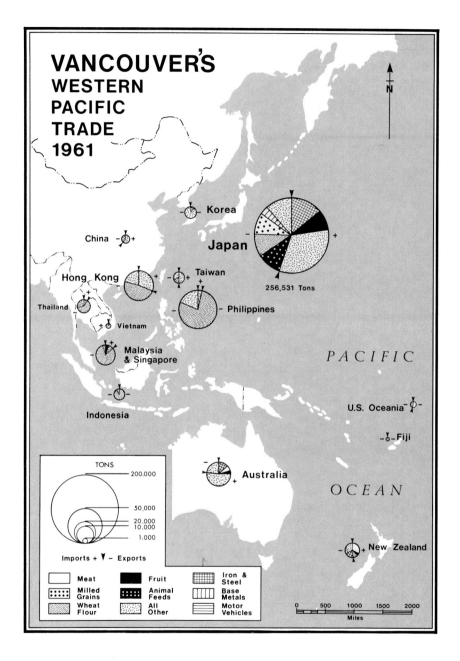

FIGURE 7,8 Leading general cargo commodities by tonnage, 1961.

299

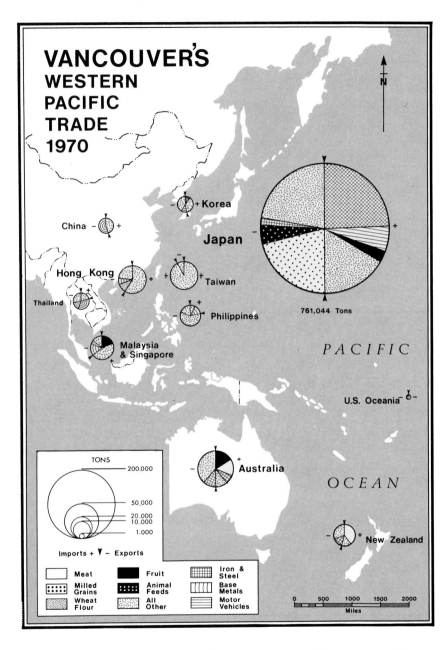

FIGURE 8,8   Leading general cargo commodities by tonnage, 1970.

preponderance of trade has been outbound from Vancouver, chiefly wheat and wheat flour in the early 1960's, replaced largely by potash, sulphur, malt, and zinc toward the end of the decade (Figures 5,8 and 6,8). Only Malaysia and Singapore originate a substantial import flow, and this has come about recently. Molasses, fruit and rubber are the three main products involved. Several other countries, the Khmer Republic (Cambodia) and Laos, Vietnam and Indonesia have entered the records with small shipments in certain years, mostly wheat flour or potash outbound. It has been noted that Canada has not managed to sell in quantity to Southeast Asia even those products in which she might be expected to have a natural advantage, such as apples, canned fish, newsprint and plywood.[32] This has been attributed to foreign exchange difficulties in some countries and relatively high ocean freight rates from Vancouver to Southeast Asian destinations relative to rates from Europe or South America.[33]

Australia and the Southwest Pacific

The growing trade with Australasia is characterized by a predominance of tonnage outbound from Vancouver, except in the case of Fiji (Table 4,8 and Figures 3,8 and 4,8). This has resulted from recent substantial exports of sulphur and potash (Figures 5,8 and 6,8). Even exports of general cargo have increased proportionately (Figures 7,8 and 8,8). In 1961 over three-quarters of the non-bulk cargo exchanged with Australia was imported, while by 1970 that trade was in balance. The Fiji Islands have shipped increasing quantities of raw sugar to the British Columbia Sugar Refining Company in Vancouver, a trade that dates back to the last century. Australia is exceeded only by Japan in the variety of goods exchanged with Vancouver, handling 80 basic product categories in 1970, compared with 107 for Japan. No other country in the western Pacific rim exchanged more than 17 categories. Vancouver's trade with both Australia

301

TABLE 4, 8   VANCOUVER'S SHIPPING TRADE WITH AUSTRALIA AND THE SOUTHWEST PACIFIC IN TONS, 1961-1970

Country	1961			1965			1970		
	In	Out	Total	In	Out	Total	In	Out	Total
Australia	41,193	27,476	68,669	28,558	172,493	201,051	76,777	245,812	322,589
%	51	60	54	29	58	51	44	47	46
New Zealand	4,159	6,194	10,353	2,498	119,605	122,103	11,255	264,635	275,890
%	5	13	8	3	41	31	7	51	40
Fiji	35,075	273	35,348	63,466	778	64,244	84,438	601	85,039
%	44	1	28	65	–	16	49	–	12
U.S. Oceania	50	11,952	12,002	1	3,223	3,224	4	11,697	11,701
%	–	26	10	–	1	1	–	2	2
French Oceania	2	4	6	2,379	176	2,555	0	6	6
%	–	–	–	3	–	1	–	–	–
British Oceania	4	6	10	6	445	451	0	2	2
%	–	–	–	–	–	–	–	–	–
Total	80,483	45,905	126,388	96,908	296,720	393,628	172,474	522,753	695,227
%	100	100	100	100	100	100	100	100	100

Percentages are rounded to whole numbers and a dash indicates zero or less than one percent.

Source: Shipping Report, Part IV, Dominion Bureau of Statistics, Ottawa, 1961, 1965 and 1970.

and New Zealand involves similar commodities. Sulphur, potash and fertilizers have been the most important bulk exports, while pulp, newsprint, iron and steel have led non-bulk exports (Figures 8, 8 and 9,8). On the import side the leading products have been meat, fruit and sugar. Except for grain shipped regularly to island territories of the United States, trade with Oceania is sporadic and of very small proportions.

FUTURE PROSPECTS

The recent burgeoning of western Pacific rim trade through Vancouver seems likely to continue (Plates 68 and 69). The immense population of the nations under consideration, approximately 1.5 billion, constitutes a gigantic consumer market and an important source of products, both raw and manufactured. The growth of trade with Japan is indicative of the possibilities for large-scale commodity exchanges with other countries as they become more industrialized. Trade with Japan seems destined to escalate in coming years. Japan requires increasing amounts of raw materials to supply its extensive manufacturing industries and Canada stands as a major world source of such resources. A large share of future trade likely will move through Vancouver, but other British Columbia ports may handle an increasing portion, especially of bulk commodities. The Roberts Bank bulk terminal, a few miles south of Burrard Inlet, was opened in 1970 and will originate most of the coal shipments. Being under the control of Vancouver's port authority, the National Harbours Board, Roberts Bank can be considered as an extension of that port. The development of another bulk port in southwestern British Columbia has been proposed. The planned expansion of facilities at Prince Rupert may enable that port to capture more of the trade generated in the north. Although efforts are being made to increase the processing and manufacturing of raw materials before export, this will be a slow process. Eventually, it is expected that

303

PLATE 68
Vancouver Harbour and the commercial core.

British Columbia Government Pho

British Columbia Government Pho

PLATE 69
The Japanese vessel "Otowasan Maru"
loading grain at Ballantyne Pier.

305

Canadian exports will be in a more highly processed form than are many of today's shipments. Vancouver probably will remain the focus of most of the non-bulk trade, especially that which is containerized. The Vancouver container terminal began operations in 1969 and services to Vancouver were introduced by a consortium of six Japanese lines and by the Blue Star-East Asiatic Company. Most of the container trade is with Japan and it gives promise of continuing increases. More common use of the container may have the effect of bringing about a better balance of trade, because balance maximizes economy in container exchanges.

Future estimates of a specific port's shipping trade are most difficult to make, in view of the uncertainties in world trade and the effects of port competition. One authority has ventured an estimate for the Port of Vancouver of approximately 85,000,000 dry cargo tons to be handled by 1990.[34] This represents a threefold increase in a twenty-year period. If the ratio of western Pacific rim to total Vancouver shipping trade as of 1970 continued to prevail, two-thirds or 57,000,000 tons would be attributable to that region in 1990. Even granting a large margin of error, it seems reasonably safe to predict a considerable increase in Vancouver's western Pacific rim trade.

CONCLUSION

The relationship of the Port of Vancouver with a particular foreland, the western Pacific rim, has been examined both in the historic context and in the present circumstances. Vancouver's port history may be divided into three broad phases spanning the century 1870 to 1970. The first half century was characterized by the dominance of lumber in the shipping trade and the development of strong relationships with Pacific rim countries. The completion of the Panama Canal and the establishment of bulk grain handling facilities at Vancouver were key elements of change that ushered in a second phase about 1920. The shipping trade increased substantially in the 1920's, with grain becoming the dominant commodity. The scope of Vancouver's trade was widened greatly as Europe and the east coast of North America became significant forelands of the port. Conversely, the dependence on Pacific rim trade subsided. The volume of trade plateaued in the 1930's, shrank significantly during World War II, and rebounded to previous levels in the early postwar period. The third phase dates from the mid-1950's when the rapid escalation of bulk commodity shipments began and the pattern of great imbalance between export and import tonnage was established. Bituminous coal entered the picture as a major export commodity, even challenging the leadership position of grain at the beginning of the 1970's. In that period Vancouver asserted its primacy among Canadian ports and achieved a far more important role in the shipping world than it enjoyed previously. Western Pacific rim shipments assumed major proportions and a dominant position within Vancouver's foreign shipping trade. The turn of the century prophecies of high trading volumes finally were realized, but the expectation that Vancouver would evolve as a manufacturer of products for the Orient has not yet come to pass. At least the Port of Vancouver may confidently expect a continued growth of trans-Pacific trade.

REFERENCES

1. The research grant support of the Canada Council and the assistance of Diana Hocking, who collected statistical information and prepared maps, are gratefully acknowledged.

2. DEFIEUX, C.M. "Birth of a Port," in COLLIER, R.W. (ed.) Proceedings of a Symposium on the Port of Vancouver. Vancouver: Department of Extension, University of British Columbia 1966, p. 10.

3. Ibid., p. 11.

4. STEVENS, L. "Rise of the Port of Vancouver, British Columbia," Economic Geography, 12 (January 1936), p. 63.

5. DEFIEUX, C.M., op.cit., p. 9.

6. Ibid.

7. MORLEY, A. Vancouver from Milltown to Metropolis. Vancouver: Mitchell Press, 1961, p. 98.

8. STEVENS, L., op.cit., p. 63.

9. DEFIEUX, C.M., op.cit., p. 9.

10. Greater Vancouver Illustrated. Vancouver: Dominion Illustrating Company (circa 1908), p. 42.

11. Ibid., p. 45.

12. STEVENS, L., op.cit., p. 63.

13. Ibid.

14. Ibid.

15. KERFOOT, D.E. Port of British Columbia: Development and Trading Patterns, B.C. Geographical Series, No. 2. Vancouver: Tantalus Research 1966, p. 69.

16. Great Vancouver Illustrated, op.cit., p. 45.

17. Ibid.

18. Vancouver, British Columbia. Vancouver: Vancouver Tourist Association (circa 1902), pp. 2-3.

19. Greater Vancouver Illustrated, op.cit., p. 45.

20. STEVENS, L., op.cit., p. 63.

21. Ibid.

22. GIBB, A. National Ports Survey 1931-32. Ottawa: King's Printer, 1932, p. 155.

23. KERFOOT, D.E., op.cit., p. 95.

24. GIBB, A., op.cit., p. 160.

25. Ibid.

26. KERFOOT, D.E., op.cit., p. 45.

27. Ibid., p. 48.

28. Ibid., p. 98.

29. Government of Canada, Shipping Report, Part IV. Ottawa: Dominion Bureau of Statistics.

30. Ibid., 1961 and 1970.

31. Ibid.

32. Government of British Columbia, Canada's Exports to South-East Asia: A Study of Trade and Transportation. Victoria: Department of Industrial Development, Trade and Commerce, November 1963, p. 4.

33. Ibid., p. 37.

34. ROSS, I.S. "The Port of Vancouver," Ports and Harbors, 14, No. 3 (March 1969), p. 16.

THE CONTRIBUTORS

Rudolph Wikkramatileke, B.A., M.A., Ph.D., Professor, Department of
Geography, University of Victoria. From 1948 to 1955
Dr. Wikkramatileke was a member of the faculty of the
University of Ceylon. He then moved to the University
of Singapore, becoming Chairman of the Geography
Department there until 1968 when he came to the Uni-
versity of Victoria. His degrees are from the University
of Ceylon, Clark University and the University of London.

Bryan H. Farrell, B.A., M.A., Ph.D., Director, Centre for South Pacific
Studies, University of California, Santa Cruz. Follow-
ing several years of teaching at the Southern Methodist
University and the Universities of Auckland and Alberta,
Dr. Farrell became the first Head of the Geography
Department at the University of Victoria in 1963. He
held this position until 1970, and during that time and
until his move to Santa Cruz in 1974, pioneered and
became Director of the Pacific Studies Programme. His
degrees are from the Universities of Canterbury, Washington and Auckland.

Chuen-Yan David Lai, B.A., M.A., Ph.D., Associate Professor, Department of Geography, University of Victoria. Dr. Lai
join the university in 1968 after several years of lectur-
ing and teaching at the University of Hong Kong in his
native city. His doctorate is from the University of
London, and his other degrees from the University of
Hong Kong.

Michael C.R. Edgell, B.A., Ph.D., Assistant Professor, Department of
Geography, University of Victoria. Receiving both
of his degrees from the University of Birmingham, Dr.
Edgell also spent a year attending a post graduate
course in Conservation at University College, London.
Joining the University of Victoria for the first time in
1965, he moved to Australia in 1968 to teach at
Monash University and returned to Victoria in 1972.

Malcolm A. Micklewright, B.A., Ph.D., Assistant Professor, Department
of Geography, University of Victoria. Before joining
the Department of Geography at Victoria in 1971, Dr.

Micklewright taught for two years at Memorial University, Newfoundland. Both of his degrees are from the University of Washington.

Charles N. Forward, B.A., M.A., Ph.D., Professor and Head, Department of Geography, University of Victoria. For a period of eight years before coming to Victoria in 1959, Dr. Forward was engaged in research with the Geographical Branch, Ottawa. His first two degrees are from the University of British Columbia, and his doctorate from Clark University.

BJJJ
